RUNNING WITH THE MACHINE

A Journalist's Eye-Opening Plunge Into Politics

To Kelly,
the very image of grace under pressure.

RUNNING WITH THE MACHINE

A Journalist's Eye-Opening Plunge Into Politics

Dan Lynch

Whitston Publishing Company, Inc.
Albany, New York
2001

Library of Congress Control Number 2001-132595

ISBN 0-87875-533-0

Printed in the United States of America

Photos by Jerry Vitagliano
JCV Studios
Clifton Park, NY

Also by Dan Lynch . . .

Deadly Ernest

A Killing Frost

Deathly Pale

Brennan's Point

Bad Fortune

Yellow

Contents

PREFACE

This is a book I'd never imagined I would write.

After three decades in the newspaper business, with six novels in print that I'd cranked out hurriedly during stolen moments between daily deadlines, my plan had been to spend my post-newspaper career writing all the other novels I had mapped out on wrinkled, gray, remote ridges deep in my brain. I'd planned to spend the rest of my days mainly spinning tales peopled by imaginary characters living out their imaginary lives in ways that might entertain readers, make them laugh, frighten them and possibly enlighten them a bit along the way.

Instead, here's a nonfiction book about a political campaign for the New York State Assembly—my campaign. Here's a book about what it's like to run for the Legislature in any large state. Here's a book about real people in often surreal situations. Here's a book about how government really works and why the conventions of political life require it to work that way.

Here, in short, is a book I felt needed to be written before I moved on to more fiction. After a life in journalism, then, here's one final piece of journalism—a story told from a personal perspective that illustrates just why journalism is so crucial in a democracy and why the proper, thoughtful execution of journalism's role is so vital if that democracy is ever to keep its promises to itself and to its citizens.

As we all know, our democracy isn't in the best possible shape. If it were, fewer people would be so repelled by it and more would be willing to participate in it. Fewer public policy problems would remain unsolved. More of this fabulous country's commitments to all its citizens would be kept.

Every two years, thousands of state legislative races are conducted across the face of this nation. A substantial number occur in small states where lawmakers serve as part-time public officials meeting for brief periods to pass laws and to apportion public money. The rest of their time they spend as ordinary citizens tending to their farms, their shops, their law offices and to their lives as real human beings. In the big states, however—and New York is the quintessential big, industrialized state—state lawmakers are professional politicians, like members of Congress. They practice politics for a living.

These professional politicians in big state capitals earn generous salaries compared to what most of the taxpayers who support them bring in. They solicit and spend staggering sums on their political campaigns. They make laws and dispense tax dollars primarily in response to political and financial pressures that are poorly understood by the millions of Americans whose lives these professional politicians touch daily in ways that few citizens appreciate. Moreover, professional politicians on the state level exist and function in a complex world not fully grasped even by the state house reporters who deal with these people on a daily basis. Life in politics in a large state is, in many ways, like life in some secret society where unique rules prevail and where ethical and moral values hold sway that bear little relationship to those of the larger universe.

Much of what's wrong in American politics stems from

the special culture that permeates political life. During the political campaign recounted in this book, that culture was revealed to me in ways I'd never expected. The experience provided me fresh insight into a set of mores and a value system that I'd never fully grasped, even though I'd been reasonably certain that I'd understood it all.

As a newspaper columnist and broadcast commentator, my obligation was to call things as I saw them—to recount events as I witnessed them, to communicate to readers and listeners how those events and the people involved in them struck me, and to pull few punches in the process. I've done that here as well. I've tried to present the reader with candid accounts and honest assessments in simple, vivid language that fairly summarize what I saw and heard and felt as the events this book recounts unfolded.

My thanks go to countless friends, family members, journalistic colleagues and political comrades in this adventure who are too numerous to name here but whose devotion, dedication and concern made this experience entirely memorable and worthwhile, for all its hardships.

Dan Lynch
April 2001

1

OFF AND RUNNING

"You know what ought to happen in this country to even things out?
Reporters ought to have to run for office."—Gary Hart

For June in upstate New York, the day was scorching. All across the sprawling, grassy expanse of the Altamont Fairgrounds in suburban Albany, a milling mob of several thousand gushed sweat in the harsh spring sunlight.

As the afternoon swelter reached its peak, Democratic Party operatives began prowling through the multitudes to round up the local candidates, who were glad-handing in the crowd. Hillary's plane had touched down at the airport. She was on her way. It was showtime.

I was standing outside one of the fairground pavilions, promiscuously pressing the flesh of dozens of strangers as they milled by. I was waving and smiling and feeling more than a little ridiculous. That's when somebody nudged me on the arm. "It's time, Mr. Lynch. Everybody has to get to the stage now."

"I'm on my way," I promised. It then occurred to me that I wasn't sure where I had to go, so I asked. A finger pointed down the tree-studded hill. That was the direction in which I dutifully headed.

Television cameras and crews already were posted in front of the outdoor stage at the hill's base. So were a few print reporters I knew. These were the local, Albany-based media people. Out-of-town reporters would arrive on Hillary's press bus. They would show up in evil moods. I'd ridden enough press buses to understand why.

For reporters, the boredom of a long political campaign can be mind-deadening. The candidate always delivers the same speech. The crowds always applaud at the same lines. During the 1976 presidential campaign, a *New York Times* reporter, Jim Naughton, had grown so desperate for amusement that he'd used *Times* expense money to bribe the mascot of the San Diego Padres. Naughton bought the head of the kid's chicken costume. Thereafter, whenever President Ford stood for reporters' questions, the *New York Times* was represented by a guy wearing a huge chicken head. To his credit, Ford pretended not to notice, but the chicken head eventually wound up in his presidential library in Michigan.

The outdoor wooden stage at the Altamont Fairgounds was painted brown and well worn. Many a vote had been won on that stage, and a more than a few lost as well. The Albany County Democratic Committee's annual fundraising picnic was where the party faithful got their first chance to inspect the year's crop of candidates. This year, seven candidates were running for office in Albany County—an incumbent congressman, four incumbent state legislators and a judicial candidate whose election was assured.

And, for the very first time, me.

I was the outsider in this crowd, the newcomer running against a three-term Republican incumbent in a New York State Assembly district where I faced an enrollment disadvantage of nearly 2-1. I also was the guy who'd vigorously criticized the Albany County Democratic machine for years in my daily newspaper column, on my radio program and in countless television appearances. I was the guy who'd played a large role in sending one of the party's key elected officials to federal prison a few years earlier, after the politician had become infected with a terminal case of sticky fingers.

Also, I wasn't a Democrat, although I'd been enrolled in the party until 14 years earlier, when I'd begun writing my column. Once I began expressing personal views in the newspaper, along with running the news operation day-to-day as managing editor, I felt that the combination of authority and visibility obligated me to abandon party membership. Readers were entitled to understand that I wasn't expressing partisan views, even though my father had been an active Democrat in the town where I'd grown up and I'd always felt closer to the Democratic Party than to the GOP.

More to the point, though, I was the guy who'd spent a media career bemoaning politics as usual and calling loudly for reform at every opportunity. And here I was that afternoon—the Albany machine's endorsed candidate, awaiting an appearance with Hillary Clinton, whom I'd both praised and attacked before many thousands of members of the greater Albany reading and listening audience.

I had the nomination because I'd been willing to run and because the party bosses suspected that my high profile in the Albany area news media for years had made me enough of a celebrity to give them a chance at victory in a Republican district where conventional Democratic candidates always had fallen tantalizingly short on election day. I was acutely aware that, except for my wife, nobody at that party picnic that afternoon really loved me. Many of them respected me, albeit grudgingly. A number of them loathed me. On the other hand, a substantial percentage of them loathed one another, too. The most conspicuous aspect of political life—in Albany, New

York, or in any other town in America—is the stark degree of personal hatred that so many political people harbor for one another. The second most conspicuous aspect of political life is the willingness of political people to sublimate those intense hatreds for the sake of their own livelihoods and ambitions.

Because of history and custom, political culture tends to be startlingly indirect. Despite what you see on television or in the movies, politicians tend not to confront one another over matters of principle or personality—except in public, that is, during an election. And those confrontations generally are pure theater, staged not to educate the voters but to mislead them. In private or in small groups, political people who hold one another in utter contempt routinely disguise their true feelings. Frontal attacks conflict directly with the ingrained cultural values of the political process.

That was probably the way it was inside Independence Hall in Philadelphia during that moist, muggy summer in 1776. I can imagine Thomas Jefferson and John Adams smiling and shaking hands while each schemed to stab the other in the back at the earliest possible opportunity. And there was Benjamin Franklin, despising both of them and trying to figure out which guy would make the more valuable friend or the more implacable enemy.

Mike Burns was waiting for us near the stage. A burly, gray-haired guy in his late 50s, Burns ran the Albany Iron-workers local. He'd ascended, after years of faithful subservience to whomever had been in charge at the moment, to the chairmanship of the Albany County Democratic Committee. Burns clearly was nervous. He wanted this show to go well, and he was worried that not all his candidates could be found in time for Hillary's arrival.

"We all gotta go inside here," Burns told me, a hamlike hand pressed on my shoulder and directing me toward a looming storage structure near to the stage. "She'll be here in a few minutes."

We candidates were herded into a big, metal building. We were joined by local elected officials not up for election that year but obligated nonetheless to show the flag for the party faithful. Already inside the building was Jerry Jennings, Albany's mayor and the Albany County Democratic party's unquestioned emperor. There was taciturn Mike Breslin, the humorless Irish lawyer who served as Albany County executive. There was Assemblyman Jack McEneny and Assembly-man Ron Canestrari and Congressman Mike McNulty. Most of us were accompanied by campaign aides and family members. My wife, Donna, stood with me along with Jerry Vitagliano, a friend and volunteer who was serving as my campaign's official photographer.

As the crowd milled noisily outside, the doors to the building were slammed shut with a sharp, metal clank. Almost immediately, the temperature inside soared to steambath level. Luckily, all the candidates were in casual clothing—no suits and ties for this appearance at the fairgrounds. As the doors closed, Secret Service agents took up silent sentry positions inside the building. Wires snaking out of their suitcoats and into their ears, they were poised at each entrance like nervous Dobermans. Hillary was still nowhere in sight. As the First Lady of the United States as well as the New York Democratic party's endorsed candidate for the U.S. Senate, Mrs. Clinton kept her own schedule, and everybody else adjusted accordingly.

Kate Doyle was the party's candidate for surrogate judge, backed also by the Albany County Republicans and therefore guaranteed victory in November. She was running for a crucially important position in terms of political patronage. The surrogate is charged with dispensing estate appointments to lawyers throughout the county, who then respond by making hefty political contributions. For that reason, in all 62 counties in New York, the custom is for party bosses to get together to cross-endorse someone who'll willingly spread around the wealth and ensure that a substantial portion of it goes back to both major parties. Voters are offered no choice as to who'll serve as surrogate judge. Generally, only one name appears on the November ballot on the line of either major party.

Kate was a tall, lean, good-humored blonde woman in her mid-40s. After a few minutes inside that storage shed, with perspiration flowing down her brow and into her eyes, she turned to one of the Secret Service agents.

"Hey," she suggested, "open the door and let some breeze in here. I've been coming to this picnic for years. Anybody out there with a gun will be too full of beer by now to hit anything."

The request was met with silence and a cold, baleful stare. Kate Doyle smiled nervously at the Secret Service agent and backed away to stand beside me.

"These guys don't laugh much," she grumbled.

"You noticed," I said.

For me, the grim demeanor of Secret Service agents was nothing new. I'd covered a number of national political conventions and presidential campaigns. I'd once been frisked while entering the White House for a luncheon in the State Dining Room after my car keys had set off a metal detector. I'd stolen a White House memo pad beneath the very eyes of a Secret Service agent during an interview in the Cabinet Room with Ronald Reagan. I'd had Richard Nixon make me a gift of a presidential fountain pen in the Oval Office. Years earlier, at a campaign appearance by a presidential candidate, I'd bumped into a Secret Service agent who'd gone through Air Force basic training with me. As the candidate droned into the microphone, the agent and I had stared at one another, wide-eyed, each mouthing the same silent sentence: "What the hell are *you* doing here?"

Before that afternoon at the Altamont Fairgrounds, I'd met Hillary Clinton several times. Five years earlier, we'd sat at adjoining tables and chatted pleasantly during a luncheon in the Rayburn Building in Washington. During the previous year of her candidacy for the U.S. Senate, I'd covered a number of her appearances in Albany before deciding to abandon my news media jobs and run for office myself. The Secret Service agents assigned to her campaign knew me by sight. If they were surprised to spot me that afternoon in a crowd of local politicians awaiting a private audience with the First Lady, they gave no sign. They simply eyed me with the same level of suspicion with which they eyed everybody.

Well, not quite everybody, actually. They now seemed to direct an even loftier level of distrust at Kate Doyle, who'd uttered the word "gun" in the presence of the security detail. A word of advice: never, ever say "gun" to a Secret Service agent on protective duty. It's a little like shouting, "Hi, Jack," to some friend you might spot at the airport. It's a sound that unsettles some people, and the people it tends to unsettle are carrying guns of their own.

In just a few more minutes, a door on the side of the building swung open. Hillary swept in, perfect teeth flashing beneath the sculptured skullcap of blonde hair. She was clad in a salmon-colored pants suit and was surrounded by a separate gaggle of Secret Service agents. Jennings availed himself of his prerogative as the most powerful politician in the room by immediately stepping forward to greet her. Hillary smiled up at him and warmly grasped his hand.

A few months before, a writer for *Esquire*, traveling with Mrs. Clinton, had taken note of the chemistry between the

U.S. Senate candidate and the Albany mayor. Jennings was a ruggedly built guy a few years younger than Hillary. With his pompadour haircut and deep tan, the mayor looked like a bigger, beefier, graying version of Sylvester Stallone, and women were prone to like him. He and Hillary behaved as though they had the hots for one another, the *Esquire* writer had noted. After the article appeared, Jennings was needled incessantly about the piece, which he airily dismissed as press hype. Clearly, though, he'd been flattered by the suggestion that the First Lady found him attractive. And, clearly, Hillary was doing nothing that afternoon to downplay that impression.

Donna and I stood in a semi-circle of local politicians as Hillary moved around the storage building, greeting each person with a grin, an outstretched hand and a bouncy, "Hi!" Jennings had his personal photographer on hand to record the occasion; the mayor seemed somewhat annoyed that one of my people had a camera as well. As Hillary made her rounds, I suddenly found myself concerned that Jerry Vitagliano would shoot a photograph of me with her. I suspected that she was pure poison in the heavily Republican district in which I was running. A poll taken a few months later confirmed that. It showed her with a high negative rating in the four suburban towns where I was standing for election. If a photo of Hillary and me together ended up in print somewhere, it would do me no good with the voters of New York's conservative 107th Assembly District.

I had to be polite, though, and Jerry Vitagliano already was stepping back to raise his camera as Hillary came my way. I made a mental note to send a copy of this photo to my older brother in Maryland. He was a devoted Republican who'd had to be talked out of wearing his NRA pin in his lapel at the announcement of my candidacy the previous month. Mention Hillary's name in my brother Tim's presence, and you could watch the blood vessels begin to throb in his forehead.

"Hi, Dan," Hillary said, extending her hand. "Having fun?"

I laughed. "Well, I've been a candidate for a month now, Mrs. Clinton. Believe me, it's been sheer frenzy."

Her smile never wavered. "Tell me about it. This is my third stop of the day. I have a dinner speech tonight in Buffalo. You'd better get used to it. This is what it's like."

I figured that I'd had a pretty good idea of what it would be like when I'd decided to do this. I'd been around politics for decades, studying the process much more closely than most people or most reporters, for that matter. I'd understood from the beginning that media people view the process from a sanitized perspective—that most of the work of an election is performed far from the lens of any television camera, that most of it is grunt work, chaos and total disorganization.

I understood also that I faced an uphill fight in this race, not because my opponent was an imposing candidate—he was, in fact, a fairly notorious dodo in political circles—but because the enrollment disadvantage in my district was distinctly daunting. And, unfortunately, most people vote party, period. Ronald Reagan could never have been elected mayor of Albany, with its 11-1 enrollment advantage for the Democrats. John F. Kennedy would have struggled mightily as a Democratic Assembly candidate in New York's heavily Republican 107th State Assembly District.

Hillary wished me luck. I wished her the same. Then, for the rest of the campaign, I made certain that we never came within 100 feet of one another—and certainly not in the view of the same news camera at the same time. I never bothered to explain to her why I avoided her, but a politician's first duty in an election season is to look out for Number One. I suspect that Hillary Clinton possessed a sharper appreciation of that harsh reality than anybody else I'd ever met.

In a few moments, the candidates were assembled into a line for presentation on the stage to the crowd at the Albany County Democratic picnic. I made it a point to be at the end of the line, far away from Hillary. In formation, we marched out into the sunlight, ascended the stage and listened to Hillary deliver her standard stump speech while the television cameras whirred and the crowd cheered. Afterwards, she shook hands at a rope line while I made my way back into the crowd. She had work to do, and so did I.

Money is the mother's milk of politics, and every candidate needs to raise it. After I'd announced my candidacy, I'd squeezed a few thousand dollars out of friends and relatives to get my campaign rolling. I needed more, though—a lot more, actually—and a key ingredient in raising campaign cash is the composition of the candidate's campaign committee.

You might have seen the official stationery of some candidate for public office. Down one side of the stationery, always listed in alphabetical order, appear the names of various politicians who've publicly lent their support to that candidate's efforts. Those names are key to raising money. When those names appear on invitations to fundraising events, they let potential contributors know that the candidate inviting them to kick in money is a legitimate contender, backed by people with the power to reward those contributors through passing legislation or blocking it or through the awarding of government contracts.

I'd already convinced some serious people to lend their names to my fundraising efforts. Sheldon Silver, the speaker of the state Assembly, had agreed to be on my committee. So had Chuck Schumer, New York's junior U.S. Senator. So had Attorney General Eliot Spitzer and State Comptroller H. Carl McCall. So, too, had former Governor Mario Cuomo. Cuomo had called me from his Manhattan law office the day he'd received my request in the mail.

"Why are you doing this?" Cuomo had asked me. "Are you mentally ill?"

"Well, you ran for office," I pointed out.

"Yes," Cuomo said, "but I now realize that I was mentally ill at the time, and I've since recovered."

Having prominent state politicians on my committee would help, but I knew that initially I would need to raise money from local contributors. I needed people like Jennings and Mike Breslin on my committee, too, but they'd been conspicuously slow in responding to my written request. After Hillary's speech, I cornered Mike Breslin up the hill from the stage. The county executive saw me coming and visibly winced. I pretended not to notice.

Mike Breslin was a bespectacled West Point graduate in his late 50s. He enjoyed a reputation as a totally straight arrow, an able public official and a distinguished veteran of Vietnam, where he'd commanded a company during the roughest combat of the war. The Breslins were a political family. Mike's younger brother, Tom, was a criminal court judge. His other younger brother, Neil, also a lawyer, was a member of the New York State Senate.

From my personal experience, Neil and Tom were more or less regular guys, warm and gracious and easy to talk to. Mike, however, had always struck me as a total stiff. He was one of those rare people in politics without a shred of geniality, humor or style. His brothers referred to him as "the colonel." I'd tried, but I'd never managed to warm up to the man.

I went straight to the point. "I'd like you on my committee, Mike."

"You're an independent," he responded coldly. "I think there's a difference between Republicans and Democrats."

Instantly, I found myself in an odd position—odd for me, anyway. As the Albany metro area's leading newspaper columnist, I'd made a comfortable living by writing and saying precisely what I'd thought. I'd never asked people like Mike Breslin for a thing. I'd needed no favors from politicians. If anything, they'd hoped for favors from me—a favorable mention in my column, public agreement with their policies, condemnation of their enemies.

Many of them had received such favors, too. They'd received them not because I was in the business of dispensing favors but because I'd made a judgment on some public policy issue strictly on the issue's merits. When I decided to run for office, I'd presumed that those years of taking honest, informed, often unpopular stands on public issues would have earned me a measure of personal respect from the Mike Breslins of the world. Now, I was learning that wasn't the case. They'd figured that they'd merely been kissing my ass all those years. Now, they expected their asses to be kissed in return.

I had a response in mind to Breslin's crack. I was inclined to point out to Mike Breslin that there were, indeed, differences between Republicans and Democrats. One difference was that Breslin ran for office in a county where Democrats outnumbered Republicans by 2-1. He ran where waving the party flag was an essential part of his campaign strategy. I, on the other hand, was running in a legislative district where Democrats constituted precisely 25 per cent of the electorate. Given that unpleasant reality, I'd remained an independent on the advice of Mike Burns and others. Now Mike Breslin was using that strategic decision, despite my endorsement by the county committee, to avoid having his name appear on my campaign committee. Moreover, he was doing that not out of any deeply felt political conviction but simply because he could do it. After all, I'd given up my column and my radio show. What was I going to do about it?

It was a temptation to say that aloud, but I restrained myself. Instead, I merely pointed out that I'd filled out a new voter registration card that would enroll me as a Democrat. The card, I assured Breslin, would go into the board of elections when and if I deemed the moment appropriate.

"I didn't know that," Mike Breslin told me.

"So," I asked again, "are you on the committee or not?"

"Call me next week," the county executive suggested.

Which, in fact, I didn't do. I'd been aware for a solid month that a number of key players in the Albany Democratic Party who'd promised me their backing not only had no plans to help me in this run but could be presumed instead to help the Republican I was running against. I regarded that as treachery; they, however, regarded it as business as usual.

I wasn't sure precisely where Mike Breslin stood. My guess was that he wouldn't work openly against me, but that he also planned to do nothing in particular to help me, either. After all, I'd come in from the outside. I wasn't a party guy. Besides, now that I could no longer help or harm him, I wasn't anybody he had to concern himself with. Like most political people, Mike Breslin seemed to divide the world into friends and ene-mies. His friends were people who could do him some good. His enemies were everybody else.

So, rather than phone Mike Breslin and give him the opportunity to refuse to return my calls, I instead complained bitterly to Burns and other party officials. I merely asked, "Am I the endorsed candidate or not? Do or do not elected officials of the Democratic party feel any obligation to support the party's candidates?"

I wanted Mike Breslin to feel some pressure. He could always ignore that pressure, but it really made no sense for him to do that. Then, a few days later, I called Breslin's deputy, a shrewd political operative named Chris Andreucci with whom I'd done business in my former life as a reporter.

"Just what the hell is wrong with your boss?" I asked Andreucci politely.

"It's taken care of," Andreucci assured me. "Mike will go on your committee."

"That's very nice of him," I said.

So, it began. After decades of covering politics and criticizing the venality of both the process and the people in it, I now found myself running for public office as the machine's candidate.

And, not surprisingly, not every part of the machine seemed to be working all that smoothly.

2

FEW ARE CHOSEN

"Forgive your enemies, but never forget their names."
—John F. Kennedy

So, was Mario Cuomo right? Was I mentally ill because I wanted to serve in the New York State Legislature?

Fred LeBrun thought so. For years, LeBrun had been a friend and, most recently, my column-writing colleague at the Albany *Times Union*. A few weeks after I took early retirement from the newspaper, and after word had begun circulating in Albany political circles that I was toying with running for the Assembly, LeBrun published a column headlined, "Dan, don't jump into that sewer."

In his reporting, LeBrun had gone to the newspaper's library and pulled out a few of my columns on the shortcomings of the Albany lawmaking process. It was certainly true that, as a columnist, I hadn't been especially kind to legislators. LeBrun pointed out that I'd described the Legislature as "211 shameless hustlers, hopeless dopes and well-intentioned inno-cents. . . ." He reported that I'd also referred to the Legislature as a "rowdy collection of towering egos, insecure approval seekers and shameless vote whores."

"So," LeBrun wrote in that column urging me to stay out of politics, "why would any reasonably sane adult with a few bucks in the bank, the kids grown and a load of writing talent want to join a club of shameless hustlers, hopeless dopes and well-intentioned innocents? Beats me."

LeBrun told his readers that I lacked the proper temperament for political life. Yes, LeBrun wrote, the incumbent, a longtime political hack named Bob Prentiss, was "asleep in the seat." LeBrun warned, however, that, "Dan does not suffer fools easily or for more than 10 seconds. The hackles go up, his neck gets red and the bile flows. That, in fact, is one of his charms. The traits that can make for a good columnist—outrage, indignation, a sharp tongue coupled with analytical clarity—is exactly the opposite of the traits that make for a successful, run-every-two years, self-deceiving, back-slapping pol. Suffering fools is virtually a job description for an assemblyman, then you get to ask the fools for a contribution. They're called constituents."

At the root of LeBrun's objections was the firm conviction that it doesn't really matter who holds public office. That's where he and I disagreed. Thirty years of covering public life, as well as a lifelong preoccupation with history, had convinced me that individual people can and do make a difference in the human condition. World War II took place because a raving lunatic had seized power in Germany. The war had been won because of the courage and fortitude of two extraordinary men named Winston Churchill and Franklin Delano Roosevelt. Abraham Lincoln saved the union and freed the slaves after previous Presidents had dawdled for decades over moral questions of enormous gravity. Certain things have happened in history because certain people were in place who did certain things that other people would not have done.

I'd also experienced, first-hand, the power of government to make people's lives better. I'd come from a relatively poor family. My father had never seen the inside of a college classroom. His father had never gotten past the seventh grade.

My older brother had been an academic genius who'd gotten through college on merit scholarships. I'd been less bright, however. Moreover, my own scheme to finance my college education via football scholarships had been derailed by an unfortunate lack of size, speed and talent. At the time, though, the federal government had in place a student loan system that had enabled me to go to college and then take a full decade after graduation to pay the government back. That loan program had changed my life. It had made possible for me a career I could only have dreamed of otherwise. Now that loan program was long gone, a casualty of misguided government economy. The taxpayers had made a hefty profit on the financing of my education, but there was nothing like that program available to New York students. As a legislator, I wanted to put something in place that could do for others what that federal program had done for me. I wanted to do some good, and I'd come to the conclusion that I'd done whatever good I was going to do in journalism.

Not much was left for me to do in newspaper work. I'd started as a student at the Temple University School of Journalism, working my way through college by laboring nights and summers covering local government, bloody car crashes and the occasional domestic murder for two Gannett newspapers in New Jersey. Once I'd gotten my degree and finished active military duty, I'd lucked into a terrific job covering politics for the *Philadelphia Inquirer*. It was a vastly better job than I deserved at the time, but I loved the work. I loved the window on the world it provided me. I loved also being part of a building effort at the *Inquirer*, which was in the process of transforming itself from one of the country's worst big-city newspapers into one of the nation's very best.

During my fifth year at the *Inquirer*, I decided that my professional goal was to become editor of a daily newspaper that needed work. I would transform that newspaper into a quality publication that fought fearlessly for government integrity. Like a good many journalists of my generation, I was a steadfast believer in journalism as a force for good in a democracy. I had the good fortune to learn my craft at the *Inquirer* during the golden age of newspapering—at a time when newspapers, specifically the *Washington Post*, were redefining the role of the press in society.

The *Post* had taken an aggressive look at a corrupt presidency and, at considerable risk to the company's fortunes, had demonstrated the courage to reveal that presidency for what it was. A wounded nation was better for the loss of its political virginity, and newspapers were learning that real news was more than mere accounts of what had happened the day before. It was more than press conferences and official pronouncements and box scores on the baseball page. News was what mattered to people, even when reporters had to seek it out rather than have it dropped into their laps. And official corruption mattered enormously.

With the *Post* as an example, the *Inquirer* was doing the same kind of reporting in Philadelphia. It was auditing government. It was measuring the performance of public institutions and the people who ran them against the stated goals of those institutions. Meticulous, courageous examinations of government corruption and mismanagement—and of the police brutality for which Philadelphia was justifiably famous—later helped earn the *Inquirer* 18 Pulitzer Prizes. By then, though, I was long gone. I'd moved to Long Island's classy tabloid *Newsday* to receive intense training as an editor. I spent five grinding but hugely productive years there, learning how to manage staff, make reasoned news judgments and to function effectively in a leadership role in a quality newspaper environment.

That's when the headhunter looked me up. I met him at the Waldorf Astoria. A medium-sized newspaper in the Northeast is looking for a managing editor, the headhunter told me. There's a new editor in place, a guy with a serious reputation, who wants to build. Would you like to be part of a building effort like that, the headhunter asked?

I loved *Newsday*, but I didn't feel particularly needed there. *Newsday* would continue to be a top-quality operation with or without me. There were perhaps a half-dozen up-and-coming *Newsday* editors who were the right age to be considered when the editor's job opened up in a half dozen years or so. We were headed toward a tight corporate bottleneck. Moreover, if I'd been placed in command of *Newsday* that very day, I would have taken no sweeping steps to modify the operation. In general, things worked pretty well there. Here was a chance to make a difference—a chance to build a quality newspaper as number two in the operation—and, eventually, to assume the top newsroom job and refine what already had been done.

This move would constitute a step down in weight class—from a career in large, mass circulation newspapers to a smaller, less significant journalistic environment—but I was 33 years old and ready to make a move like this. Yes, I told the headhunter, I would relish the opportunity to be a part of such a building effort.

A few weeks later, I was back at the Waldorf, eating breakfast in Peacock Alley with Harry Rosenfeld, the new editor of the Albany *Times Union* and *Knickerbocker News*. The combined daily circulation of the two newspapers was roughly 110,000, down from *Newsday*'s half million-plus. That meant a smaller staff and working with people whose skills were less impressive than those of *Newsday* people.

Rosenfeld was, however, a legendary figure in American newspapering at the time. He'd been the metro editor at the *Washington Post*, the guy who'd supervised Bob Woodward and Carl Bernstein during their coverage of the Watergate Scandal. Jack Warden had played Harry in the movie *All the President's Men*, although Harry had always complained that he thought that Robert Redford would have been more deftly cast as Harry Rosenfeld than as Woodward.

Rosenfeld was gruff, outspoken and famous for his towering tirades. He tended to behave, alternately, as a benevolent father figure or a raging, Old Testament prophet, depending on his mood. There existed, though, no better daily newspaper editor in the country, and I eagerly accepted his offer to become his key deputy as managing editor. I ended up spending 16 marvelous years in that role. The *Times Union* underwent a stunning transformation. Painstakingly, we built a quality staff, a number of whom later moved on to solid careers at the *Inquirer* and *Newsday*.

Under Rosenfeld, the *Times Union* was fearless and energetic in its coverage. When Albany County decided to build a downtown sports and entertainment arena a few blocks east of the State Capitol complex, Rosenfeld authorized me to assign a team of reporters to monitor the project—to make sure that this huge building project was erected with integrity. We soon discovered that the vast construction project was anything but honest. In open violation of the law, contract specifications were drawn around favored products and suppliers. Contractors complained bitterly, and privately, of having to pay kickbacks.

The Albany County executive, Jim Coyne, was the Democratic party's golden boy—handsome, gregarious, charming. Unfortunately, he also seemed to be running one of the most corrupt public construction projects that anybody had ever seen. The Albany County district attorney, Sol Greenberg, made a point of looking the other way, as had been his lifelong custom when confronted with official corruption. Ultimately, after three solid years of hard *Times Union* reporting on this official thievery, the U.S. attorney's office finally got into the picture. Both Coyne and the architect who'd run the project for him were convicted on corruption charges and shipped off to federal prison.

We'd done that—Rosenfeld and me and our colleagues at the *Times Union*. And we'd built circulation in the process. Readers wanted that kind of reporting. Unfortunately, Rosenfeld's time as editor was running out. He was nearing retirement age just as the newspaper business was undergoing a disturbing transformation, both in Albany and across the country.

The golden age was over. Chains were gobbling up independent newspapers all across America. In 1980, roughly 80 per cent of weekday daily circulation came from newspapers published by chains with centralized decision-making and tight cost controls. Today, it's closer to 90 per cent. Most of these chains were publicly held, and Wall Street was demanding bigger profits every year. Jim Squires, who'd served as editor of the *Chicago Tribune*, summed up what was happening in the newspaper industry in a perceptive but truly depressing piece in the *Washington Journalism Review*.

"Each year," Squires wrote, "the operating departments of the newspaper were forced to do more with less, while the demands for ever-increasing profits never ceased. . . . Enough would never be enough. The kind of reinvestment needed to stop the decline in market penetration and advertising share would not be made. . . .

"Each day, [editors] tried to serve up both good journal-

ism and whatever cash flow corporate management wanted. . . . Of course, such a strategy can't produce anything but
declining market penetration."

In short, the large, multi-media companies that own
most newspapers in America had decided that daily newspapers
are a mature industry, that prospects of market growth are bleak
and that newspapers should serve primarily as revenue sources
rather than as forces for civic reform. Traditionally, daily newspapers had been two to three times more profitable than most
businesses. Now, because of declining circulation caused by
increasing profit pressures, newspapers had been reduced to
being only one or two more times as profitable as most businesses, and the decision had been made—quality costs too
much. No more kick-ass reporting that might disrupt the revenue stream.

Nobody ever put it in those terms—not precisely and
certainly not publicly. The newspaper business would continue
to prattle about its devotion to its journalistic obligations. One
by one, though, all across the country, the crusading editors of
America faded into retirement—Bill Woo in St. Louis, Gene
Roberts at the *Philadelphia Inquirer* and Harry Rosenfeld at the
Albany *Times Union* among them.

Rosenfeld's successor was named. Given my well-
known views on the need for newspapers to overturn rocks and
to tightly monitor the conduct of the local power structure, that
successor wasn't me. Instead, the Hearst Corp., the parent
company of the *Times Union*, brought in as the new editor an
executive of a recently defunct Hearst newspaper in Texas. Jeff
Cohen was a career Hearst guy, several years younger than I
was, and not at all from the same school of journalism.

So, I found myself facing several choices. I could serve
as a managing editor in an industry where newspapers now
seemed to be viewed as cash cows. I didn't think I could do that

well. I could uproot my wife and kids and move to some new newspaper in some new town, where much the same sort of thing was happening. Or I could re-invent myself. I could get out of newspaper management entirely, with all its frustrations, and return to pure journalism. In the end, that's what I decided to do.

I went to Tim White, then the publisher of the *Times Union* and Cohen's boss, and asked for a column. I'd been writing a weekly column for years for the newspaper's Sunday edition. I'd demonstrated that I could do this work well. Moreover, the prospect of a doing a daily column had been made suddenly more attractive to me by Hearst's affiliation with the *New York Times News Service*. All of a sudden, my column would be going out to 660 or so daily newspapers across North America instead of merely the dozen newspapers that constituted the Hearst chain.

So, my decision to ask for a daily column provided me with a new opportunity. At the same time, it solved a thorny problem for the *Times Union*. I'd been a capable managing editor. Nobody was going to fire me or demote me. At the same time, Cohen was entitled to name his own deputy. Clearly, he and I saw the world and the newspaper business too differently for either of us to be entirely happy with the other.

I had to stay on as managing editor for more than a year until a successor was found. Then, one day in June, 1995, I began my daily column in the *Times Union*. I told the readers that, "I'm going to write about what I see and hear and think and how I feel about it. As we go along, you can decide for yourself whether I'm a liberal or conservative or even if that matters much. You have this promise from me—I'll try to tell you the truth, always.

"The truth isn't always pretty, and sometimes it makes people mad. But it's a commodity increasingly hard to come by in the duplicitous age in which we live. I figure you have at least that much coming for your 50 cents a day and your $1.75 on Sunday."

Writing that column was, in a word, terrific. I've never had so much fun. I used the column to do tough, hard-edged reporting on political venality, on official corruption and on government ineptitude. With the column as a platform, I also became, in short order, a fairly prominent media celebrity in Albany. I started doing a daily talk radio program on WROW, the Albany metro area's top news-talk radio station. I did regular television appearances on local TV stations. It was great fun for five years. There was only one problem. I'd come to feel, finally—after more than three decades in the news business—that I really wasn't accomplishing much of value.

That sentiment was crystallized for me in February of 2000, as I covered a major criminal trial in the snow and slush of downtown Albany. Four New York City cops were on trial on murder charges for the killing of a totally innocent young guy in the Bronx who'd been stopped and frisked by the cops. The cops had thought he was reaching for a gun. Forty-one police bullets later, they discovered that Amadou Diallo had been reaching only for his wallet.

The cops eventually were acquitted. Diallo's death had been the most tragic of accidents, but an accident nonetheless. Every day, though, in the snowy little city park across from the Albany County Courthouse, furious demonstrators gathered to complain that the cops were getting away with murder. Standing in that park, drowning in those howls of pain and outrage, I felt . . . well, I found myself feeling utterly useless. I summed up those feelings in a column in the *Times Union* announcing that I was abandoning daily newspaper work. I'd taken early retirement to do one column a week on a contract basis, to expand my radio time a bit and, primarily, to work on books. My kids were grown, educated and into their own careers in the news business. I was there, finally; I loved newspaper work, but I now had other things to do. In that column, I wrote:

> A strange guy has been hanging around my house lately. I see him in the mirror when I shave. He looks like me, only older. Lately, he has been muttering the same thing over and over.
>
> He has been saying, "It's time."
>
> It took a while for his words to sink in. That's because my mind generally is occupied with producing this column. What should I write for tomorrow? To whom should I speak to better understand some issue? Where can I run down those people? How do I get the truth out of them?
>
> Or, I'm out in the street, as I was during the Diallo trial, watching the news and the people who make it and trying to sort out what I think about it. Or, I'm stalking the marble halls of the Capitol trying to learn who's burying what dagger between whose shoulder blades. Or, I'm being bounced out of some politician's fund-raising affair because people with money don't want it known that they're buying influence. Or, I'm talking to some poor, helpless schnook whose life has been ripped apart by the bungling incompetence of some government agency or some cold-blooded ward-heeler.
>
> Writing a daily newspaper column gives you a box-seat on the world. Sometimes, what you see from that vantage point is compelling, intriguing and touching. Sometimes it's exciting. Sometimes it's funny. Sometimes it's sad.
>
> Most often, though, you're getting a prime view of the world's warts. You're gazing upon all its imperfec-

tions, up close and personal. And many of those imperfections seem positively immortal. . . .

For me, it's time to say goodbye to daily newspapering. . . . A guy I once knew, the late Tom Fox of the
Philadelphia Daily News, wrote a marvelous daily column for a few years. He gave it up, comparing the job to
being married to a nymphomaniac—great fun in the
beginning but nothing that anybody sane wants to sustain
in perpetuity. I now know what he meant.

So, finally, I was out of the newspaper business. But,
despite my desire to focus more on books, I wasn't quite out of
public life. I still had my weekly column in the *Times Union*. I
had the option of increasing my time on WROW, and I enjoyed
talk radio. Moreover, during the previous five years, people in
both political parties had held conversations with me on the
possibility of me running for public office. I'd listened and pondered the possibility and figured that perhaps one day, down the
road, I might consider it seriously. My wife, Donna, thought it
might be a good idea. Also, every reporter figures that he or she
could do a better job in public office than the people those
reporters cover. That's because reporters who cover politicians
quickly come to understand, as voters do not, what hopeless
boneheads many of these people are.

The summer before I took early retirement, I'd had separate lunches with two figures in Albany County Democratic
politics—County Chairman Burns and Assemblyman Jack
McEneny. These two guys represented two distinctly different
wings of the party. Burns was the classic, up-through-the-ranks
machine pol. McEneny was a thoughtful government professional who'd earned the loyalty of the party's reform wing. He
was a bright guy in his mid-50s who'd won his Assembly seat
and held onto it despite machine opposition. He'd also displayed the temerity to mount a vigorous but unsuccessful pri-

mary challenge against Jennings for mayor, which had earned him the undying enmity of the conventional Albany Democratic Party apparatus. Each man had offered support for me if I decided to run for office at some point. I seemed to be one of the few things that both Burns and McEneny could agree upon.

I'd also had conversations with Tom Bayly, the Democratic party chairman in adjoining Saratoga County, where I lived. Bayly was an aging man in failing health with a firm dedication to traditional liberal principles. He'd lost a leg to diabetes, and his party was badly outnumbered in the county voting rolls, but Tom Bayly fought on, year after year. A few years earlier, he'd urged me to run for Congress. No way, I'd told him. But when the question of my running for the Assembly had come up, I'd told him, "Maybe somewhere down the road. As long as I'm in the media, though, I really shouldn't even talk about it."

Now, finished with my newspaper career but still deeply concerned with public affairs, I suspected that I could have the Democratic nomination for either the Congressional district or the Assembly district in which I lived. I also could have the State Senate nomination, although I felt no particular urge to run for that office. My state senator was Joe Bruno, the State Senate majority leader and a guy pumping millions of state dollars into the community in which I lived. My instinct was that nobody should run against anybody in Bruno's position. And, in the end, nobody did. Joe Bruno returned to office in 2000 unopposed.

I pondered it, but I could see no real purpose in running for Congress. My congressman, John Sweeney, was new in the job, but we'd been on cordial terms for a number of years. He was a conventional Republican, a guy who'd come up through the party system. Sweeney was too partisan for my taste, and he literally reeked of ambition. But Sweeney sat relatively secure in a 2-1 Republican congressional district, and I didn't think I could do a better job in office than he was doing. His party was in the majority. Moreover, Sweeney was a decade younger than I was. Entering a seniority-based system at age 54 where only a few members of the House of Representatives knew me as an individual struck me as a waste of everybody's time. What could I accomplish in that job, even assuming that I could win it, that Sweeney couldn't accomplish?

That left the Assembly. The incumbent, as LeBrun had put it, really was asleep in the seat. Bob Prentiss was 64, a member of the minority party and generally viewed by the Capitol press corps as the single dopiest man in the Legislature. That was a title for which there existed real competition, too. Prentiss was the classic, central-casting version of the hack professional politician. He'd been on the public payroll in one political job or another for better than three decades. He'd accomplished nothing in three terms in the Assembly and was in no danger of accomplishing anything if he got a fourth term.

Moreover, I felt I might be able to play a useful role in solving some genuine problems. Like most of the older, industrial states, New York is in horrible shape. Yes, New York was benefitting enormously from the presence of Wall Street and that eruption of tax dollars that was spewing up to Albany from south of Houston Street in Manhattan. The financial services industry comprised only 2 per cent of the state's work force but had provided 58 per cent of the growth in Gross State Product during the 1990s. The explosion of state tax revenue from Wall Street, however, hid some long-term, structural problems on which a thoughtful legislator might have impact, especially serving the two-year term before reapportionment kicked in. As many as 25 per cent of the members of both houses of the Legislature would be in their final terms. They would retire rather than run in new districts in 2002. That meant that some of them, at least, would be eager, on their way out the door, to get something done and to remedy some long-standing problems.

Was it really necessary, for example, for New York to have the highest local taxes in America—70 per cent above the national average? If you adjusted for income differences by measuring per capita state taxation by each thousand dollars of income, New York ranked only 42nd in America in state tax load. And, at that, New York spent more than it should on the state level. New York's annual state budget nudged up against $85 billion for 19 million citizens while California's was only $100 billion or so for 34 million residents.

Why did New York have the highest debt level of all 50 states? State government and public authorities were in hock for a combined $100 billion. Was it really crucial to maintain a state aid to education formula that shortchanged urban districts trying to educate the kids who needed the most help—especially when New York had the highest youth poverty rate in America, topping 25 per cent? Was it logical for New Yorkers to pay the nation's highest energy costs at a time when manufacturing jobs were moving south and west? What could be done to keep younger, better-educated New Yorkers in the state, attracting high-tech employers, as the percentage of the Empire State's elderly continued to climb?

Moreover, why couldn't New York lawmakers produce a budget on time and, by so doing, get better interest rates when the state borrowed? Why did New York have the nation's 49th worst credit rating? The answer, I knew, was largely because the Legislature hadn't managed to adopt a budget by the statutory April 1st deadline in a decade and a half. The lawmakers refused to pass a timely budget because the moment the budget passed the political contributions from lobbyists dried up. Those 2,200 lobbyists were contributing, after all, for the purpose of influencing the spending of state tax dollars. The lobbyists spent roughly $70 million a year in lobbying expenses to wield that influence, and why kick in to lawmakers' campaign warchests once all the decisions had been made for that year? Also, individual lawmakers collected $116 a day in tax-free expenses every day they were in session. Nobody in the Legislature wanted that flow of personal cash to dry up too early in the year.

So, yes, I wanted to serve. There was work I wanted to do. Did I want to run, though? I'd already spoken to a few people about putting together a political organization on short notice. Donna said that if it was what I wanted, she would support my efforts. I'd even given a detailed memo to Mary Gilson, a woman I'd come to know well as a columnist when I'd determined that the New York State Police had accused her husband, just after he died in a hunting accident, of a crime that he'd never committed. Mary had both the time and contacts in the volunteer community in the town in which I lived, and she was grateful to me for setting the record straight on the crime her husband had mistakenly been accused of committing. She was poised and ready to help.

Running for the Assembly, however, meant leaving both my media jobs and going completely without income for the duration of the race. It would be a hugely expensive proposition from a personal standpoint. Moreover, if anybody knew how tough it would be to win election in such a heavily Republican district, it was me. I well understood how tightly stacked the deck is against challengers to incumbents in elections for the New York Legislature.

Virtually every one of the state's 211 districts was heavily gerrymandered. In 55 of the 61 State Senate districts, for example, one party had an enrollment advantage over the other of 10,000 votes. In the Assembly, 135 of the 150 districts were slanted the same way, and the one I would be running in was one of them. The result of this system was that in the previous two election cycles—a total of 422 separate state legislative elections—only one incumbent had lost.

So, were I to run, I would face long odds, even against a candidate as dismal and uninspiring as Bob Prentiss. Nonetheless, I was thinking about it, and seriously. Donna had taught high school government for a long time. It was her view that citizens have obligations. When you're in a position to do some good, she felt, then you have a duty to make the effort. I found that a compelling argument for me to run, but I hadn't fully and completely made up my mind.

Which was when the party found a way to make up my mind for me.

3

ORGANIZATION MAN

"Since a politician never believes what he says, he is always astonished when others do."—Charles DeGaulle

The *Times Union* always had insisted that I maintain an office in the building, but I seldom had used it. My reporting style was to be on the scene of events worth writing about or visiting people in their offices or homes, where they tend to be more at ease and speak more freely. If I needed to bring in somebody for a meeting, I could always grab a conference room in the newspaper building.

Also, I printed my phone number at the bottom of my column four days a week. That was a crucial mechanism for attracting reader feedback and for picking up tips that could grow into columns. That meant, however, that I could count on the phone in that office ringing, quite literally, 50 to 100 times a day. Such a high volume of phone traffic made it impossible for me to report or write from that office.

Besides, with a laptop computer and a cell phone for picking up voice mail messages, I felt no need to tether myself to that office in an Albany suburb, far away from the often bruising political action in the State Capitol downtown.

Moreover, too many reporters tend to waste their work days and nights hanging around the office. That was always one of my favorite gripes as managing editor. Apparently, some reporters view the newspaper building as some kind of giant, concrete mama. I knew that neither reporters nor columnists are likely to find news in the office. So, I generally filed my four-day-a-week column from wherever I could find a phone. Sometimes, that was the bar of a restaurant called The Bleecker, only a block west of the state capital complex. Or, if I'd finished my reporting early in the day, I would file from a small office in my house just before knocking off work for the day.

Just before 5 p.m. on a gray, dismal Tuesday in late March—during my final week as an employee of the newspaper—I was in my home office filing my column for the next day's paper when the phone rang. It was Lara Jakes, a woman in her mid-20s who worked out of the State Capitol covering politics for the *Times Union*.

"I'm reporting a story," she told me. "There's a rumor floating around here that you're running against Bob Prentiss."

I'd insisted that news of my impending retirement be closely held at the newspaper. There's nothing lamer than a lame-duck newspaper columnist. I wanted to retire quietly and be out the door when news of my departure made its way around town. Clearly, however, with a rumor like this floating around, that wasn't going to happen.

"I've heard that rumor," I said. I explained that Fred Dicker, the state editor of the *New York Post*, had called me several weeks earlier with the same question. I'd told him it was nonsense and asked him where he'd gotten the tip. From a lobbyist, Dicker had told me. At the time, I'd merely been puzzled. Now, about to retire, I was more intrigued.

I told Lara, "I told Dicker that I'm actually going to run for Congress against Sweeney, but I was only hoping that word would get back to Sweeney and make him crazy. Actually, now that I think about it, you're the third or fourth person in the past few months to raise with me the question of whether I would ever run for office. I've told everybody the same thing—'I already have a job, thank you.'"

"Well," Lara said, pressing, "is it true? Are you going to run against Prentiss this year?"

"Look," I said, "I've been asked to run for office for several years now. Everybody with any media prominence in this town gets asked. I've never said yes; I've never said no. I just haven't done it, is all. Yes, I'm retiring as an employee of the paper this Friday, and the paper will have a story to that effect once I'm out the door, but I'll continue a weekly column on a contract basis. I would have to give that up if I ran for anything. Also, I'm not even enrolled in a political party. I haven't been in a party in nearly 15 years. If I were to run for office this year, I couldn't even vote for myself in a primary. I've taken none of the really complicated steps that I would have to take to become a candidate for anything. I also would have to give up my radio show, you realize."

I added, however, that I wasn't ruling out anything once I left the newspaper a few days later. I might apply for a job as a television anchor, I said. I might go to Hollywood. I might buy a burro and go prospecting for uranium in Nevada. Nothing, I assured her, was set in stone except my plans to write more books. That was my top priority.

"Did you talk to Judith Hope?" Lara asked, still pressing.

She couldn't see it, but I was shaking my head wearily at the other end of the phone. Judith Hope was the chairwoman of the New York State Democratic Party. No, I replied. Apparently, this conversation would not end unless I answered with a yes or a no each time a question was asked. Lara then asked if I'd spoken to Jasper Nolan, the Republican chairman of my home county, Saratoga County, about running in the fall for the Assembly. That was a relevant question because the Republican Party leadership openly regarded Prentiss as an embarrassment. Twice, they'd endorsed primary opponents against him. Twice, Prentiss had beaten the party organization with the aid of right-wing fundamentalist Christian activists who sent shivers up and down the spines of regular organization Republicans. No, I told her, I hadn't spoken to Jasper about running that year.

Satisfied that she had no story, Lara finally let me go. After I got off the phone, I sat at my desk, my unfinished column flickering on my laptop's screen, pondering the situation. I now harbored some suspicions about how and why this rumor had begun. Somebody, it seemed, planned to ask me to run for this office and wanted me thinking about the prospect before the question actually was posed. Having fielded a number of queries on whether I might run for some office—two of them at this point from reporters—I realized that I really wasn't sure what I would say if and when the question came up for real.

The 107th Assembly District in which I lived was made up of four towns in two counties. About 39 per cent of the district was comprised of three towns in Saratoga County. I lived in Clifton Park, the largest and most prosperous of those. The bulk of the district, though, was in Albany County, and the Albany County Democratic organization would decide who the party's nominee would be. It was simple math, really.

Moreover, the Albany County Democratic organization was one of the nation's longest lived political machines with a rich, ancient history of shady activity and—in the old days, anyway—fairly open corruption. It traced its roots to the O'Connell family—specifically to the late Dan O'Connell, who'd died at nearly 100 years of age in 1977, two years before I'd arrived in Albany as Rosenfeld's managing editor. "Uncle Dan" O'Connell had been a legendary figure—taciturn, bespectacled, chain-smoking and famous for a broad-brimmed fedora he wore constantly, indoors and out. For a political boss, this guy apparently had been classic in personal style. O'Connell had led the charge to toss out a corrupt Republican machine early in the century and then had presided unchallenged as the county's Democratic potentate for decade after decade.

O'Connell had run the classic urban political machine —tightly disciplined and not overly concerned by the niceties of the law. Routinely, the machine manipulated taxes, judges, grand juries, the electoral process, patronage and government contracts. It was O'Connell's theory that good government meant government with many small jobs for party workers. If that translated into many families tied economically to the machine, then that meant good politics, too, in his mind.

Upon O'Connell's death, leadership of the party had been assumed by Erastus Corning 2nd, a shrewd, charming, Yale-educated aristocrat O'Connell had installed as Albany's mayor before World War II. Corning died in office in 1983, after more than four decades of presiding over city hall. With both O'Connell and Corning now the property of historians, the once-invulnerable machine, as it was so proudly called by so many ordinary Albany citizens, was no longer the potent force it had been during the O'Connell-Corning era.

The Democratic party still maintained a 2-1 enrollment advantage countywide. That number was sustained by an 11-1 Democratic advantage in the city, where Republicans were little more than a rumor. The Republicans had firm control of some key suburbs, however, and had taken two countywide

races in recent years. Moreover, the party chairmen who'd suc-
ceeded Corning had not been strong figures. Unfettered by
control of a rock-solid party structure, County Executive Jim
Coyne had run wild in office—living a frantic life of drinking,
wenching and gambling before a federal jury had tossed him
into prison. Burns was the fourth county chairman since
Corning's death, and he was not a strong leadership figure.
Power and patronage was diffused between the Breslins on the
county level and Jennings in the city, with Jennings holding a
decided edge. Iron control from the top of the Albany County
machine had become a thing of memory.

　　Still, for all the changes, the Albany County Democratic
organization was not at all culturally inclined toward backing
reformers with independent streaks, which is what I certainly
would be in office, and everybody knew it. I therefore found it
difficult to believe that I actually could be the favored candidate
of party officials in the Albany County Democratic organization. Still, I was well known. I had decent relationships with
many key party leaders. And something clearly was afoot, with
my name figuring into whatever it was. I would have to sit
back and wait to see what developed.

　　The following evening, around 9 p.m., I received a call
at home from Liz Bishop, the anchor at Albany's CBS television
affiliate, WRGB-Channel 6.

　　"I hear you're running against Prentiss," Liz said.

　　"Well, it's true that I'm retiring. I have books to do.
Beyond that, though, I'm not sure what else I'm going to do."

　　I then called Cohen at home and warned him that the
Channel 6 news would have a story at 11 on my retirement. I
also told him about the questions directed to me by Dicker, Liz
and Lara about an Assembly run. What are you going to do, he
asked? At this moment, I have no idea, I told him. I'm ending
a three-decade-plus newspaper career this week, and at the

moment that's all I'm focusing on.

Only minutes after I got off the phone with Cohen, I had a call from Jim Brennan, the anchor at Albany's ABC affiliate, WTEN-Channel 10. Are you running, he asked? Who the hell knows, I responded? Then, bowing to family obligation, I called my daughter, Kelly. A few years out of college, she was a reporter and weekend anchor at Albany's NBC affiliate, WNYT-Channel 13.

"Your station's competition will have the story of my retirement," I told her. "They also asked me about whether I'm running for the Assembly. I said I have no firm plans."

So, that night, all three television stations ran the story of my impending retirement. Only Liz mentioned anything on the air about politics. She told viewers that when asked that question, I'd been "non-committal."

The next day, my retirement was a topic of some attention on talk radio. Paul Vandenburgh was the program director and morning drive-time host for WROW AM-590, the station on which I did my one-hour, four-day-a-week talk program beginning at 11 in the morning. As a political moderate, I was what passed for the house radical on WROW. Vandenburgh argued vociferously for conservative Republican principles in a medium where the audience is disproportionately male, middle-aged, affluent and conservative. Nonetheless, Vandenburgh was must-listening for anybody of any political persuasion in government or politics in Albany. He heard everything. There are rumors this morning, Vandenburgh told his listeners, that Lynch is running for the Assembly. Once Vandenburgh announced the existence of a rumor, it was official.

Finally, the following evening—after I'd finished my last work day as an employee of the *Times Union*—the call I'd been awaiting came in on my home phone. On the line was a man I'd never met. That was Tony Catalfamo, chairman of the

Democratic party in the Town of Colonie, which comprised 61 per cent of the 107th Assembly District.

"I heard on Vandenburgh," Catalfamo said, "that you might have some interest in running for the Assembly."

"Yeah, I've heard that, too. I just can't imagine how that rumor got started."

Tony only laughed into the phone. "Well, can we get together?"

Sure, I said. I agreed to call him the following week. That night, I was too exhausted and worn down emotionally from leaving newspaper work after all those years—and from the frenzy of that last, loony week—to consider anything else. The following day, as I savored my first moments of less than full-time employment since my senior year of high school, I had a call from Mike Conners. He was the Albany County comptroller and a guy about my own age whom I liked enormously. Conners was bright and capable and delightfully rowdy—almost nutty enough to be a newspaperman. He also was the son of an assemblyman. His late father, Dick Conners, had served in the seat that Jack McEneny now held.

"Are you going to do it?" he demanded.

"Well, yeah, I might. I'm not making any rock-hard decisions just yet, though."

Conners said he rated me as a 51 to 49 per cent favorite over Prentiss, despite the incumbent's heavy enrollment advantage. He told me that I would have to raise $100,000 to make the race. He noted, too, that my columns over the years had so badly annoyed the legislative leadership that I probably would end up with an office in the basement of the Legislative Office Building, right next to the boiler room, but that I would make a hell of a state legislator.

"I know the routine in the Assembly," Conners told me. "My dad served for years and years. I would love the job, but

I'll never run for it. I stay on as county comptroller because I don't ever want people comparing me with my father. You know, if you pull this off, you'll enter that body with the stature of a 10-year veteran. Everybody will know who you are, and you and the leaders won't be strangers to each other. You'd be one of those rare people in the Assembly—somebody who might actually get something done."

That same weekend I made a call to Mike Burns. If you're with me, I told him, I'm now inclined to do this. I'm with you, he assured me, but Tony has a good deal of say in this because his town of 80,000-plus citizens makes up most of the district. You also, he told me, will have to line up the support of the three Democratic party town leaders in Saratoga County and of Tom Bayly, the Saratoga County Democratic chief. Somebody in the party in Saratoga County, Burns warned, also wanted the nomination.

That somebody, he informed me, was Paul "Butch" Lilac, the supervisor of the Town of Stillwater. I'd never met the guy, but I knew who he was. Lilac was a recently retired high school teacher and coach who'd won routinely as a Democrat in a solidly Republican community, although his margin of victory in local elections had been slipping precipitously in recent years. I took Burns' advice and got on the phone. Bayly was in the hospital, recovering from surgery. His key aide, another party official named Paul Rickard, whose daughter had attended high school with my daughter Kelly, said he would get word of my interest to the county chairman.

I then called Jan Lemon, the chairwoman of the Democratic Party in my own town, Clifton Park, and told her that I was interested in running. I'd known her for years, both from her political involvement and because her son, Josh, and my son, Kevin, had played basketball together as kids. Jan was bright and, by nature, fiercely combative. With her party down nearly 2-1 in enrollment in Clifton Park, she needed those fighting instincts. The night I called her, though, the guy she wanted to fight with was me.

"Did you quit the newspaper so you could run?" she demanded.

No, I told her, I'd retired for other reasons. But now this has come up, and I feel an obligation to pursue it. She informed me that she'd already committed her support to Lilac. How would I like to wait a year and run for town board? No thanks, I told her. What I would like to do instead is come before your town Democratic committee. I would like the chance to explain to your committee people what I have to offer as a candidate in a race like this. I understand the issues, I told her, and I enjoy unusually high name recognition.

"Oh," Jan informed me, "you'd be surprised at how many people have never heard of you. After all, nobody reads newspapers any more, do they?"

So, all of a sudden, I was encountering a bump in the road in exploring the possibility of running for the Assembly. That bump's name was Jan Lemon, and—if I really decided to do this—it would have to be rolled over.

Two nights later, I got together with Tony Catalfamo and some other people. We gathered at a downtown Albany restaurant for a meeting of Albany's left-leaning Robert F. Kennedy Democratic Club. State Comptroller Carl McCall, widely rumored to have his eye on the governor's mansion, was the club's speaker that evening. Once McCall finished a rousing talk on the evils of Republicanism, the group I'd hooked up with then moved out to Colonie Democratic Party headquarters in offices less than a mile down the road from my old professional home, the *Times Union*.

Tony Catalfamo turned out to be a smiling, soft-spoken guy who held down a day job as chief of maintenance services for the Albany School District. With him were Conners, McEneny and two key members of the Colonie Town Democratic Committee, Shirley Brown and Joe McElroy. Shirley was an experienced political operative who'd been in politics for decades. McElroy was a ruddy, good-natured guy who operated a successful vending machine business and had served as a ward leader in the city before bumping heads with Jennings and moving his political activities to the suburbs, where McElroy now lived.

We sat around a conference table and talked for 90 minutes. Yes, I said, I guess I did want to run for this office if the path were open. I felt, as Conners had told me over the phone, that I had a chance to do some good if I could win a seat in the Assembly. I sat there, responding to questions about public policy matters and outlining my views on what needed to be done in the Legislature.

Finally, Tony Catalfamo told he that he would back me and would urge his committee members to do the same. He also volunteered to call Butch Lilac and tell him that. Tony didn't say so directly, but that call would signal to Lilac that he would face a primary battle if he pressed for the nomination. And, since three in five of the district's Democratic voters lived in Colonie, Lilac would face stiff odds in any such primary fight.

If you're going to do this, McEneny advised me, then you'd better immediately check with every major elected official in the party and make sure that you have each and every one of them behind you. Those rings must be kissed, he warned.

"Every elected official wants to be the first person told," McEneny explained, "and he or she can take offense if he or she isn't in the loop early on. It's a simple matter of respect."

I nodded, digesting the advice. Culturally, I was coming to realize, the process of getting into politics seemed to enjoy certain similarities to joining the Cosa Nostra.

4

THE GANG'S ALL HERE

"Politicians are the same the world over. They promise to build a
bridge even where there is no river."—Nikita Khruschev

Like Albany politics—at once profoundly venal yet infused with the loftiest of rhetoric—New York's ornate, red-roofed State Capitol building and the sleek, modern, sprawling Nelson A. Rockefeller Empire State Plaza that is the Capitol's strange bedfellow represent the starkest of contrasts.

The Capitol itself occupies the crest of a high, steep hill, looking out east over Albany's 300-year-old downtown and the Hudson River beyond. The Capitol is classic political architecture. It's clearly a turn-of-the-century government building and conspicuously less elegant than the neo-classic, Greek revival State Education Department building to its north, with its soaring white columns and the block-long cascade of steps linking it with the sidewalk of Albany's Washington Avenue.

The Empire State Plaza, though, is something else entirely. Stretched out to the south of the Capitol, across the narrow strip of pavement that is State Street, the Plaza both sprawls through the City of Albany and towers over it. It's a gigantic mall flanked on both sides by soaring modern buildings girded in white marble, the tallest of which is the 40-story-high Corning Tower. In 1983, it was named after Erastus Corning 2nd as the mayor lay on his deathbed in a Boston hospital.

"We're pushing this name through in a hurry," then-governor Mario Cuomo told a *Times Union* editorial board meeting one afternoon. "The reason for the rush is obvious."

"Yes," said one editorial board member, "but wouldn't it be more appropriate to name a non-bid contract after him?"

Actually, Corning's name on such a contract would have been utterly appropriate, but the tower was the perfect monument nonetheless. Without Corning, there would have been no Empire State Plaza. The project was hatched during the 1960s in the fertile mind of Nelson Rockefeller. At a time when New York's 18 million citizens constituted a full 10 per cent of the nation's population—when New York truly was the Empire State, with a huge voting block in the 435-member House of Representatives—Rockefeller was the classic bricks-and-mortar chief executive. He built like an Egyptian Pharaoh whenever he could push a construction project through the Legislature. Rocky taxed and spent lavishly, secure in the conviction that he would end up President sooner or later and could then pay off all the state's bills as they came due with federal dollars. New York's governor, legislators complained, seemed to suffer from an incurable edifice complex.

The Empire State Plaza dwarfed any of his other building projects. Rockefeller envisioned an Albany Brasilia—an incongruously modern government complex that would eradicate several old, ethnic Albany neighborhoods and displace between five and 10 per cent of the city's population. Aside from its skyscrapers, the plaza also would boast a cavernous underground concourse with shops, restaurants, parking lots and a convention center. It also would feature a structure housing several theaters that Rocky wanted to call the Empire State Performing Arts Center.

When the architects brought Rockefeller their model of the project, he was eating breakfast in the governor's mansion on Eagle Street. He studied the model closely. Then, without a word, Rockefeller reached out and removed one small, monolithic model of a skyscraper and replaced it on the model with his soft-boiled egg in a cup.

"That's what I want," the governor rasped out.

That's what he got. Today, the Empire State Performing Arts Center is a massive, oblong structure—a concrete dirigible with a conspicuous weight problem resting at a sharp angle atop a slim stem of concrete. Nobody calls it the Empire State Performing Arts Center. Instead, the building is simply referred to as The Egg. For a long time, the plaza itself was known locally as the South Mall because of Rockefeller's plan to eventually build another version of it on the north side of the Capitol. He never did, and the plaza is referred to today, as often as not, as Rocky's erection.

When Rockefeller first proposed the project, the leaders of the Legislature were apoplectic. No, they said; we won't approve bonding for any project so monumental. Blithely, Rockefeller walked right around them. He persuaded O'Connell and Corning to have Albany County issue the bonds.

Corning's reward? The private insurance agency he owned received an exclusive, non-bid contract from the Rockefeller administration to insure the entire project. The bulldozers began rolling, and the fat premium checks began to be deposited in the bank account of Corning's insurance agency.

The modernistic, marble-coated Legislative Office Building across the Plaza from The Egg is where I was prowling the day after the meeting with Tony Catalfamo and the others. Line up all the elected officials, Jack McEneny had advised, so that's what I was doing. I hadn't been able to reach the all-powerful speaker of the Assembly, a New York lawyer named Sheldon Silver. Shelly had been in budget meetings all day. By phone, however, I'd touched base with Jennings, who'd said he would support me for the nomination. If anybody was key to making this work, it was Jennings, but we'd long had a cordial relationship, and I figured that I could count on him. I'd left a call with the office of Mike McNulty, the metro area's Democratic congressman. Now, I was running down all the Democratic state legislators from the Albany metro area for face-to-face meetings.

The five-county Albany metro area, with just under a million people, was represented by nine state legislators. Five were Republicans, including Bob Prentiss, and four were Democrats. One of the Democrats, McEneny, was already in my corner. Another of the Democrats, Assemblyman Ron Canestrari, was a key figure in the Assembly political structure. He was co-chair of the Democratic Assembly Campaign Committee, generally referred to as DACC, the majority party's political organization. Him I saw first.

Canestrari was a slim, soft-spoken lawyer in his mid-50s. He was the former mayor of Cohoes, a small, fading industrial city just north of Albany on the Hudson's west bank. I knew him, although not well, and his backing was crucial.

"I'm pretty sure," I told him, "that Lilac has already spoken to you."

"He has," Canestrari confirmed.

"Well," I said candidly, "if he hangs in on this there could be a primary, Ron."

"I certainly hope not," Canestrari said.

Canestrari was careful not to commit himself either to me or Lilac, but I was certain that the moment I left his office he would be on the phone with Burns, who'd already assured me of his support if I ran. So, I figured that, ultimately, I could count on Ron Canestrari, too. Assemblyman Paul Tonko, a gregarious engineer who chaired the Assembly's energy committee, was openly and gladly supportive. That left only State Senator Neil Breslin, the younger brother of Mike Breslin, the Albany County executive. I'd put in a call to Mike Breslin, too, and he got back to me on my cell phone as I left Tonko's office.

"I'm probably going to run, Mike," I said into the cell phone.

"Then I'm with you," Mike Breslin assured me.

A few moments later, as I reached the hallway outside Neil's office, my cell phone beeped in my pocket. Once more, it was Mike Breslin.

"Now, look," he said. "I know I told you I'd back you. But you did check with Mike Burns, right?"

"He's on board," I replied.

"Good," the county executive told me. "In that case, I'm still with you."

Neil Breslin gave me forty-five minutes of his time. He overflowed with both warnings and advice. Canestrari and DACC, he said, would be glad to help me in this race, but there were conditions. I would have to raise $15,000 as quickly as possible and use it to hire DACC's approved pollster, a Boston firm called Kiley & Company. If the poll showed that this was a competitive race, then DACC would leap into it with both feet. They would design and deliver my direct mail pieces, which constitute the primary form of advertising in a state legislative race. They would handle my broadcast advertising. They would supply capable campaign management. I would not, he stressed, have time to manage my own campaign. I would be too busy meeting voters and raising money.

Fund-raising, Neil Breslin told me, was a horrible experience. I would find it humiliating and demeaning. I would

have to impose on friends and relatives and complete strangers
as well—and for specific amounts. He also warned that, with
me as the Democratic candidate, the Republicans might hold
their noses and decide to find some cushy, high-paying job for
Prentiss in state government so they could put up a better candidate and save the seat. Neil was gracious and informative and
said they he would be happy to put a Lynch campaign sign in
the window of the Breslin brothers' highly visible campaign
headquarters on Albany's Central Avenue.

I returned to my home office to spend the rest of the day
on the phone, talking to leaders of the Independence Party, the
Conservative Party and the Liberal Party, all of whose parties
were on the New York ballot and whose ballot lines could be
useful to me in varying degree. I merely wanted them to know
that I probably would be doing this and urged them to consider
cross-endorsing me if I did. Later on, I left a voice mail message for Prentiss. I thought it was time to let him know where
I was on all this.

I'd known Prentiss casually, as I'd known most of the
other legislators from the Albany metro area. He was a stocky,
bald guy in his 60s who'd always struck me as a reasonably
jovial political hack—short on intellect and ability but possessed of no conspicuous malice. He was famous in the
Assembly for his interminable, incoherent floor speeches and
for an incident a few years earlier in which, during a debate
over an anti-abortion bill, Prentiss had turned to an Assembly
staffer and asked how many months were contained in a
trimester.

For years, he'd operated an employment agency on the side while holding down various political jobs as his real source of income. He'd served 19 years as one of Albany County's 39 part-time county legislators when he'd suddenly decided to challenge incumbent Arnold Proskin in a primary election for the Assembly.

Proskin was a shrewd, smiling suburban lawyer who'd always had surprising success running in a Democratic county. He'd served briefly as district attorney and a judge and had been enjoying an undistinguished career as a minority member of the Assembly when Prentiss had gone after him. Arnie had been savaged by some *Times Union* stories on his law practice. The stories indicated that Proskin might have exerted undue influence on some rich, elderly clients and ended up improperly benefiting from their wills.

At the time, nobody had given the virtually unknown Prentiss a chance against a proven vote-getter like Arnie Proskin. Prentiss had, however, enlisted the support of a quiet but startlingly powerful group of fundamentalist Christians who were convinced on the basis of his voting record that Proskin was insufficiently anti-gay. In a general election, Proskin would have won handily against the bumbling, inarticulate Prentiss. In a primary, however—with a lower voter turnout— the Christian Coalition types seemed particularly enthused about taking out Proskin, a Jew, and outhustled the regular Republican organization. Two years later, the regular GOP ran a bright, attractive Republican lawyer named Peter Crummey against Prentiss. Again, the Christians defeated the old lions of the Albany County Republican Party.

After that, Prentiss cruised. In Saratoga County, GOP chief Jasper Nolan was worried about stirring up the Christian right any more than absolutely necessary, so he became Prentiss's new best friend. In 1998, because of problems with a key state employees union, the Democratic Party was unable to field a strong candidate against Prentiss, and he essentially got a free ride from both parties to a 2-1 reelection win.

As I awaited Prentiss's return call, I finally got a call-back from Shelly Silver, the speaker of the Assembly. Silver was one of the three people, along with the governor and the State Senate Majority leader, who actually ran the state on a more or less equal footing. I'd known Shelly only slightly. He was a solemn, thoughtful man not widely noted for his sense of humor. As such, he was an incongruous leader in any law-making body, but especially in the New York Assembly.

Shelly Silver presided over nearly 100 of the most diverse and varied politicians in the state—from moderate, white-bread upstate Democrats to far-left representatives of the minority community in the five boroughs of New York City, who made up more than half of Silver's Democratic conference in the Assembly. The speaker, therefore, was pulled in several different directions at once every day of the week. Where his predecessors had tended to deal with such pressures with jokes, back-slapping and—sometimes—by outright bullying, Shelly was serious and stoic and known for playing his cards close to his vest.

Typical of the way he dealt with opposition was the way he'd responded to me the previous year, when I'd been report-ing out a column on hate crimes legislation. Silver was for it. I had reservations about the bill's language. It was my policy as a columnist, before criticizing anybody or opposing any posi-tion on an important public policy issue, to give the other side a chance to change my mind before I committed my own thoughts to print. In a private, face-to-face conversation in a meeting room in the Capitol, after a Silver press conference in which he'd backed the hate crimes bill, I'd explained to him my concerns with this proposed law.

"I admire the bill's intent," I told him. "But, the way it's written, it punishes people not only for what they do but for what they were thinking at the time. It's one thing to punish criminal intent—say, with the law against assault with intent to kill. It's another thing entirely to punish a person's motives, what's in his heart rather than what's in his head at the time of the crime. I would rather see a law that forces a judge to take those motives into account in arriving at a sentence rather than a law that makes thinking a particular thought or feeling a particular emotion a crime."

I'd expected an argument, but he'd only shrugged.

"Well," said the Speaker of the New York Assembly, "that's a point of view."

So, when Silver called that afternoon, I expected him to be non-committal, but he wasn't—not quite, anyway.

"We would love to have you with us," he said. "We would love to have you as a member of the Assembly. But we have rules."

He then explained to me what Neil Breslin had explained earlier—that there was this little matter of raising 15 grand and then doing well in the poll paid for by that money. If I did that, then fine, Shelly and his campaign organization would line up behind me. If not, DACC would give me two mailings, each worth about $8,000, and wish me a lot of luck in the general election. The staffer who ran DACC, Shelly told me, was one of his key aides, a guy named John Longo. I should get the check for $15,000 to Longo, the speaker said.

Shortly thereafter, I heard from Prentiss.

"I'm tilting toward running against you," I told him, "and you have my pledge that if I actually do it, I'll run a positive, gentlemanly campaign and behave toward you with respect and consideration."

Prentiss was subdued in his response. He said he'd

heard a rumor of my interest.

"Isn't this sort of a come-down for you?" he asked me. "Wouldn't you be happier in Congress?"

I explained to him my reasons for considering the Legislature rather than Congress. I also told him that I was headed for South Carolina later in the month to play some golf, sit in the sun after the long Albany winter and to think this thing through. I said I would let him know my decision before I made any public announcement.

"What's holding me back," I said, "is your reputation as a ferocious campaigner and the fear that, if I actually do this, you'll kick my butt."

He thanked me for the call. He hung up pretty sure that we would be going up against one another in the fall. I suppose that, at this point, I was pretty sure that was how it all would work out, too.

A few days later, I found myself sitting at a restaurant table awaiting lunch with Paul Vandenburgh of WROW, U.S. Rep. John Sweeney and Bill Powers, the New York Republican chairman. I liked both politicians on a personal level, and this lunch had been scheduled some time earlier, before all this political business with me running had come up. A slave to punctuality, I'd arrived at the restaurant first. Sweeney showed up a few minutes later. Congress was out of session, so he—like me—was in jeans and a sport shirt.

"So," my representative in Congress told me, "we get to have lunch one last time before you run against us."

"Maybe I won't do it," I said. "Maybe I'll say the hell

with the Assembly and run against you instead."

Sweeney smiled. "Yeah, but you won't. Do everybody a favor and talk to Bill before you do this, okay?"

"I will," I promised.

Which, in fact, I later did by phone. Why run with them, Powers asked me? If I'm going to do this, I explained to to the state GOP chief, I want to serve in the majority conference; I see no purpose in doing what Prentiss does—sitting around with nothing to say about anything and collecting a public paycheck every two weeks just for taking up space. Well, you might win this, Powers told me. It could be done, he said. But I wouldn't like the people I would be dealing with, he assured me.

These Friday luncheons with Vandenburgh and various political figures were a fairly regular occasion. The group varied, but the topic was always the same—politics. Well, politics and sports. Okay, politics and sports and women. Sweeney was divorced and a relentless playboy. Needling him with threats about writing about his love life was one of my great recreations.

"John doesn't care what you write about him," Powers said at lunch that day. "After Clinton, who the hell cares any more?"

Later in the day, back in my home office, I received a call from Bill Hammond, the Capitol reporter for the *Daily Gazette*, one of the three daily newspapers in the immediate Albany metro area.

I'd competed against the *Gazette* for 21 years. When I'd

finally left the *Times Union*, the newspaper's circulation had grown by 36 per cent while the *Gazette*'s had declined by 19 per cent. I certainly couldn't take credit for all that, or even most of it, but those numbers represented many millions of dollars of revenue lost to the *Gazette* and its owner, a guy named Jack Hume, who'd achieved such remarkable success in the newspaper business in a time-honored fashion—by inheriting the newspaper from his family. I'd met Hume once or twice over the years. I didn't recall him being particularly friendly, so I wasn't at all sure how my candidacy, if one actually developed, might be treated by Jack Hume's newspaper.

Hammond asked me if I were running. Could be, I said; I'll let you know when I get back from South Carolina. I was pleasantly surprised on Sunday when his story came out. It seemed complete, more or less accurate and—more crucially—fair. Hammond wrote:

ALBANY—Longtime newspaper columnist Dan Lynch confirmed Friday that he is considering running against Assemblyman Robert Prentiss, R-Colonie, in the fall election.

"It's possible," Lynch said Friday from his home in Clifton Park. "I feel very strongly both ways at the moment."

Lynch, 54, said several people have urged him to run since March 28, when he announced his retirement from the *Times Union* of Albany after 33 years as a full-time journalist. He said he has had "very preliminary conversations" with party officials but has made no decision about a candidacy.

"I'm not going to say no to anything right now, and I'm not going to say yes," he said. "I'm going to go to South Carolina and play some golf, is what I'm going to do right now."

Prentiss said he learned about the possibility Friday morning when Lynch, whom he described as an old friend, called to say he was thinking of seeking the Democratic nomination in Prentiss' 107th Assembly District.

"He said he was going on vacation for a few days, down to the sunny beaches of South Carolina, to do some reflecting, and when he returned he would let me know his final decision," said Prentiss, now in his third two-year term in the Assembly. "If he did decide to go, he pledged, as I recall, a positive, gentlemanly, issue-based campaign."

The story ran 16 column inches over four columns. It quoted McEneny on what a terrific candidate I would be, and pointed out that the Public Employees Federation, an important state workers union, had scheduled a "Dan Lynch Night" to thank me for some columns I'd done supporting state workers in their fight for a fair contract with the George Pataki administration. Hammond managed to have me working at the *Times Union* for 24 years instead of 21. Beyond that, however, the story contained few errors.

There's an old saying in newspaper work. It goes like this: "Everything you read in the newspaper is totally accurate and fair in every minute particular, except for that rare item of which you have personal knowledge. That article will be invariably screwed up in some way, large or small." I had reason, later in the campaign, to understand what a dead-on truth that was.

The following day, I had a call from Tim O'Brien, a *Times Union* reporter I'd been involved in hiring some years earlier. I told him pretty much what I'd told Hammond. The *Times Union* story ran the same day as the *Gazette*'s. It was shorter, 10 inches instead of 16, but it contained no errors.

Even though I was no longer a warrior in that particular journalistic battle, I took some satisfaction in that.

After the newspaper reporters started calling, though, I
placed a call to Kevin Dailey. He was my lawyer and a personal
friend of some year's standing. Kevin had been the supervisor
of Clifton Park, switching back and forth between parties during his career in local politics. He'd been the Democratic
party's candidate against Prentiss in 1996, coming within a
hair's breadth of knocking him off. I was well aware that Kevin
was bitter about the election loss. He'd grown up in Clifton
Park and had felt betrayed by his neighbors and local constituents.

"Should I do this?" I asked him.

Don't do it, he warned. You'll lose narrowly, as I did.
DACC is made up of a bunch of left-wing nuts. They have a
nearly 2-1 party advantage in the Assembly, and they don't care
about this seat. The Colonie organization is worthless. Butch
Lilac will try to screw you in Stillwater. Jack McEneny and
Ron Canestrari will view you as a rival and won't help. Jan
Lemon will do nothing for you in Clifton Park. The *Times
Union* will bend over backwards to avoid the appearance of
favoritism and won't cover your campaign.

"Well, yeah," I said to Kevin, "but do you really think I
shouldn't do it?"

A few days later, as I was driving home from the radio
station after doing my program, Jack McEneny called me on
my cell phone. He'd just pulled the district's enrollment numbers from the new registration booklet. I'd known that the

107th was the state's fastest-growing district. It now contained roughly 137,000 people when all the Assembly districts had been drawn a decade earlier for 120,000.

"These new numbers are pretty grim," Jack told me. "The growth is all in Saratoga County, where it's solidly Republican."

Total enrollment in the 107th: 93,367. Total Republicans: 39,129, or 41.9 per cent. Total Democrats: 25,716, or 25.5 per cent. Independents: 25,716, or 25.6 per cent. Another 4,000 or so voters were scattered among the minor parties, with half of them enrolled in the Conservative Party, which was virtually certain to endorse Prentiss.

"That's a steep hill," Jack said.

Which it was, certainly. The fact is that few of the people who hold public office ever face real fights. No incumbent Democrat or Republican representing the Albany metro area ran without a distinct enrollment advantage. If I won election in this Republican district, that feat would constitute a stunning upset against long odds.

So, no matter how strongly I was being urged to run and no matter how useful to the public I thought I could be in office, this was a tough decision.

Just before I left town for South Carolina, Lilac gave an interview to the *Gazette*, complaining about the interest in my candidacy by party bigwigs.

"I've been an office-holder in the Town of Stillwater for 25 years," Lilac fumed to the *Gazette*'s Bill Hammond. "That's half my life working for the principles of the Democratic Party.

I would be insulted if I didn't get the nomination over an independent, to be honest with you."

Lilac's attitude was pretty much what I'd expected. One of the huge problems with the political system—one of the key reasons so many office-holders in New York and elsewhere tend to be such substandard people, devoid of ideas and depressingly short on brains or basic integrity—is the enduring belief in political organizations that the only people worthy of serving in public office are party people who've devoted their lives to partisan causes. Like Lilac, most party people tend to be horrified by independent reformers who've achieved notoriety and prominence in some other field coming into the system from the outside.

That's one of the key factors keeping capable people in business or academia out of politics. The political hacks who've lived off the system for years simply don't want them. Whatever those outsiders might have accomplished in the real world, they haven't paid their dues to the party organization.

Phone calls from Albany to South Carolina kept us informed on events back home. The weekly newspapers in the district were running stories on my interest in running for the Assembly. If I decided to run, this publicity would have real value. Also, I was told in one call, Lilac was now under heavy pressure to get out of the race. In a *Times Union* story, his tone was markedly different from the one he'd exhibited in the *Gazette* piece before I'd left town. Lilac now was saying that he would make up his mind on running in a few weeks and wanted to meet with me before deciding. Joe McElroy called to inform me that both of us were scheduled to appear the following week before the Colonie Democratic Committee.

"You're sure to get the committee's endorsement," McElroy told me. He added that Tony wanted to make that endorsement public immediately to send a message to the

Saratoga County Democrats, like Jan Lemon, who were backing Lilac. The message would be that I had 61 per cent of the Democratic vote behind me and that a primary would be sheer futility on Lilac's part. I'll be there for that meeting, I assured McElroy.

Later in the week, Jan Lemon called Donna at our rented beachfront condo to ask about Donna taking a crowd of her high school government students to the state Democratic convention, which would be held later that month in Albany. Gee, Jan said, there sure has been a lot of publicity about Dan considering this run. Rather gleefully, Jan noted that LeBrun and Channel 10's political commentator, John McLoughlin, were saying in print and on the air that it would be a mistake for me to run—that the process is too dirty and that I was too reform-oriented and stiff-necked to tolerate it. Jan seemed to think that was bad publicity for my candidacy. I didn't see it that way.

I returned home to Clifton Park more inclined to do it than not. I watched tapes of the television discussions on the race that had been aired during my absence. Channel 10's McLoughlin seemed to think the entire matter hilarious. A journalist contemplating running for office? How laughable, he was saying.

I'd made regular appearances on McLoughlin's Sunday morning program until some months earlier, when it had finally occurred to me that his program was not an environment in which I felt comfortable professionally. McLoughlin had never met a politician or law enforcement figure he wasn't eager to fawn over. He seemed to lack any functional grasp of a journalist's obligation to fairly assess the conduct of people in power in public institutions. McLoughlin's idea of enterprise reporting was to go out on the street with a camera operator and conduct unscientific interviews with ordinary people as they passed by on the sidewalk, asking their views on various public issues, usually minor ones. I expected that, if I did run, he would openly be an enemy. Part of that suspicion was fueled by my knowledge that McLoughlin was trying to position himself for a job with the State Senate Republicans if his contract with Channel 10 wasn't renewed.

Before I'd left town, I'd spoken to Joe McElroy about managing my campaign. McElroy was a seasoned political pro. He'd managed one of Jennings' campaigns before he and the mayor had suffered a falling out. McElroy was favorably inclined, and Jack McEneny spoke highly of his skills. We were to meet to discuss terms upon my return from Myrtle Beach. First, though, I had three chores to perform. One, I had to meet with Lilac face-to-face. Two, I had to see if the Colonie Democrats really would endorse me. Three, I had to tell the *Times Union* that my conversations about running were growing serious now. It was time for me to suspend my column until I knew for sure where this was going.

Lilac and I met for lunch at a diner. He turned out to be a thick-set guy a few years older than I was, pleasant enough but not at all polished. I told him that I'd once met his brother, an Air Force officer, at the White House, when his brother had been an air attaché in the Reagan administration. Butch's brother had later retired and moved to the Middle East to run the Saudi Air Force. Butch confided to me that his brother had loaned him $7,000 to help him meet the DACC figure.

"I won't wage a primary fight against you," he told me over a tuna fish salad sandwich. "But I'm unhappy about this. I gave the party a lot of service over the years."

"Butch," I told him, "I've provided public service myself—not to the party but to the people, as a journalist. There are a good many ways to serve, after all."

I urged him to get out of the Assembly race and, instead, to run for Congress against Sweeney. After all, I pointed out, half the congressional district's voters were in the county where Lilac had run for office for a quarter century. Hillary Clinton would be running for the Senate, which would bring out every Democrat on election day, even during a nuclear attack. Lilac said he would think about it. If he did, I knew he wouldn't run. Sweeney had only one term under his belt, but he also enjoyed a district with a 2-1 enrollment edge. All the incumbents did.

None of these political people was willing to take a chance on a real fight.

That evening, Butch and I showed up separately in Colonie for the meeting of the town Democratic committee. I waited outside in a conference room while he made his pitch for a half hour. We shook hands as Butch left. Then it was my turn.

About two dozen committee people were seated, classroom-style, before an open area in a meeting room. I spoke briefly, telling them that I was glad for this opportunity to address them and that I was interested in running because I thought I could be instrumental in solving some of the long-term problems that afflicted the state. I spoke to them about tax load, energy costs, failing schools and the need to create more and better jobs. I talked to them about the coming crisis in health care for the elderly, who were already 20 per cent of the state population and would be nearer to 25 per cent in another decade or so.

"The sun is shining economically," I said. "The time to fix the roof is now, before it starts to rain again."

I took questions for a half hour. After that, as I was leaving, Tony came out to catch me before I got in my car.

"You were endorsed unanimously," he said. "You're our candidate."

And, as I pondered what had happened, I realized that I was really in this thing now. I called the newspaper the following day. I told Cohen that these conversations about my running were getting serious and asked that my column be suspended until I made a formal decision. I needed the paper's permission to suspend the column because my contract permitted immediate suspension only if both sides agreed. To my surprise, Cohen was opposed. Think it over, please, I suggested. Later in the day, he got back to me. The newspaper had received a press release from the Colonie Town Committee that the committee had endorsed me as its candidate for the Assembly.

Yeah, Cohen told me, I guess we should think about suspending the column.

5

WINGING IT

"Politics has got so expensive that it takes a lot of money even to get beat with"—Will Rogers

❖   ❖   ❖

Once reporters began calling for her response to my endorsement by the Colonie Democrats, Jan Lemon went nuclear. For starters, she regarded reporters as vermin. She couldn't control what they wrote, and she felt they usually missed the point of whatever might be going on. Two, they were calling today for Jan's reaction to a development that was news to her.

She immediately got on the phone with Tony to express her displeasure. She did it in the sort of vivid terms generally reserved for a dog who embarrasses himself on the living room rug. Well, Tony told her in his most placating tone, I'm sorry you're upset, but what's done is done. By the time Jan got me on the phone to invite me to a meeting of her own town committee, she'd calmed down somewhat. In our conversation, she was merely seething.

"We here in Clifton Park wanted to go first," she complained. "Colonie always dominates the district, and it's not right. Nobody told us we couldn't go first. After all, both candidates are from Saratoga County, not Albany County. And, by the way, who told the press?"

"Jan," I said, "I don't tell the Colonie Democratic Committee what to do. What do I know?"

Actually, I knew enough to understand that if Jan had managed to convince the Clifton Park Democrats to endorse Lilac—which, I suspected, was pretty much what she'd had in mind—then the Colonie Democrats would have been less likely to support me. The Colonie people would have understood that backing me after Clifton Park had backed Lilac would mean a primary fight for the Assembly seat, and nobody wanted actual bloodshed. With Colonie endorsing first, however— and backing me instead of Lilac—Jan was now faced with the chore of convincing her committee to reject that endorsement and to throw themselves into a primary battle they probably would lose.

In an effort to settle her down, I phoned Joe McElroy and asked him to call her and take the rap for the press release. He got back to me to say that Jan was more subdued after that conversation. She'd admitted to him, he said, that I was the better choice.

"She said that with you as the candidate," Joe told me, "the Democrats have a chance to win in November."

Later in the day, however, Joe called me again. He'd spoken to Jan one more time. Her committee would listen to what I had to say that night, he said, but they wouldn't endorse. Jan had re-thought the whole situation, apparently, and had gotten mad all over again.

Later in the day, Cohen called. Yes, he said, the *Times
Union* would go along with my request that my column be suspended until I made up my mind on running. He then read me
a proposed editor's note that the paper would print that coming
Sunday. The editor's note informed readers that the decision to
suspend the column had been made by the newspaper's management.

I don't like the language, I told him. That wording
makes it seem that I've been guilty of some ethical breach by
continuing the column while I considered the prospect of running. It sounded as though the paper had discontinued the column as punishment. If I do end up running, I explained, that
faulty interpretation surely will be used against me, and it's
neither fair nor accurate. The notice must say, I told him, that
the suspension of the column was initiated at my request.

No, Cohen said. His top deputies had urged him for
weeks to suspend the column. The act of finally doing so, he
argued, had been the result of an internal decision. I told him
that I was utterly unconcerned with what anybody but me had
advised him. The decision to continue running the column after
my name was mentioned for this office, I pointed out, had been
solely Cohen's decision; it never had been the decision of his
deputies. What's important here, I told him, was what I'd told
Times Union publisher Dave White several days earlier and my
direct, personal request to Cohen the day before that the column
be suspended—a request that Cohen initially had refused to
honor. Cohen remained adamant. I remained bent on protecting myself.

"Why won't you print the truth?" I demanded. "Why are
you so intent on misrepresenting this?"

Well, Cohen suggested, let's split the baby and say it
was a mutual decision. No, I replied. This is about me, and I
insist on publication of the truth, the whole truth and nothing

but the truth. He said he would get back to me. I immediately placed a call to the publisher, asking that he return my call on a matter of some importance. Instead, it was Cohen who got back to me. He'd revised the notice. It now read:

> Editor's note: Dan Lynch, whose commentary appears in this spot each Sunday, is considering a run for the New York state Assembly. In the interest of neutrality, Lynch requested and the newspaper agreed that his column will be discontinued until he makes a final decision about a candidacy.

"Thank you," I said.

That evening, the Clifton Park Democratic Committee met in a hotel conference room. Lilac spoke to them first. As he left and I entered, I counted roughly two dozen people in the room, only one of whom I knew—Jan Lemon.

I spoke to the group for 10 minutes or so, pointing out that I'd lived in Clifton Park for two decades, had raised two children in that community and felt that the town that was my home deserved better, more effective representation in the Assembly. I then took questions.

Immediately, one guy got into my face. Why, he demanded, was I unwilling to leave the Assembly seat to Lilac? Why wouldn't I run instead against Sweeney for Congress or Joe Bruno for the State Senate? I explained that entering the House of Representatives at nearly 55 years of age wouldn't leave me time to gain enough seniority to do much for the congressional district. Also, I explained, were I to run for the State Senate and were somehow to beat Bruno as a Democrat in that overwhelmingly GOP district, I would enter that body as a member of the minority party with no say whatever over anything important.

"Running against Bruno," this guy argued, "would constitute a service to the party. The Democrats don't need another assemblyman; we need another Democrat in the State Senate."

I responded to a number of questions about issues—about the need to lower local taxes and electricity costs, about economic development and school funding. Throughout all that, however, this guy kept at me, loudly and with gleeful bellicosity, making the same point over and over. Finally, I said to him, "I appreciate the intensity of your conviction. I really do understand your suggestion. Now, it's time for you to understand that I'm rejecting that suggestion—unequivocally."

At the end of the session, Jan informed me that the committee would not take a vote that evening—nor ever, I concluded. Maybe Jan couldn't stop me from getting the nomination, and she seemed to realize that she couldn't, but she would be damned if her committee would actually endorse me.

And they never did.

The following evening, Lilac and I were again on stage. Separately, of course, we went before the entire Saratoga County Democratic Committee.

The meeting took place in a large dining room in a diner in Malta, one of the three Saratoga County towns in the

Assembly district and a community in which the Democratic Party was badly outgunned. The entire Malta Town Democratic Committee consisted of precisely two guys, Rick Morse and Skip Carrier. Both were full-time employees of the Assembly Democratic majority who prudently maintained this local political involvement to ensure the continued flow of state paychecks.

By the time I'd arrived, Lilac was finishing his presentation and hustling out the door. When my time came to speak, I found myself at the head of a U-shaped table gazing out on about 35 people. Jan was on hand, as was Saratoga County Democratic Chairman Tom Bayly in his wheelchair. I'd been trained as a reporter and writer, not as a speaker. Three years of babbling extemporaneously on radio, though, seemed to have left me with vastly improved public speaking skills. I did about 10 minutes on the reasons for my interest in making this race. During the question and answer session that followed, I was asked if I'd been taken on as a client by DACC.

"They first insist that I raise 15 grand," I explained. Then, with considerably more confidence than I actually felt, I added, "So, I will."

Unlike the session with the Clifton Park Democrats the night before, I found myself treated courteously by the Saratoga County committee. I was asked probing questions, but I wasn't dragged into combat with anybody. As I left the diner, Paul Rickard caught up with me. I'd done well, he assured me. I'd demonstrated a strong command of the issues. Lilac, on the other hand, had responded to questions about issues by promising to form a committee to help him formulate his positions. Lilac also had promised the committee that he wouldn't wage a primary fight against me, Rickard said. If Butch lost the nomination, he'd pledged to return to Stillwater and serve as the best supervisor he could be. I recalled my lunch with Lilac and harbored doubts that he would accept any loss with such grace.

"Well, we'll see," I told Rickard.

When I got back home, I called McElroy and briefed him on the session. He was pleased. He also informed me that it wasn't necessary that the Saratoga County Democrats formally endorse me, as long as they didn't endorse anybody else. What was necessary, he said, since I wasn't an enrolled Democrat, were the signatures of both Mike Burns and Tom Bayly on a legal document known under New York state election law as a Wilson-Pakula Proclamation. Both county chairs had to sign that document before they could put on the Democratic ballot a candidate who was not a member of their party. If the county chairmen signed that document, he said, it didn't matter what the county committee did or did not do.

The following day, I attended one of our regular WROW luncheons. A dozen people were on hand—media people, assorted politicians and their hangers-on. The moment I entered the restaurant, the needling began.

"Hey, Jerry," New York state's Republican chairman, Bill Powers, said to Jennings, "are you going to let this guy into your party?"

"Hell, no," replied the mayor of Albany, "not until we take a vote, anyway."

"Just make it a point not to endorse me personally," I urged the mayor. "Do that, and you'll destroy my candidacy right from the start."

"You won't like running," Sweeney warned me. "You won't be able to go to the supermarket without people staring at you. It's very difficult."

I turned to Carl Strock, the *Gazette's* daily columnist and a once-a-week talk show host on WROW. I said, "If Sweeney can get people to like him well enough to get elected to Congress, then how tough can it be, right?"

As we left the restaurant after lunch, Sweeney gave me a hug and wished me luck if I actually decided to run. Despite that gesture, I was acutely aware that he would do everything in his power to defeat me. It would be both his party duty and no more than prudence. The last thing my congressman needed was a strong Democrat holding down a state legislative seat in his district. The first lesson every successful politician learns is to watch his back.

And to ruthlessly strangle every potential challenge, no matter how remote, in its cradle.

Late that afternoon, a *Times Union* reporter named Dennis Yusko called me. Butch Lilac had scheduled a press conference for 2 p.m. the following day. Did I know what it was all about, Yusko wanted to know? Butch didn't speak to me about it, I replied. Maybe he's getting out, I suggested.

The fact that Lilac hadn't given me a heads-up before announcing a press conference, however, indicated that whatever he planned to do the next day probably wouldn't be the last thing he did. By late afternoon the following day, Yusko had called me back. I'd also heard from a *Gazette* reporter. Lilac had, indeed, dropped out of the contest for the nomination, citing newly discovered family considerations. He'd done it, however, in a fit of conspicuous pique.

In a prepared statement handed out to reporters, Lilac had said, "The Colonie Democratic Committee, whether intentional or unintentional, clearly undermined the integrity of this selection process . . . I've given all I can to the Democratic Party. I can't give much more."

He told Yusko, "They flawed the process by jumping the gun. It's an old political trick—get your guy out there first—and that's not the way this process is supposed to work."

No, I thought as I later watched Lilac grumbling on the television news, it wasn't supposed to work that way at all, was it, Butch? It was supposed to be you who got out there first so you could stiff me, only you didn't manage to pull it off.

I'd told Yusko when he called, "The discussions are now serious and formal. Obviously, the fact that Butch doesn't want to have a battle over this makes it easier to make a decision. I'm going to have to make a decision in a week or two."

I wasn't kidding myself, however. Lilac was no longer opposing me for the nomination. That didn't mean, though, that he wouldn't do everything he could to keep me from winning the election. After all, I was the outsider coming in from outside the party structure to take what he'd figured his years of party service had made his personal property by divine right.

I knew that Lilac, at every opportunity, would try to hurt me and to help the Republicans who'd been his sworn enemy for a quarter century.

Once again, and seriously now, I was asking Joe if he had any interest in managing my campaign. Sure, he was saying during a meeting around Mary Gilson's kitchen table.

McElroy wanted $1,200 a week for doing the job—to be paid only if I won. He left me with the distinct impression, however, that he wasn't wild about the project.

"You don't really need me," he said. "You have the advantage of being a celebrity in this town, and that should be enough to overcome Prentiss's enrollment advantage."

McElroy added that he operated a successful private business that took much of his time. His wife had little enthusiasm for his political involvement, and he'd promised her a summer trip to Las Vegas. All right, I suggested, then stay out until September. It'll be those last two months that I'll really need help anyway, I told him. Fine, McElroy said.

I felt good about having him on board. The problem was that, even after all those years of covering politics, I didn't realize that this would be my first lesson on how the system really works, up close and personal. Politics has its own language. It's a world in which the simple English words "yes" and "no" actually translate to something else entirely.

In politics, they mean: "Maybe."

The media buzz on the possibility of my running was intensifying. Talk radio was alive with discussion of it. The *Record*, the Albany metro area's third daily newspaper, ran a six-column story on my interest in the race across the front of the paper's metro section. I did two half-hour television interviews, one with Liz Bishop on Channel 6 and another on WMHT-Channel 17, Albany's public television station, in which I explained that I was pondering the race and would soon decide. At the same time, a widely circulated weekly newspaper in the district, the *Spotlight*, ran a front-page story on the race topped by a painfully alliterative headline: "Pundit ponders pursuing Prentiss post." The paper also ran an editorial demanding that I get off the air while I even considered the prospect of a candidacy. I responded with a letter to the editor that read:

> . . . as I've said repeatedly on WROW, were I to decide to run—a decision I'll make soon, by the way—I would immediately leave my program and devote myself to full-time, unpaid service as a candidate. The novel idea set forth in your editorial—namely, that any media figure who's even approached about running for public office should immediately quit his or her job until he or she decides—would result in the immediate resignations of a good half-dozen media people in this town every year.

A few days later, my phone rang again. It was Peter Kermani, the Albany County Republican chairman.

I'd expected the call, actually. I'd heard Vandenburgh on the air predicting that the Republicans soon would invite me to run for Congress on their ticket against Mike McNulty. I lived in Sweeney's congressional district, not McNulty's, but the U.S. Constitution doesn't require a member of Congress to live in his or her district, only in the state in which that district is located. Also, Sweeney hadn't lived in his district when he'd first run in 1998. He'd moved in during the campaign.

Vandenburgh's on-air remarks, however, meant that the

routine rumor had been started before the phone call was made. Also, I'd already had a call from Joe Sullivan, the City of Albany GOP chairman, asking me to run as a Republican for the State Senate against Neil Breslin. The entire Republican party in the City of Albany consisted more or less of Joe Sullivan and six other people, so I'd written off that call to sheer desperation. I didn't live in Breslin's district, either. Politely, I declined. In the end, Joe himself was forced to run against Breslin that year.

"You're just the kind of guy who ought to be in public office," Kermani told me over the phone. "You're a better man than Prentiss, and you'll beat him in an Assembly contest, but you should be in higher office."

We talked for another 10 minutes. I'd never met Kermani, although I knew who he was and knew several of his family members. Kermani was not a career pol. He was a successful businessman who virtually ran the Albany Symphony Orchestra on a volunteer basis because he believed that the metro area needed to maintain that cultural resource.

"I agreed to serve as county chairman for one reason and one reason only," he told me, "to get good people into public office—like you."

I told him that I appreciated the flattery but that if I was going to this dance it would be with the people who'd first invited me. When I got off the phone with Kermani, I immediately called Congressman McNulty and assured him that, despite any rumors he might have heard, I most definitely would not be running against him.

"Glad to hear it," McNulty said.

The fact was that McNulty, like most legislative officeholders, held down the safest of seats. He enjoyed a huge enrollment advantage. Two years earlier, he'd won virtually all the 400-plus election districts in his congressional district. If

Abraham Lincoln had somehow risen from his grave and decided to run against Mike McNulty in that district, McNulty
would have kicked Honest Abe's butt. So, Mike McNulty
might well have been glad to hear that I wasn't running against
him.

Frankly, though, he couldn't have cared less.

A few mornings later, I arrived at an Albany hotel to
deliver a breakfast speech to a crowd of a few hundred retired
state employees. The speech had been scheduled many weeks
earlier. The retired state workers were looking for automatic
cost-of-living increases in their pensions. That already was law
in 39 other states, and I'd supported the bill both in my column
and on my radio show. I found myself sitting at the same table
with Assembly Republican leader John Faso, a calculating
lawyer in his late 40s from the Albany suburbs, and, of all
people, Bob Prentiss. Prentiss said little during breakfast,
although he eyed me during my speech as though I were holding a gun on him.

During the question-and-answer session that followed
my talk, I was asked if I would be running against Prentiss. I'm
not sure yet, I replied. I praised Prentiss as a fine guy
(*applause, applause*) and reported that, when I'd been asked to
run, he'd been the first person I'd called with the news that I was
considering it.

If I thought Prentiss is such a great guy, somebody
asked me, then why would I run against him? I explained that
Prentiss sat in the conference of a minority party outnumbered
nearly 2-1 in the Assembly. Republicans in the Assembly, I

explained, had nothing to say about anything of consequence. If I were to win election, I said, I would sit in the majority conference with real power to benefit the community in which I lived. I explained that I intensely disliked the fierce partisanship of the system, but that it was a fact of life and that I would deal with it.

As I spoke, I glanced over at Faso and Prentiss, both listening intently.

With broad, phony, professional politicians' smiles plastered across their faces.

Within a few more days, I came to realize that my mind was made up. Donna and I had one last, brief conversation. Go ahead and do it, my wife told me. So, yes, I really was running. I'd been inching along toward that conclusion for some weeks. Now it was time to move.

I called some relatives and friends to let them know that this run for office was a definite go. I informed people who'd expressed interest in working with me that we were about to start rocking and rolling. I touched base with all the party leaders. I told Vandenburgh that I would be leaving my radio program at the end of the week. I called Dave White at the *Times Union* and said there would be no more columns.

We reserved a meeting room in a Colonie hotel for the following Saturday and sent out press alerts to every media outlet in town that I would have an announcement to make at that time. I'd selected a Saturday for the announcement because I wanted the story to make the Sunday newspapers, which had more circulation than the weekday editions. By an odd quirk of fate, that meant that my daughter, Kelly, would read the news of my announcement on Channel 13, where she was the weekend anchor.

Before I announced, the media buzz grew louder. Mark McGuire, the *Times Union*'s broadcast columnist, explained to readers the essential difficulty that media outlets, particularly that newspaper, would face with me as a political candidate.

"Write something flattering," McGuire said in his column, "and we're sucking up; write something derogatory and we're hammering him just to demonstrate our impartiality. . . . If Lynch runs, and odds are he will, I have no doubt the media will make every attempt to be objective. I'm also sure we'll fail at times. News flash: We're not perfect."

Which I'd already known.

I hadn't realized at that time, though, just how stark those imperfections could be.

Just before I announced, I touched base with the two largest state workers unions, the Civil Service Employees Association and the Public Employees Federation. I got good vibes from CSEA, which represents the clerks and snowplow drivers and blue-collar workers throughout state government. PEF, however, was another story. Its members were generally well-educated, higher-paid professional people—state engineers and physicians and the like—and the Republicans essentially controlled PEF's regional political action committee. PEF could be tough to crack, I was warned.

Hell, I replied, I'm running as a Democrat in a district where three in four voters aren't Democrats. On the cosmic scale of worries, PEF's endorsement ranked fairly low.

The week before announcing my candidacy, I appeared before a screening panel of the Working Families Party. That was one of the minor parties on the New York ballot, begun by the unions and devoted to fairly left-wing, pro-union causes. The WFP had few party members in my district, but I wanted their ballot line regardless. The more places my name appeared on the November ballot, the better off I would be.

The WFP had sent me a questionnaire. It asked my position on a number of specific bills that had been introduced into the Legislature that year. I was asked if I would vote for those measures and if I would co-sponsor them. By the time the election was over, I'd filled out easily a dozen such questionnaires. I'd also refused to fill out a good dozen of them for reasons I explained carefully to the WFP screening committee.

I can support most of these bills in principle, I told them. My goal in serving in office, though, I explained, would be to serve in the majority conference as a moderate, independent, nonpartisan voice for compromise—for playing a meaningful role in actually solving a few of the problems those bills were designed to address. What I did not want to do, I told the WFP screening committee, was to commit myself to supporting specific language in a bill that would never pass the GOP-controlled State Senate. I wanted to be part of the solution, I explained, not part of the problem.

The WFP was looking for allegiance on four key issues—continuing rent control in New York City, health care expansion, campaign finance reform and a hike in the minimum wage. I'm for campaign finance reform, I said, and also for a rise in the minimum wage. I also want to see more people with decent health care. I told them, however, that I was not with them on rent control, which I knew was a huge issue for the city-based contingent of their party. I realized that the WFP would never back Prentiss, who was way too far to the right for their taste, but this issue was a flash point that could keep this group neutral, and one guy on the screening panel immediately bristled. Why not, he demanded?

"Look," I told him, "I could say I'm with you on this. Only a minuscule number of voters in my district care about this, since they're not directly affected, so standing with you on rent control wouldn't hurt me a bit. Instead, though, I feel compelled to be honest with you. That's how I plan to conduct this campaign—even though so many people assure me that it's not possible to run successfully for an office like this and still remain honest on the issues."

It's simply not fair, I argued, to have, say, an eight-unit apartment building where half the tenants are in rent controlled apartments with artificially low rents while the tenants of the other four apartments are paying rents above fair market price to subsidize the beneficiaries of rent control.

"That doesn't happen," the guy on the screening panel insisted.

"Really," I replied. "Then how does the landlord make a profit? And if he doesn't make a profit and can't sell the building to get out from under the loss, then he'll abandon it, won't he? Isn't that what happened in the South Bronx? I can't support that system. What I could support is a 50-year phase-out with current tenants protected for life but with new tenants in those same buildings paying fair market rate rents."

It was a tense moment. Like most pressure groups, these people wanted their way and generally insisted on complete loyalty to their point of view before endorsing candidates and supporting them with either money or campaign workers. If you insist that each and every legislator sign on to these specific bills, I told them, then you'll end up with the loyalty only of lawmakers from New York City. You'll end up with only the support of lawmakers who run in districts where they beat the Republicans 6-1 in general elections and fear only primary challenges from the left. They'll sign on to your bills and refuse to compromise on any comma or paragraph, and the Republicans in the State Senate will refuse to pass them. So, the problem you're trying to solve will continue indefinitely without a solution of any sort.

Doesn't it make more sense, I argued, for you to also back moderate candidates in tough districts like mine who'll be free to work for constructive change? Does it make sense to insist that everybody you back adhere to rigid positions that have the effect of keeping the problem in place eternally? Or would you rather see hard right-wingers like Bob Prentiss in seats like this? Would you prefer to see in office people who actively oppose the goals you support instead of working effectively toward them?

Everybody was pleasant enough, but I left that meeting pretty much convinced that I wouldn't have their backing. To my surprise and pleasure, the Working Families Party endorsed me a few weeks later. Other such groups, though—most notably the trial lawyers and the gay lobby—never forgave me for refusing to promise to support every word in their favored bills. Generally big contributors to Democratic candidates, those groups demanded fierce loyalty to every minute item in their agendas. They would back candidates, of course.

But only if they owned them.

❖   ❖   ❖

6

THE FIRST STONE

"Now and then an innocent man is sent to the Legislature."
—Frank McKinley Hubbard

During my final week on the radio, just before my announcement was scheduled, the *Gazette* decided to print yet one more story on my weighing a run against Prentiss. That was fine. I was eager for all the publicity I could get. What was not fine was what the story ended up saying.

During my telephone interview with Bill Hammond, I'd gone into voluminous detail with him on how I'd come to request that my column be placed on hiatus until I worked through the decision-making process. I'd laid out the whole business—the call I'd gotten in South Carolina inviting me to a formal meeting of the Colonie Democratic Committee, my phone call a few days later to Dave White informing him of that development. I'd told Hammond in cursory fashion about my conversation with Cohen and, quite emphatically, of my request to Cohen that my column be suspended until I made a final decision on running.

So, I was disappointed when Hammond wrote, "The *Times Union* has already suspended his weekly column while he considers becoming a candidate. . . ." Moreover, that same phrasing had been used a few days earlier by the weekly *Spotlight* newspapers. I'd kept quiet about the misinformation in the story in the weekly. I figured it was a bit early to start irking reporters with complaints about their failure to get facts straight. This time, however, I left Hammond a voice mail message informing him that he'd gotten it wrong—that the *Times Union* had agreed to suspending the column only after I'd insisted on it and pointing out that the editor's note had said that explicitly.

The Hammond story served to heighten my suspicions that the *Gazette* not only wouldn't be my friend in this campaign but might even gear its coverage to do me harm. Carl Strock, the *Gazette*'s columnist, had told me explicitly at the most recent WROW luncheon that his bosses were urging him to bash me. I wasn't happy about that because I knew that even reporters with the most benign of intentions could harm candidacies. Thirty-plus years in newspaper work had taught me that too few reporters really listen, and they tend not to get quotes right.

That was one reason I'd always taped people when I interviewed them. I made certain that nobody could ever accuse me of printing inaccurate quotes. After reading Hammond's story, it occurred to me that I probably would be prudent to turn on that tape recorder whenever I was interviewed during the course of the campaign. I also took the time to fax off letters to the editor to each paper, to ensure that the record was set straight on the circumstances surrounding my abandonment of my newspaper column.

If that irked anybody, too bad.

A few days before I announced my candidacy, I had lunch with Richie Stack, chairman of the Albany County Conservative Party. That ballot line, I knew, was worth about 3,000 votes in the general election. In a close race, that could be the margin of victory. Should I even bother to try for your party's endorsement, I asked? Well, he explained, Prentiss's daughter is on our executive committee. That was answer enough for me.

Later that same day, while prowling the Capitol, I bumped into Joe Bruno, the State Senate majority leader. Bruno was a handsome, silver-haired millionaire, a decent guy for whom I had some regard. Bruno had done well in private business. If he'd ever been in politics for the money, he clearly was no longer. Moreover, at 70, he wasn't hustling for higher office. He seemed, at this stage of his life, to be in this game out of a sense of public service, and I respected that.

Run as a Republican against Neil Breslin, Bruno urged me. Thanks, but no thanks, I said. I told him I'd heard a rumor that Prentiss might end up running against Breslin for the State Senate and that some other, stronger candidate would be fielded against me for the Assembly. No, Bruno assured me, Prentiss was staying where he was. Clearly, Bob Prentiss was nobody Joe Bruno was eager to have as one of his members.

Nonetheless, that information gave me pause. I'd been reliably informed that the moment rumors of my potential candidacy had begun circulating, the rolling-in-dough Republicans had polled in the district, testing my strength as a candidate against Prentiss. If they were leaving him in place against me, then he must have done reasonably well in the poll. Since I'd raised not a dime and had done no polling whatever, I was only guessing at how I might do in a poll. Yes, I knew it was a conservative district, naturally tilting toward any Republican. Given my high name recognition, though, my instinct was that

Prentiss and I would start off reasonably close in the polls. Maybe the GOP poll had shown him stronger and me weaker than I'd figured.   That prospect was not encouraging. Nonetheless, I was now committed.

Later in the day, I drove to the *Times Union* office, went to the publisher's second-floor office and hand-delivered to him this letter:

> Dear Dave:
> After spending some time pondering the opportunity the Democratic Party has offered me to run as the party's candidate for the New York Assembly this fall, I've decided that the most appropriate action for me to take at this time is to exercise the cancellation clause in my contract with the *Times Union* and to sever all business connections with the newspaper. This letter constitutes that cancellation. This has not been an easy decision to make. I very much appreciate the newspaper's patience as I've fought my way through this process for the past six weeks.

Then, with all ties to the news media severed and invitations to my announcement in the mail, I called Prentiss a few days before my formal announcement.

"I'll probably announce by the end of the week," I told him. "If you were in the majority, I wouldn't be doing this. As it is, though, I feel an obligation to our mutual neighbors in this district to do this. I'll treat you with both dignity and respect throughout the campaign."

Prentiss said, "I really wish you lived in a different district, but I'm proud to be a participant in the kind of campaign you want to run. That's the sort of campaign I want to run, too, and the voters will be the better for it."

And, of course, news of that conversation was all over WROW the following morning. Vandenburgh told me that he'd gotten a call from somebody high in the Republican organization that I'd called Prentiss. I presumed that the call had come from Powers or Sweeney. If they'd been trying to take the edge off my announcement that coming Saturday by leaking the news to Vandenburgh, they'd played it wrong. The buzz was all over drive-time radio, merely setting the stage for coverage of the formal announcement.

The next evening, I attended the New York state Democratic Convention at Albany's Pepsi Arena—going to an event like this for the first time not as a reporter but as an "honored guest." At least, that's what it said on my ticket. I was approached by people who wanted to help in the campaign and by lobbyists promising support. At the convention, I also learned that I had a meeting set the next day with Arnold Proskin, the former Republican assemblyman that Prentiss had knocked off in a primary six years before. The meeting had been set up by a Democratic lawyer tied in with the Colonie organization. I wasn't sure what Proskin wanted, but I certainly was willing to listen.

The following afternoon, Joe McElroy and I met with Shelly Silver's campaign organization, the Democratic Assembly Campaign Committee. Or, more specifically, we met with John Longo and Mike Kane, DACC's two top people.

Since it was not an arm of government but an arm of the party, DACC was headquartered in a basement suite of offices in a privately owned office building near the Capitol complex.

DACC's offices included a sophisticated print shop and banks of both phones and computers. Longo and Kane were in casual clothes and mirror images of one another—both 40ish, both bearded, Longo dark and Kane with reddish hair.

They were explaining the deal to us—namely, that it took 15 grand to get DACC into the game, and that I had to do well in the poll before they would consider throwing DACC's resources behind my campaign. Not 20 minutes into the meeting, however, Longo was called out to take a phone call. He never returned.

It wasn't until that evening, as I attended a Women's Press Club dinner honoring Channel 6's Liz Bishop, that I picked up a voice mail message from Hammond, called him back and found out what was going on. Silver had learned that the Assembly majority leader, Mike Bragman of Syracuse, was planning a coup. Bragman had lined up a giant squad of Democratic members of the Assembly to depose Silver as speaker. The vote was scheduled for the following Monday, two days after my announcement.

"Which guy do you like for speaker?" Hammond asked, doing his best to put me on the spot.

"I think I'll wait until I'm a member before I get into fights like this," I replied.

Actually, this was a bad situation for me. Bragman would need the votes of Faso's Republicans to pull this off. And Faso held no particular affection for me.

The year before, Faso's chief of staff had received a call from a constituent, a motel and general store operator named Joe Cavallaro. She'd treated the guy rudely before hanging up on him. He'd called back. When she hung up on him again, he continued calling—a few dozen times. When nobody would take his calls, he called Faso's home number, which was listed in the phone book. Faso's chief of staff promptly had Cavallaro arrested, dragged before a judge in cuffs and charged with aggravated harassment.

The poor guy was a small businessman with no criminal record. He'd called on a legitimate matter and been abused. He ended up spending five grand on legal fees before a judge had thrown the silly case completely out of court.

I'd been highly critical in my column of Faso's personal role in the incident. He'd refused to drop the charges because, he told me, he feared a false arrest suit. That struck me as a shabby reason for an assemblyman to have a constituent prosecuted, and I said so in vivid terms in my column. Faso, I'd been told, was still furious over that column and lusting for vengeance. If Bragman managed to knock off Silver as speaker with Faso's help, I figured I could forget utterly about DACC's help, regardless of whether I came up with the 15 grand and regardless of how well I might do in any poll. Part of Faso's price for helping Bragman pull off his assassination of Silver would surely be a hands-off policy by DACC regarding my race.

Two days later, though, Silver was out of the woods. He'd used his pals in the lobbying community to put pressure on individual Democratic members of the Assembly to renounce their support for Bragman. A good many members of the Assembly had told Bragman yes. When the people who financed their campaigns threatened them, however, most of those promises to Bragman evaporated like morning mist in the noonday sun.

It was just one more example—and a rare public example, at that—of how little the commitments of politicians really mean.

The following evening, I dutifully appeared at the home of Ken Champagne, the Colonie leader of still another of New York's minor political parties—the Independence Party.

New York's Independence Party was composed of rabid moderates. It was an affiliate of H. Ross Perot's national political organization. It had been started by a Rochester millionaire named Tom Golisano, who thought it might be nice to be governor. He hadn't won, of course, but he'd attracted more than 300,000 votes, and his party now occupied an important line on the ballot.

I wanted that line, and so did Prentiss. He'd been scheduled to appear before the party's screening committee at 7 p.m., with me showing up an hour later. I figured that Prentiss would take as much time as he could, so I arrived 20 minutes early to put pressure on the screening committee to send him on his way—and, also, to turn on the charm with Champagne's wife, Kay, telling her how cute her young daughter was. The kid was cute, too.

The ploy worked. Prentiss got to stay only 15 minutes over his allotted time. When he'd been dismissed, I managed to stretch my time out to two hours. The screening committee consisted of Champagne; a guy named Paul Caputo, who ran the party in a neighboring Albany suburb outside my district, and Larry Rosenbaum, an insurance man who served as the Independence Party's Albany County chairman and vice chairman of the state party.

"I want your line," I told them, "because a good many Republicans who might vote for me will never do it on the Democratic party line. I want to give those voters a place to cast a ballot for me."

Prentiss had won the Independence Party's backing in the past, but these guys were interested in what I had to say. We talked issues for all two hours. I assured them that my goal was to serve only two or three terms, do as much good as I could in those four to six years, and then get out. When I left, I felt reasonably confident that I would have their backing. Of course, you never could tell.

Ask Mike Bragman.

Arnie Proskin's office on Route 9 in Colonie's upscale Loudonville section was an elegant converted church. Proskin was in his 60s, prosperous and professionally friendly. He also seemed to enjoy hearing himself talk. At one point in his monologue, I tried to ask him how he could help me in this race.

"Let me finish my sentence," he snapped.

I smiled in response. "Yes, sir."

Proskin was saying that his law practice included some judicial duties that prevented him from actively involving himself in politics any more. He assured me, however, that I would get a good many Republican votes. He knew that from his friends in the regular party organization, who despised Prentiss.

"I'll vote for you," Proskin told me, "but don't let that go to your head. I'd vote for the Frankenstein monster over that creep Prentiss."

A few days before I formally announced my candidacy, Channel 13's news director, Paul Conti, put out a memo to his staff.

"We have an unusual situation developing," Conti wrote. "Dan Lynch is going to formally declare his candidacy for the Democratic party's nomination to seek an Assembly seat. Everyone here knows that his daughter is our weekend anchor. Not much mystery. Some of our viewers know that, too.

"Normally, I would just forbid Kelly from having any contact with the story and that would be that. It's not that simple. She's the weekend anchor. Stories will come up. She has to read them. I've already discussed this with Kelly at her instigation. The purpose of this note is to lay out publicly what we have decided so that there isn't any question about it later from outsiders."

Conti then went on to set forth the rules—that Kelly would not report in any way on my race, that she would edit nothing that had to do with my race, that if a story on my race broke on the shift she was anchoring, she would read precisely what the producer wrote for her.

Both the *Times Union* and *Gazette* later ran stories on Conti's rules to avoid conflict of interest. He hoped that memo and those rules would insulate both my daughter and his station from irresponsible partisan attack.

He turned out to be wrong.

To my pleased amazement, the announcement came off without a hitch.

The event was orchestrated in a frenzied rush by Bob Berry. Like Joe McElroy, Berry was the proprietor of an independent business, a large-scale commercial landscaping and grounds maintenance operation, who had a sideline as a political consultant. Berry was a tall, lean, bespectacled guy who'd worked with McElroy on several campaigns. He wasn't exactly Mr. Charm, and vast multitudes in the Albany County Democratic organization disliked him intensely, but he was as smart as hell, and he knew what he was doing.

The announcement was held in a meeting room at the Desmond, a large hotel in Colonie, New York—and, its primary allure, a unionized one. The hotel happened to be located only a few hundred yards from the *Times Union* building. Peggy Fossaceca, a cousin of mine living in my home town of Elmira, four hours west of Albany, had been enlisted to have printed up—in total secrecy and a great rush—100 "Dan Lynch for the Assembly" signs, green letters on white background. These were prominently displayed around the room. On a table outside the door were large green buttons with white letters touting my candidacy that Mary Gilson had ordered made up at the last minute. I'd chosen that color scheme because McEneny had told me that the 107th had more voters of Irish descent than any of the state's 150 Assembly districts.

"Lose the green as soon as you can," Berry said when he saw the colors. "Green on lawn signs doesn't show up well against grass. Also, anybody who cares that you're Irish already knows, and all that green will just piss off everybody else."

My older brother, Tim, and his wife, Sandy, flew in from Maryland for the occasion. Tim was the most conservative of Republicans, and this was not a crowd he would find particularly congenial. My younger sister, Eileen Farrar, drove up from Westchester County. Our son, Kevin, was too busy chasing movie stars as a reporter for the *National Enquirer* in

Florida to make it to the announcement. Kelly, of course, made it a point not to show. She and I both were acutely aware that it would be utterly improper for her to play any role whatever in the campaign, and she never did.

We got more than 100 people in that room—party people, friends we'd invited and a mob of press. I later learned that Prentiss had sent a spy to my announcement as well, one of his campaign workers who'd been a regular caller to my talk radio program during the six weeks in which I'd been trying to decide whether to run. This guy's job had been to hector me over the air until I cut him down with my machine gun sound effect, but he caused no trouble that day.

As per Berry's instruction, Donna and I hid in a hospitality room in the hotel until he called us out. We entered the room hand-in-hand and took the stage, where Berry had lined up behind us a bevy of party leaders and elected officials. Two people I'd expected, and who'd pledged to me that they would back me, had failed to show—Mayor Jennings and Congressman McNulty. I filed that away for future reference.

Berry had approved my wardrobe for the occasion—a navy blue suit, green tie with navy stripes and light blue dress shirt. No white shirt, he'd warned; it makes you look washed-out on TV. I delivered a brief speech. Because of the need to get an accurate text to media outlets that didn't have representatives present, I was forced to read what I had to say rather than delivering the talk off-the-cuff, which was my preferred style of delivery. With the TV cameras whirring, I said, "In my newspaper column and on my radio program, I've tried for years to encourage common sense and high ethical standards in the conduct of public affairs. I've never been a partisan figure, and I've never approached these issues from a partisan perspective.

"I recently retired from the *Times Union*, and I've given up my program on WROW radio. Today, I'm announcing my candidacy for the New York Assembly seat in the 107th district, which covers Colonie, Clifton Park, Malta and Stillwater. I'm taking this step for several reasons."

I then recited the litany of troubles facing both the state and the district—an aging population, an economy lagging behind the national average, the stark failure of New York's urban schools, the highest per capita tax rate in America, etc.

"I believe the New York Assembly to be in desperate need of new ideas, new approaches, new blood and new solutions to old problems," I said. ". . . I'm not a politician. . . . For years, I've enjoyed the enviable privilege of a public voice. I've tried to use that voice to stand up for people who've been pushed around by the system and who perceive that system often to be unresponsive, unfair, uncaring and working not in their best interests—but, instead, in the interests of the career politicians who run it.

"Now, I've given up that voice. I'm now asking my neighbors to grant me the honor of both a voice and a vote in representing them and their families in the New York Assembly."

I'd never once mentioned party affiliation in my announcement speech. In fact, I'd made a point at one juncture in the talk of saying that I remained an independent devoted to nonpartisan solutions. As applause sounded, as per Bob Berry's instructions, I moved off to the side for a press conference. It went on for 10 minutes. I ended up with good news coverage—stories on all the TV stations and the big radio stations, a metro-front piece in the *Gazette*, a page one story and photo in the *Record* and—in my alma mater, the *Times Union*—a story and photo tucked neatly inside the local section, deep enough into the paper to prevent anybody from accusing the *Times Union* of overplaying my announcement. The Associated Press ran the story on both the state and broadcast wires. The following week, the weeklies made a big deal of my announcement.

It came as no surprise to me, however, when Carl Strock, in his *Gazette* column the day after the announcement, took a shot at me. I figured that his bosses had suggested to him that it would be a good idea.

"He was . . . at pains to declare that he remains 'an independent voter enrolled in no party,'" Strock wrote. "But in this he seemed to me like a maiden eager for a roll in the hay who also desires to remain a virgin, for we all know he was recruited into an Assembly run by the Colonie Democrats, who endorsed him before he declared, and he allowed that if elected he expects to be a member of the Assembly's Democratic conference. So, is he partisan or non-partisan? Is he independent or is he a Democrat?"

Later in the column, Strock wrote, "Now what? He wants to become one of those career politicians who run [the system]?"

It was the predictable cheap shot, and it wouldn't be the last one, I suspected, from the *Gazette* or from other quarters. Still, for better or worse, I finally was in this race.

Now it was time to boogie.

Although he'd never really gotten in, Joe McElroy was now out of the campaign. In a meeting around Mary Gilson's kitchen table—our unofficial campaign headquarters, until we found a real one—he explained why. He had private business concerns. His wife wanted more of his time. Also, he told me, there was a reason McNulty and Jennings had ducked the announcement.

"They figure that you'll win the hottest local race this year," he said, "and if I'm your campaign manager they're afraid that I'll get credit for it and then take on Mike Burns for county chairman."

"Do you want to be county chairman?" I asked McElroy.

"No, but Jerry doesn't believe that. . . . If I'm publicly associated with your campaign, then Jennings and Burns will work against you."

Also, he added, Jennings seemed convinced that Tony Catalfamo was in on the coup to unseat Burns, so Jennings planned to run Albany school board candidates whose main job, if elected, would be to get Tony fired from his job with the school district. It was a job that Tony's father held before him, Joe said, and McElroy would have to devote most of his attention in the fall to the Albany school board elections to ensure that Tony's job was safe. McElroy went on and on. I didn't need him, he said. My positive name recognition would carry me through.

I had no idea whether any or all of this was true. What did seem to be true, however, was that Joe wanted out. Bob Berry, who was also at the meeting, said he didn't want to be involved unless McElroy was involved. Berry had never run a campaign completely by himself. You can do it, Bob, McElroy assured him.

Clearly, this whole business with Jennings, Burns, McElroy and Berry was a swamp. These animosities apparently ran deep and were the product of a history I'd never been part of and had no way to evaluate. I really had no clue as to what was going on, and I had to take McElroy's word for everything. If this was all an act, I didn't like it. If it wasn't an act, well, I didn't like that either.

A few days later, Berry agreed to come on as campaign

manager. He would take $600 a week as his fee—$200 a week to be paid as the campaign went along and $400 a week more only if the campaign was successful. The problem, of course, was that whatever animosity Jennings harbored against McElroy, he could also be presumed to harbor at least as much against Berry. I needed a campaign manager, though, and nobody else was available. Besides, whatever his feelings toward McElroy or Berry, I knew Jennings would help me win this election, now that I was in it with both feet.

After all, the mayor had given his word.

A few months earlier, before the question of me running for office had arisen, I'd agreed to speak at a fund-raising breakfast for a non-profit group called the Volunteer Center of the Capital District. This organization rounded up volunteers to work for other non-profits that did charity work in town.

Also, long before I announced my candidacy, I'd accepted an invitation to serve as a dinner speaker for another non-profit called the Center for Independence. That organization worked with disabled people. I'd had an uncle, a man who'd really been a second father to me in many respects, who'd suffered gallantly through life as a polio victim. I'd planned to speak to the dinner about his boundless courage and unflagging optimism in the face of such hardship.

In every town across the country, local media figures routinely are asked to help such groups raise money. The idea is to sell tickets to these events by having somebody well known locally put on an entertaining talk for people willing to shell out cash to support such worthy causes. I hadn't realized it when I'd accepted the speaking engagement, but one of Channel 13's anchors, John Gray, had been scheduled to be master of ceremonies at the Volunteer Center breakfast. Only now the Republicans were howling that Channel 13 was effectively endorsing my candidacy by permitting Gray to sit at the same head table with me. The complaint was made in a press release issued by Mike Lisuzzo, the Clifton Park Republican chairman, a guy I'd never met, and—as of this writing—still haven't.

The press release was headlined: "Is Assembly candidate Dan Lynch trading cash for votes?"

It read:

> It has come to the attention of the Clifton Park Republican Committee that Assembly candidate Dan Lynch will be participating in a fundraiser for a nonpartisan community group on June 14, 2000.
>
> Committee Chairman Mike Lisuzzo said, "The appearance of impropriety and potential media collusion is staggering. The fact that an announced candidate for political office is a headliner for a $35 per person fundraiser warrants a full investigation."

Lisuzzo went on in his press release to accuse Channel 13 of taking sides in the race and demanded that I be replaced as the featured speaker. He again called for "a formal investigation."

By whom, I thought—the FBI? What was this loon talking about?

The complaint clearly was nonsense. In no way were these appearances political. I wouldn't be hustling for votes, and it wasn't as though I needed the publicity. I'd been invited to speak precisely because I was so well known. Lisuzzo's attack served only one purpose—to make life uncomfortable not for me, but for my daughter, who wasn't a candidate for anything. Moreover, there was no way Lisuzzo was acting without Prentiss's approval or without his direction. Candidates were, as Bob Berry routinely reminded me, "pieces of meat" whose appearances and words were subject to review, criticism and direction by campaign managers. Nothing happened in a campaign, however—especially the issuance of a press release or statement—without the candidate's knowledge and okay. None of the town Democratic chairs, for example, would have taken any such action on my behalf if I'd opposed it. That was an integral part of political culture. The candidate always has veto power.

What I'd presumed to be only harassment of my daughter, however, turned out to be something considerably more sinister. I soon received a call from Laura Hagen, the executive director of the Center for Independence. Could you come see me, she asked?

So, the following morning, I was in her office on Albany's Central Avenue while she set me straight on the true meaning of Lisuzzo's call for "a formal investigation." Her group was tax-exempt, she informed me. Lisuzzo was demanding an investigation of the center's continued tax exemption. And, since the state agency that controlled the issuance of tax exempt certificates was controlled by Lisuzzo's party, this press release was a threat, plain and simple, and enormously serious to her and her board of directors. Therefore, she said, she was forced to withdraw the invitation for me to speak at her group's fund-raising dinner.

I was simply aghast. Prentiss had been so emphatic in his agreement when I'd pledged a clean campaign. He'd sworn that was the sort of campaign he wanted to run, too. Now, here he was, threatening the tax exemption of a group devoted to serving the needs of people in wheelchairs. And he was doing it solely in an effort to deny me a speaking audience.

"And you're going to cave in on this?" I said to Laura Hagen.

She explained that Lisuzzo had not only issued his press release. He'd also delivered the threat orally to a guy named Doug Sauer, who served as executive director of the Council of Community Organizations, the umbrella group for all the nonprofits. Sauer had instructed her to keep me off the dinner program at all costs. Meanwhile, of course, Prentiss would be attending the dinner. All the incumbent state legislators had been invited.

"What would you do if you were me?" she asked me.

I said, "You've read my column for years. You've heard my radio show. You know what I would do. But we all have to make these decisions for ourselves, don't we?"

I left her office furious. What a column this would have made—only I didn't write a column any more. When I got back to my home office, I called Strock at the *Gazette*. If this isn't a column, I said, then what is?

"I lose on anything I write about you," Strock told me. "If I support you, then I'm supporting a former colleague in the media. If I criticize you, then I'm criticizing a former competitor."

I told him, "Carl, it's not about me; it's about the nonprofits. When it was just about me, I didn't call you, did I?"

Nonetheless, Strock refused to look into the story. I then called a radio talk show host I knew. She was horrified, but she ended up doing nothing with it either. These nonprofit groups were strictly on their own against the politicians who controlled their tax exemptions and much of their funding. Nobody in the media was willing to protect them against Prentiss's naked bullying.

        Over the weekend, Laura Hagen called me. Her board,
half of which was composed of the disabled, wanted to fight.
Please speak for us, she asked. My pleasure, I told her, and I
won't show up wearing campaign buttons. I also spoke to Paul
Conti. He'd decided that he was being bullied, too, and that he
didn't like it. He'd told John Gray that he was back on the program at the Volunteer Center.

        Not too long after that, though, Laura Hagen got back to
me again. Now she was in tears. The threat had intensified. I
had to agree to cancel the talk, she begged me. I, of course, did
precisely that. I did the same when Ruth Charlesworth, director of the Volunteer Center, asked me to withdraw from the
breakfast speech. She'd been threatened with the loss not only
on her group's tax exemption, she said, but also with the loss of
her state funding.

        I did put out a press release on the situation. It said,
"The conduct of Bob Prentiss and the conduct of his shameless
political henchman, Michael Lisuzzo, vividly illustrates the
very worst aspects of political life. . . . People who behave this
way—who openly intimidate and instill fear in our disabled citizens and their selfless advocates—are simply unfit for public
service."

        Although the *Times Union* ignored the incident—
wouldn't print a word on it, in fact—my criticism of Prentiss
and Lisuzzo nonetheless received coverage in the other daily
newspapers. Unfortunately, in a fairly stunning exhibition of
the "pox-on-both-their-houses" style of coverage that character-
izes the approach of the press to so many stories about political
campaigns, the whole sordid affair was presented merely as two
competing political candidates bickering. The headline in the
Record read, "Campaign getting nasty already." The *Gazette*'s
headline was more of the same: "Finger-pointing all around as
Lynch withdraws from non-profit dinner."

Meanwhile, the *Gazette* quoted Prentiss as saying that he had no problem with my speaking anywhere. Lisuzzo had his opinion on the issue, Prentiss told Bill Hammond, and Prentiss had his. It was sheer fraud on Prentiss's part. In the same story, Lisuzzo denied making any threats to anybody and demanded that I produce evidence.

The non-profit groups had only one interest in this—keeping their heads down until the bullets stopped flying. Laura Hagen told reporters that she wouldn't specify who she blamed for the incident. All she would say was, "As executive director of a not-for-profit, I weigh very serious statements—valid or not—which could potentially affect our center."

It was as scummy and cruel a political stunt as I'd seen in 30-plus years of covering elections. It did help me understand something, though.

I now enjoyed a vastly better grasp of precisely what Bob Prentiss considered a campaign to be proud of.

7

STRANGE BEDFELLOWS

"Newspaper editors are men who separate the wheat from the chaff, and then print the chaff."—Adlai Stevenson

Jan Lemon was annoyed again.

The problem, she was telling me over the phone, was that I'd made a point of stressing in my announcement speech that I was an independent, which had perturbed some people in the party. She'd overheard the Breslins, in particular, grumbling about it.

"What?" Mike Breslin had muttered to his brother, Neil, the state senator, during my announcement speech. "This guy isn't even a Democrat?"

Well, I pointed out to Jan, I'd thought it wise to mention that fact at the announcement precisely because I was an independent. I saw no sense in having that come out as a news story rather than from me. I had visions of my former competitors at the *Gazette* calling the Saratoga County clerk's office for my enrollment and then running the story as a big investigative piece, with a screaming headline and a lead that began, "Through intrepid, enterprising reporting, the *Daily Gazette* has learned. . . ."

Also, I pointed out to Jan, under New York state election law, I could change my enrollment the next day, but I nonetheless would remain an independent until after the general election in the fall. In crafting an election code, the Legislature had taken no chances on Republicans deciding to enroll as Democrats just to sabotage the opposition's primary elections, or vice versa. A good many of New York's 211 state legislators might be small-minded, uninformed and venal, but they weren't stupid—well, not all of them, anyway.

Moreover, I informed her, both Mike Burns and Tony Catalfamo had urged me not to change my enrollment—at least not until the campaign was over. With only one voter in four in the district enrolled as a Democrat, both guys had advised me, enrolling as a Democrat wouldn't help me in November. After election day, if I was forced to enroll as a Democrat to gain admittance to the Assembly's Democratic conference, then I would do it.

That's not what Burns had told her, Jan said. He'd twice mentioned to her that he would prefer to see me enroll in the party. When I later met with Burns, he explained that he was feeling pressure from party people on the issue. I pondered that piece of information and immediately delivered a new enrollment card to Tom Bayly, the Saratoga County chairman.

"Just hang on to it," I advised Tom. "If I decide that it's necessary to become a Democrat to placate people like the Breslins, then I guess I'll do it."

I added, however, that it would be my preference to be admitted to the Assembly's Democratic conference as an independent and to serve in office without a personal party identification. If I was to serve in office the way I hoped to serve— functioning as a nonpartisan figure to the greatest degree possible and playing some meaningful role in forging sensible, compromise legislation to solve stubborn public policy problems—

then enrolling in the party would diminish my effectiveness. The Republicans would figure that I was just one of those guys, and the hell with me. Tom didn't seem exactly thrilled with my thinking, but he said he understood and filed away the new enrollment card.

Burns also was disturbed to see Bob Berry involved in my campaign. Too many people in the party dislike this guy, the Albany County chairman warned me. Well, I replied, I need Bob with me at least through the process of gathering signatures of voters on nominating petitions to get my name on the ballot. That was an enormously complex process, I pointed out, even with the party helping out, and I'd never been through it before, while Berry had. Also, I told Burns, I was acutely aware that Berry had come into this campaign with some reluctance, after McElroy had included himself out, and that Berry had a private business to run. I deemed it unlikely that he would be able to stay with me for the entire campaign, anyway.

Meanwhile, other trouble was brewing. Lilac remained furious and clearly was plotting something—anything he could think of, apparently—designed to do me harm. Also, several key people in the Albany County Democratic Party were openly proclaiming their opposition to my candidacy.

Well, not exactly openly. That's not the way politicians operate. None of these people called me for a face-to-face, man-to-man conversation. Instead, I simply received word from friendly spies that each was grumbling because the party was backing me. In each case, that opposition seemed to have its roots in some column I'd written critical of some variety of wrongdoing in the Albany County Democratic Party—or in the general hostility that the old-line party organization people harbored toward outsiders in general, the news media in particular, and toward the *Times Union* especially.

This had to be dealt with. Given the enrollment, this

race would be tough enough without treason in the ranks of the party that was supposed to be backing me. In the case of one party regular, I called Burns and—in rather emphatic terms, too—urged that the party chairman bring this guy into line. I also sent letters to every major party official, including the ones I had reason to suspect of quietly opposing my candidacy, asking them to join my campaign committee and to have their names openly displayed on my fundraising stationery. I needed a response by a specific date, my letter said, and I would be checking with them by phone if I hadn't heard from them by that date.

In short, if any of these people intended to oppose me, it would have to be done openly. The usual behind-the scenes back-stabbing would be made more difficult. As party people, they were honor-bound to stand behind the party's endorsed candidate—to the extent that honor had any meaning in the culture of politics, and I was beginning to doubt that it had much. Once they lent their names to my fundraising efforts, though, their obligation would be that much more intense.

I also called two of my rumored opponents in the Albany County party and invited them to lunch individually. In each case, in Albany's Gateway Diner on Central Avenue, only a few blocks from Albany County Democratic headquarters on Colvin Avenue, I asked: "What's your problem with me as the party's candidate?" Each guy assured me that he had no problem, that he was behind me in this race. The concern of each guy, of course, was that I would talk publicly about his refusal to back the party's endorsed candidate. Their images as loyal Democrats would be damaged by any such public statement on my part, and they knew it.

Meanwhile, John Faso was on Vandenburgh's radio program, proclaiming that I was a liberal Democrat who'd supported Shelly Silver in his fight with Bragman. I had, of course, made a point of taking no position whatever on the Silver-Bragman clash, and I was neither a liberal nor a Democrat. I figured I'd better get used to such lying, though. Election day was still many months away.

The moment rumors of my candidacy had leaked out, a good many people had contacted me by phone or by mail and asked to help out if I really ended up running. We gathered together about 50 of these people one evening at Mary Gilson's house, to munch meatballs and cheese and to schmooze with one another. We could use some of these people right away in the task of circulating nominating petitions, but our big problem was finding a place for them to work. We needed a headquarters, and we needed to raise some money to rent one.

We need to get busy on a fundraiser, I told Bob Berry. Don't worry about a thing, he assured me.

At its core, a political campaign is marketing. It consists of designing the product—i.e., the candidate—then getting the candidate's name and face in front of voters. The idea is to attract their attention and, ultimately, convince them that the candidate you're pushing is a better choice than the other candidate.

As a candidate, I'd already been designed. I was well known to a large segment of the voting public because my views on political issues had been displayed in print four days a week on the Local Front of the *Times Union* for years, not to mention my impromptu pronouncements on television and radio.

That had both advantages and disadvantages. Yes, a good many people already knew me. Unlike most politicians, however, I was in no position to tailor my positions on issues to what I perceived to be the views of most voters in my district. I had to do what few conventional politicians need to do or choose to do. I had to stand up for what I actually believed in, regardless of who that might annoy. To back off any public position I'd taken in the past would mean exposing myself as a hypocrite and as somebody that nobody should trust.

So, for a variety of reasons, I couldn't rely on my name recognition and merely sit back to await victory on election day. Moreover, this was a district naturally hostile to anybody not on the Republican ticket, so my winning the general election by acclamation was not exactly a likelihood. Instead, I had to actively market myself as what I was—as the un-politician, as an informed, conscientious guy trying to come in from outside the system to do some good. In short, well-known or not, I still had to sell myself—or, as Bob Berry so fetchingly phrased it, peddle my ass like any hooker on a dark street corner.

A good many ways exist to accomplish that—working to get press coverage, mass media advertising, direct mail. There's no substitute, though, for simply being seen by the people you want to vote for you. There's no substitute for going where the people are. And, once they see you in the flesh, they're more likely to vote for you than for some other candidate they've never laid eyes on.

For me, with a face that had been on television regularly and displayed four days a week in the logo that accompanied my *Times Union* column, that meant visiting supermarkets in the district four or five times a week, buying food and wandering the aisles, grinning like a loon at total strangers. (Berry had criticized me for not smiling enough. I'd glared at him ferociously and replied, "I am smiling.") It meant strolling through shopping centers at busy times, taking care to be seen as widely as I could. And it meant showing up at every community fair and festival in the district, wandering amid the crowd and chatting it up with whoever I could get to talk to me without being too intrusive, especially so early in the race.

So, on one sun-splashed Saturday morning in spring, a good many people were at Family Day in Stillwater, the northernmost town in the district, and so was I. Stillwater was a centuries-old, largely blue-collar community. It nestled on the west shore of the Hudson River on the outer fringe of the Albany suburbs. Stillwater was extremely Republican and conservative enough to view George W. Bush as a trifle pink. Since the *Times Union* sold fewer papers there than it did in Colonie and Clifton Park, I was less recognizable in Stillwater than in the suburbs closer to the city.

Family Day was held in a park in the Village of Stillwater. I cruised in there that morning with Mary Gilson, who was coordinating the campaign's volunteer operation; my wife, Donna, and with Cynthia Pooler, a state worker who lived in Stillwater and who'd volunteered to work in the campaign. Cynthia was a shrewd political operator. More than a decade earlier, in a district so overwhelmingly Republican that no Democrat had a glimmer of a chance to win there, she'd run for the Assembly herself, losing but developing a healthy appreciation for how a campaign works.

The four of us wore our large, green Lynch campaign buttons. As we strolled around the event, I found myself approached by a number of people who recognized me and pledged that they would vote for me. I also noticed the glares of a number of other people, who also recognized me and apparently viewed my candidacy with markedly less enthusiasm. Bob Prentiss was on hand at the event, accompanied by his wife, Marlene. She was an active politician, now holding down her husband's old seat in the 39-member Albany County Legislature. Naturally, Butch Lilac was on hand. We need to talk, I told him. I said I would call him the following day. Sure, said Lilac, you do that.

We stayed long enough for Lilac to ascend the stage, grab the microphone and introduce Prentiss to the crowd with great warmth. Yes, Prentiss was the incumbent, and it was only proper for Lilac to introduce him. Lilac, however, made it a point not to mention to the crowd that I was on hand. Clearly, that was no oversight. Then Donna and I left the event to make another stop. We dropped by Stillwater Family Day once more, later on, to catch the afternoon crowd, and once again roared off for another event elsewhere. Throughout the warm weather weekend days of the campaign, we usually dropped in on as many as a half-dozen such events both on Saturday and Sunday, from one end of the district to the other—volunteer firehouse chicken roasts, youth fairs, craft fairs, ethnic festivals, go-kart races in shopping center parking lots. The goal was simply to be seen, and seen, and seen some more, weekend after weekend.

That night, Mary Gilson and Cynthia Pooler went back to the Stillwater event on their own. Beer had flowed freely at Family Day, Mary Gilson later reported to me, and the crowd was lurching about in merry abandon. Both Prentiss and his wife had returned to the festival that evening to work the liberally lubricated evening crowd. He spotted Mary, sporting her "Lynch" button, and engaged her in conversation. Shortly thereafter, Marlene Prentiss wandered over, spotted Mary's button and proclaimed, "Oh, the enemy!"

Prentiss, Mary told me later, had promptly hustled his wife away.

The following day, a Sunday, the *Times Union* ran a story on the race. Butch Lilac, the newspaper reported, was all set to switch parties. The rumor had been out there for weeks. A few days later, Lilac actually went through with it.

In Lilac's statement to the press, he complained that he, a loyal party soldier for all those years, had been rejected unfairly in favor of "a celebrity candidacy." Tom Bayly, the Saratoga County Democratic chairman, responded to reporters that Lilac "couldn't pitch, so he's taking his ball and going home."

Oddly, it was WROW radio that led its news broadcasts for more than a day with the story of Lilac switching parties, and Vandenburgh commented on the story extensively on his morning drive-time show. Lynch had broken Lilac's heart, he told listeners. Vandenburgh even brought Lilac on the air by phone to say nothing much in particular. Then, after Lilac left the air, Vandenburgh took calls. The first caller was a Prentiss plant. It was "Mark from Latham." He was the guy who'd been assigned to hassle me during my last week on the air and to serve as a Prentiss spy at my announcement.

Lynch is unqualified to serve in the Assembly, Mark from Latham proclaimed over the air. Lynch has expressed such contempt for politicians that he could never work effectively with them to help the district.

At which point, Vandenburgh switched gears abruptly. He'd spent his entire conversation with Lilac agreeing that nominations for public office should go only to people who'd given service to the party. With this guy, however, Vandenburgh took a different tack entirely. Lynch is not only qualified, he said, he's overqualified. Lynch would do a terrific job in office.

Of course, Vandenburgh added after he hung up on the guy, Prentiss does a good job, too.

Lilac's abandonment of the Democratic Party seemed to put to rest the myth that I would be treated with kid gloves by my former colleagues in the news media. The *Record* ran an editorial castigating the Saratoga County Democratic Party for backing me and praising Lilac as a fine public official. The *Saratogian*, a small daily that circulated in the northern end of the Assembly district, also lauded him in an editorial and expressed sympathy for Lilac having "been shelved like a trusty old ornament in favor of former newspaper columnist Dan Lynch. . . . The county Democratic leaders should be embarrassed and sorry for casting off one of the rare big fish in their little pond." And the weekly *Spotlight* papers were touting my race against Prentiss as the hottest one in the Albany metro area—and, at the same time, excusing Prentiss for his failures in office.

"In announcing his candidacy," the *Spotlight* newspapers proclaimed editorially, "Lynch charged that Prentiss has been ineffective. Maybe so, but part of that ineffectiveness derives from the scandalously unfair way minority legislative members are treated. As a general rule, minority members cannot sponsor bills that have a chance of passing, and they also receive far less in member items [discretionary money for nonprofit organizations] than do their colleagues in the majority. So if Prentiss is ineffective in those ways, it's not his fault. . . ."

I'd been filling out the questionnaire for the Civil Service Employees Association, the largest of the state worker unions, when Larry Rosenbaum, the local boss of the Independence Party, called me. We're backing you over Prentiss, he said. That was terrific news. The Independence Party had only 2,100 of the 93,000 registered voters in the district, but that line was crucial to me, especially since Prentiss had the Conservative Party line locked up so tightly.

Rosenbaum told me that, as a courtesy, he'd gone to John Faso's office in the Legislative Office Building to inform him. Faso, Rosenbaum said, had flown into a rage.

"Get out of my office," Faso had roared. "You're stinking up the place."

So, any doubt I might have harbored about the intensity of Faso's opposition to me was now put to rest. The Republican Assembly Campaign Committee, which Faso controlled just as Silver controlled DACC, would be pouring big money into Prentiss's campaign.

And, meanwhile, imposing shamelessly on friends and relatives in precisely the humiliating exercise Neil Breslin had warned me I would have to endure, I'd managed to amass the princely sum of $1,150 for my campaign warchest.

Albany Mayor Jerry Jennings had been ducking me. The deadline for him joining The Committee to Elect Dan Lynch, the fundraising entity I'd registered with the New York

State Board of Elections, was fast approaching. I'd phoned the mayor four times, trying to nail down his affirmative response to my letter. He was not returning those calls.

Finally, I called Jerry Weiss. He was a lawyer and former aide to Mario Cuomo who'd managed Jennings' most recent campaign. What's the mayor's problem, I asked? Nothing, Weiss assured me; Jerry is just busy running the city. Also, Weiss added, Jennings knows that he doesn't need to worry about being eviscerated in the next day's newspaper just because he doesn't call you back right away.

Finally—after Weiss told Jennings about my call to him, I surmised—I did manage to get Jennings on the phone. Are you on the committee or not, I asked? Jennings said he would call me in a week or so for lunch—which, by the way, he never did. Yes, the mayor assured me, he would support me publicly, but he was profoundly unhappy with the involvement in my campaign of both Joe McElroy and Bob Berry.

I took careful note of the addition of that word—"publicly." It carried a distressing connotation—namely, that the mayor might be working against me privately. That was worrisome because Jennings was highly influential with certain unions whose support I was courting and whose financial backing I would need to meet DACC's $15,000 admission price.

McElroy was no longer with the campaign, I informed Jennings. And Berry would serve only a limited role—getting me through the petitioning process and helping the campaign get rolling. Berry had a business to run, I told the mayor, and he might have to opt out in the fall.

Well, Jennings said, there are certain people I don't want using my name for fundraising.

The only person who'll be using your name, I told him, was me. Did he have a problem with me, I asked? No, the mayor said, he didn't.

Nonetheless, I got off the phone nursing some serious doubts about that.

We decided to announce the Independence Party's endorsement on a Saturday—again, to get as much play as possible in the Sunday newspapers with their larger circulations. We decided also to hold the event in the northern portion of the district, in Saratoga County, since the announcement of my candidacy had been held in Colonie, in Albany County. The My Way Cafe in Malta was the perfect location.

The restaurant was a converted roadhouse—converted into a virtual shrine to Frank Sinatra, complete with old Sinatra album covers on the walls and Sinatra music piped into the place all evening. It was operated by a seasoned restaurant chef/owner named John Bove.

I'd gotten to know John when I'd been doing my *Times Union* column. He'd had a sign advertising his restaurant on a nearby state highway, on a pole from which he bought space from the New York State Transportation Department. I'd become aware that he was losing his sign because a McDonald's restaurant had opened nearby, joining another McDonald's that already had a sign on that pole. According to state transportation department rules, with a new sign going up on that pole, the restaurant farthest from the highway exit had to lose its sign. That would be John Bove's place, and losing that sign would cost him some serious business.

When I'd heard about the state's decision, I'd begun nosing around, calling officials of the state transportation department. At that point, the department suddenly decided that maybe both McDonald's restaurants could be accommodated on the same sign—a solution that hadn't occurred to the bureaucrats until they'd confronted the prospect of a critical newspaper column. It had been precisely the sort of column I'd liked to do most—a column about a little guy suffering because of the venality or ineptitude of an uncaring bureaucracy or, just as common, the arrogance or cruelty of some politician. John Faso having poor Joe Cavallaro busted for calling Faso's office was a classic example of that second phenomenon.

John was open only for dinner, so we could stage this press conference in the morning without disrupting his business. We fired off press releases. Then, on a blistering June day, Larry Rosenbaum and his Independence Party people joined me and some people from my campaign at the restaurant for the press conference. We ended up sitting around waiting for the media. Eventually, a grand total of two media people showed up. The *Times Union* sent a reporter, and Channel 13 sent a camera for some footage.

As press conferences go, this one was pretty much a bust, but the coverage itself wasn't terrible. The *Times Union* ended up running a five-paragraph item inside the local section. The *Gazette* gave the story a grudging two paragraphs, written from the press release and buried as deeply as possible inside the newspaper. The *Record*, working from our press release, ran a 15-inch story across five columns. And Channel 13 gave us less than 40 seconds of air time at 6 and 11. Again, because we'd chosen a Saturday for the event, my daughter Kelly had anchored the broadcast—dutifully reading over the air, word-for-word, the copy written for her by the broadcast's producer.

Predictably, the fact that Channel 13 had covered the event at all provided Prentiss with an excuse to attack my daughter again. For weeks, ever since my announcement, Kelly had been the target of a Prentiss inspired letter-writing and e-mail campaign designed to bully the station into taking her off the air. Now Prentiss had his flunky, Lisuzzo, issue another of his semi-literate press releases. It was headlined:

Independence Party Endorsement in 107th
Assembly District disappointing.
WNYT TV-13, employer of candidates (sic) daughter,
only station to report endorsement.

"It appears that WNYT TV-13 is no longer able to disguise their bias for Democratic candidates." Lisuzzo's press release read. "On Saturday evening news reports, only Channel 13 [who employs Lynch's daughter] saw fit to highlight this endorsement with lengthy coverage. The other two stations, TV-6 and TV-10, had no coverage whatever. Incredibly, TV-13 only covered it as if it were a breaking national news story, than (sic) ran the story in the first few minutes of their half hour report as if it were their top story. Shame on Channel 13 for demonstrating for all to witness their liberal Democratic bias in their news reporting. Clearly, those of us who want balance in our news should tune to Channel 6 or 10 for unbiased news with no political agendas seeping into their coverage."

Fallacious attacks on me had come as no particular surprise. I'd been close enough to the political process to expect that. Jan Lemon had warned me early on that if I had any skeletons in my closet, they surely would come rattling out in this campaign.

"Don't sweat it," I'd told her. "I've spent my entire adult life working like a dog and going home at night to my wife. Compared to me, Dagwood Bumstead is a swinger."

What I hadn't expected, though, were the vicious, baseless attacks on my daughter, and I was taking it personally. Even the Cosa Nostra left opponents' children alone.

I was justifiably proud of both my children. In their 20s, each had a bachelor's degree from a good college and was enjoying a successful career in the media. My son, Kevin, apparently, was fortunate that his career was in Florida and not in Albany, like his big sister's. What appalled me most about all this, though, was the fact that Prentiss was attacking my completely apolitical children when he had a daughter who was an active partisan and a son who'd pleaded guilty in a sex crime case.

That was no secret. A few years earlier, the story had received coverage in the Albany news media. Prentiss was well aware that he could attack my daughter with total impunity, however, because he knew me well enough to know that I would never mention his son's criminal record—nor would I permit anybody associated with my campaign to mention it—as this race unfolded. I would never permit a harsh word to be uttered about anybody in Prentiss's family—including his wife, Marlene, who was a practicing partisan politician holding elective office and working vigorously in her husband's campaign.

Bob Prentiss, however, held no such scruples. He was running as vile a campaign as I'd ever seen. He was, however, paying at least a small price for it. In an editorial headlined: "Prentiss should call off the dogs of war," the *Record* ripped into him for the threats against the Volunteer Center and the Center for Independence. Prentiss could deny involvement, the editorial said, but "that is no longer a credible statement."

"If the Republicans are threatening service agencies with the specter of an audit," the *Record* intoned, "Prentiss and his crew are doing his campaign and area non-profits a grave disservice."

For the most part, though, no news media outlet in town seemed to see much wrong with Prentiss's conduct. It was early in the campaign, and nobody was really paying much attention. Also, editors and news directors seemed fearful that if Prentiss were criticized in print or over the air, then their news outlets might find themselves under attack like Channel 13.

Which had the unspeakable temerity to employ my daughter.

8

ROOT OF ALL EVIL

"If men were angels, no government would be necessary."
—James Madison

Every day in this campaign was a new adventure.

I spent 90 minutes giving a talk before a group of Veterans Administration officials in a hotel conference room. It wasn't until I left the room that I realized that my fly had been open throughout the entire appearance. A full 10 days after Lilac switched parties, the *Times Union*, mysteriously, ran a story on how "shocked and disappointed" the members of the Stillwater Democratic Committee were at Lilac's defection. I couldn't figure out what that had been all about. That story should have been done a day or two after Lilac's defection, not nearly two weeks later. I had to assume that it was only a case of a reporter desperate for a story—any story—that day. Meanwhile, though, it remained impossible to get the Albany metro area's largest newspaper to touch any story on Prentiss's bullying of the Volunteer Center and the Center for Independence.

I called Kevin Dailey, the Clifton Park lawyer who'd come so close to defeating Prentiss in the general election four years earlier. I asked for his files on the race. I wanted to see his DACC poll and anything else he might deem useful. Watching the news coverage since my announcement, Dailey said, he'd revised his opinion of my chances in this contest.

"You might pull this off," he told me, "but it'll get dirty."

"It already has," I pointed out.

"Dirtier yet," Dailey warned. "You're younger and smarter than Prentiss. They have to get dirty. They have nothing else they can use to win. They'll portray you as aloof and distant and as having no connection with ordinary people."

Also, Dailey warned, nobody would really help me. The party organizations in the district were painfully weak. The unions wouldn't do much. I needed DACC to raise money, he said, but the Assembly campaign organization would accomplish nothing worthwhile otherwise. In his concession speech four years earlier, Dailey had publicly blamed his loss on DACC's ineptitude.

The following evening, Donna and I appeared at the state headquarters of the Public Employees Federation, a state workers union with 55,000 members, many of them in the 107th Assembly District. I was being honored for some columns I'd done supporting the public employee unions during a protracted contract negotiation with the state. Inexplicably, the Pataki Administration had dragged its feet in reaching a deal with the state's unionized work force, even though the unions had taken no raises for four years while the state's finances were being restored and even though the government was now awash in tax revenues once again.

I'd done those columns long before I'd decided to run, and they were consistent with positions I'd taken on such issues over the years. Like every state, New York had two governments—the temporary government, consisting of elected officials and their political appointees, and the permanent government. The second consisted of the people who actually did the work of government, year in and year out, regardless of which party happened to be in power at the moment. Whenever the politicians treated the permanent government shabbily, I tended to side with the working people.

I felt reasonably confident about the backing of the Civil Service Employees Association, the largest state workers union. PEF, however, tended to back Republicans, and this regional division of the union was more Republican than most other regions. Two years earlier, the Democratic Party's nominee against Prentiss had been a member of the PEF staff who'd dropped out of the race after his own union had formally backed his GOP opponent. That evening, Roger Benson, the union's bearded, professorial statewide president, presented me with a plaque proclaiming me "PEF Advocate of the Year."

I was quite touched by the event—although, of course, not speechless. I delivered a talk on virtues of public service and the devotion of government workers to their neighbors and their communities. Everybody was polite and gracious. Then I left, figuring that it might be possible for me to get this union's backing after all.

Probably not, though.

Joe Laux, the local boss of the Liberal Party, called to ask if I wanted his party's ballot line. He was a good guy, much further to the left than I was but not at all prepared to back Prentiss. Laux's party had about 500 members in my district. I figured that I would get their votes anyway. The question was whether I wanted my name to appear on that ballot line—the one bearing that scary label, "Liberal." How many voters in this conservative district, I wondered, would make it a point to vote against me once they entered the voting booth and spotted my name on that line?

I checked with Burns and Bayly. Ah, take it, they said; what the hell. That'll get your name on the ballot in four places. That's better than having your name there in only three places, isn't it? Besides, the Republicans were calling me a liberal anyway. I might as well get a ballot line out of that name-calling.

The *Spotlight* newspapers, which circulated separate editions in Colonie and Clifton Park, ran a story headlined: "Assembly campaign gets down and dirty." The subhead read: "Prentiss, Lynch, Lisuzzo trade barbs."

The campaign was portrayed in that story as no more than a frenzy of sordid name-calling. The story read, "Prentiss said that if the campaign has gotten nasty, it is because of Lynch's actions, not his.

"'The direction of my campaign is up, high-road, clean,' he said. 'The direction of his campaign is down, low-road, dirty. My opponent has stooped to mud-slinging. I have not.'"

The shameless old fraud once again denied any involvement with Lisuzzo's actions.

"He is not on my payroll; he does not work for me," Prentiss was quoted as saying.

The story also detailed Lisuzzo's attacks on Channel 13. Asked for his response, Paul Conti, the news director, offered the opinion that Lisuzzo had "lost his mind."

Kate Doyle, the Democratic party's candidate for Albany County surrogate judge, also was endorsed by the Republicans. She'd been attending gatherings of both party organizations, showing the flag and smiling relentlessly. At the Albany County Democratic picnic, she told me that she'd recently attended a GOP function at which Prentiss had spoken. Mr. High Road had stood up before the committee people, denounced me as a fat, Irish drunk and promised to walk me into the ground in door-to-door campaigning.

The good part, Kate told me, was that Prentiss's remark seemed to seriously annoy all the fat, Irish drunks on the Republican committee.

Struggling desperately to raise DACC's 15 grand, I'd been sending out letters to the brothers of Pi Lambda Phi, my old college fraternity at Temple University in Philadelphia, seeking political contributions. I'd been out of college more than three decades, but I had the names and addresses of every graduate of the fraternity's Temple chapter. I was asking my Pi Lam brothers to join the 211 Club—a collection of donors willing to help me become one of the 211 members of the New York Legislature. Every day, I checked my campaign's post office box. Happily, a few old friends did make contributions.

One day, I opened an envelope from the post office box containing one of my solicitation letters with a crudely scrawled message across the top. It read:

SUCK WHAT GIVE ME $211.00 AND MAYBE
I'LL VOTE FOR YOU. I DON'T EVEN LIVE IN NEW
YORK GET LOST GET A LIFE YOU FAT CAT I'VE
NEVER EVEN HEARD OF YOU!

I took that as a no.

I met with the PEF political action committee at the
union's state headquarters, a modern office building beside a
four-lane highway in Colonie. It was the same building in
which I'd been awarded my plaque as "PEF Advocate of the
Year." The group consisted of about a dozen people.
Everybody was polite. I fielded their questions for nearly two
hours.

I told them, quite candidly, "Would I like your union's
backing? You bet. If I get it, you can count on me to be supportive on state employee issues. You should also know that if
I don't get it, I'll still be supportive on those issues because the
positions I've taken on such matters in my column and radio
program over the years—and would continue to take as a member of the Assembly—have been based on genuine conviction
rather than on any desire to pander to you."

Toward the end of the session, the guy I'd been looking
for finally entered the room. He was a bulky, gray-haired man
named Dennis Anderson, a devoted Prentiss campaign worker.
Anderson hadn't even bothered to show up on time to listen to
what I might have to say. It just didn't matter to him.

He was friendly and polite. So was everybody else in
the room. Despite the cordiality, however, I left more convinced than ever that PEF would oppose me. The ideas I put

forth, what I had to say and what I might stand for in office, were simply beside the point. Most of these people were Republicans—period—and they would have supported Richard Nixon over Franklin Delano Roosevelt—period. The regional PAC could, however, be overruled by the union's statewide executive committee. That, I figured, would be my only chance at PEF backing.

The CSEA screening panel a week or so later consisted of about 25 people. They were seated around a U-shaped table in a meeting room in the Desmond hotel, where I'd announced my candidacy. I wore my navy blue suit—my "sincere suit," Bob Berry called it. I also understood that this union backed Democrats more often than it backed Republicans. A good many politicians figured it was a game that the state unions played. Each union had pretty much the same legislative agenda. If CSEA went for Democrats and PEF went for Republicans, then the state employee unions had their bases covered no matter what might happen on election day.

They gave me roughly 40 minutes. As I spoke and took questions, Prentiss was waiting outside the door for his own appearance and thus got the last word, as I'd managed to get with the Independence Party people. I would have preferred to have gone after him, not before, but scheduling is sheer luck, as is so much of politics.

I still got to deliver my basic message, although not all of it. Various members of the panel complimented the columns I'd done. I made my policy points, and I managed to get a few laughs along the way. One panel member said that she just loved Kelly on television.

For some reason, I responded, Assemblyman Prentiss seems less fond of her than you are.

I was pressing Bob Berry to get a fundraiser scheduled. I called John Longo at DACC. How soon do you need the 15 grand, I asked? Yesterday, he told me. I immediately called Bill Cunningham, a former aide to Gov. Hugh Carey and now a lobbyist for a big bank. I'd known this guy for years. When I'd announced my candidacy, I'd called him and asked him if he could help me raise money. Cunningham had said he would. Now, he wasn't returning my calls.

Shelly Silver was, however. He'd received my letter asking him to go on my committee. My pleasure, the speaker of the New York Assembly told me over the phone. I breathed a sigh of relief. Shelly's name on my fundraising stationery had to be a big help. More good news came later in the day. In the tray of the fax in my home office, I found a memo from Jennings. He would permit his name to be listed on my committee.

That Saturday morning, I met Cynthia Pooler and a Democratic committeewoman named Joanne Winchell outside the post office in the Village of Stillwater. I was there at Cynthia's suggestion to shake hands and hand out a campaign flyer I'd designed and had printed up. The eight-by-ten flyer contained a blown-up version of my face as it had appeared on my newspaper column logo, the most widely recognized printed image of me, and a sheet of text beneath the headline: "Three Reasons to Vote for Dan Lynch." All through the campaign, I kept waiting for the *Times Union* to complain about the use of that image, but it never happened. I didn't realize at that point that the newspaper paid virtually no attention to campaign literature, no matter what it said.

We stood on the sidewalk outside the busy post office and accosted people as they came out of the facility. We handed out several hundred flyers. Most people were polite. A few wanted to talk. A few were openly rude when I approached them. Either they didn't want to be bothered or were die-hard Republicans coldly furious at the sight of a Democratic candidate on the streets of their village. One jovial, bearded guy with tattoos festooned across his arms said he would vote for me if he could.

Unfortunately, he was a convicted felon.

The best way to win any election is to make sure that your opponent's name never gets on the ballot in the first place. The New York Legislature, a deliberative body with the most highly developed sense of self-preservation in American political life, had made a point of crafting laws to create the most restrictive ballot access process in the nation.

To get on the ballot as a major party candidate in any state legislative district, you needed to file with the State Board of Elections petition forms containing many hundreds of signatures of voters enrolled in that party. Since signatures could be invalidated in court on any number of specious grounds, the general rule of thumb was that a would-be candidate needed twice as many signatures as the law required to ensure that his or her name made it to the ballot in November.

Mary Gilson had turned her volunteers over to the party organizations to help obtain signatures on my petitions. The town chairs had assigned her and her people the most Republican districts in their communities—generally, places in which the town chairs didn't even have committee people in place to carry petitions. The volunteers ended up with the election districts where Democrats were few and far between. In sprawling Clifton Park and relatively sparsely settled Stillwater, that meant the most rural districts.

"I have to drive the volunteers from house to house," Mary complained to me. "The houses can be hundreds of yards apart—miles apart up in Stillwater. If I just let the volunteers out of the car to wander along the road, I could come back to find coyotes gnawing on their bones."

Petition carriers worked from voter lists. They would identify the home of a Democrat, walk up to that door, ask the Democrat residing therein to sign my petition and then check the signature against the name on the voter rolls. The name had to appear precisely as it appeared in the voting records. If I'd signed my own petition as "Dan Lynch," the name by which I was known to the public, instead of as "Daniel G. Lynch," my legal name and the one that appeared on the voter rolls, my own signature would have been disallowed. As it was, I couldn't even sign my own petitions. I wasn't enrolled as a member of any of the four political parties backing me.

Technically, even a stray pencil mark could invalidate an entire petition sheet. Moreover, if a single name on a petition sheet was knocked off in court, the entire sheet could be thrown out—good signatures as well as bad ones right down the drain. Judges had grown less restrictive since Cynthia Pooler had run for the Assembly in the 1980s and learned about this nonsensical system. Higher courts had warned ominously that these elected state judges who ran with party backing were coming perilously close to violating citizens' constitutional rights with such overly strict interpretations of the law. Construe the law more liberally, the appeals courts warned.

Still, Cynthia Pooler was taking no chances. She got one signature per petition sheet; that was it.

If a faulty signature was to be disallowed by some hack, partisan judge, Cynthia Pooler wasn't about to lose a whole sheet of good signatures along with it.

My campaign committee was coming together. Mario Cuomo called from his law office in Manhattan to say he would be happy to have his name used—although, the former governor added, he believed me to be demented to have involved myself in all this. Equally accommodating were Eliot Spitzer, the state's attorney general, and H. Carl McCall, the state comptroller.

I met Bob Berry for lunch at a diner near his office. We have all the names, I told him. Let's now get this stationery printed up, send out invitations to a fundraising affair and get DACC its money. Fine, Berry said. One small problem, though. He might not be able to stay with the campaign into the fall. He had private business to attend to.

Yeah, okay, I said; for now, though, let's just get rolling on this.

I needed a scheduler and a walking boss. Mike Mann, I knew, would be perfect for both jobs. Also, I was used to having Mike order me around.

A gentle, bearded, good-hearted guy in his mid-30s, Mike had been the producer on my one-hour show on WROW. I quickly decided that I'd never met anybody I enjoyed working with more. Mike was bright, sunny of disposition, possessed of sound, prudent judgment and never flustered.

Many months before I decided to run—and when I realized that Mike wasn't making the money he deserved at WROW—I'd made a phone call to one of Shelly's key aides and helped Mike get a job on the staff of the Assembly majority. Mike was now working in the broadcast division of the Legislature, conducting and editing interviews with lawmakers that aired on cable TV operations back in their districts.

I knew that working in a serious Democratic campaign for the Assembly could help Mike look good to his new bosses, so after I announced my candidacy I asked him to work on my campaign as a volunteer. And work he did—like a galley slave. For many months, Mike gave up every spare moment to help me win that election—and to help me retain my sanity by listening to me bitch about politicians and unions and fundraising, day after day, as we walked door-to-door throughout the 107th Assembly District. As I got deeper and deeper into this campaign, I found myself discovering new virtues in the entire concept of military dictatorships.

The scheduler in a political campaign tells the candidate where to go and when to go there. Early on in a race, the job consists of scanning every newspaper in the area and selecting events at which the candidate will show up, be seen and attract some votes. Later, the job consists of choosing which invitations to speak or appear the candidate will accept or reject.

The walking boss in a campaign chooses the neighborhoods in the district where the candidate will walk door-to-
door—disturbing people during dinner, shaking their hands,
pressing campaign literature upon them and, hopefully, getting
their votes. The walking boss also accompanies the candidate
as this grinding chore is carried out, keeping notes on voters'
reactions at each house and making sure that voters who react
favorably to the candidate are contacted by mail or phone—
and, preferably, by both methods—just before election day and
reminded to actually get out and vote.

Chris Andreucci, the chief aide to Albany County
Executive Mike Breslin, had supplied me with a list of the
swing election districts in Colonie. A computer had crunched
numbers for seven separate elections—federal, state and local.
The districts had been ranked by their relative value. With
93,000 voters in the district, it was obvious from the start that I
would be unable to knock on every door in the 107th. I would,
instead, walk in election districts where my physical presence
could have the most positive impact. That meant that walking
in hard Democratic or Republican districts, where voters tended to vote predictably on the basis of party affiliation, made little sense. Instead, I would go door-to-door in districts where
voters were less likely to vote party and more likely to vote for
the individual.

That was just the opposite of Prentiss's strategy, we later
figured out. With a heavy enrollment edge, he did most of his
walking in hard GOP districts, trying to motivate a high turnout
among Republican voters. He never got near the swing districts
until close to election day.

Mike and I began walking in late June in the Latham
section of Colonie. Late on a sweltering Monday afternoon,
ducking for shelter beneath tree limbs during periodic down-
pours of tropical intensity, we hit about 45 houses. I would go

to the door and ring the bell. If a voter came to the door, I would begin my rap.

"Hi," I would say, "I'm Dan Lynch. I'm running for the state Assembly in this district. I hope I can count on your support."

I would hand the voter my flyer and add, "This is a brief summary of what I stand for. Please look at that, and if you have any questions feel free to give me a call. My phone number is at the bottom."

Which it was. Absent a campaign headquarters—and I wasn't about to waste a dime in rent until after I'd raised DACC's $15,000 admission fee—I was listing the phone in my home office on my campaign literature. A few conscientious citizens actually called that number, too, and I always got back to them.

If nobody came to the door, I would then scrawl across the flyer, "Sorry I missed you." I would then stick the flyer, folded in half, in the crack between the door and the doorjamb. Or in the door handle. Or, in the case of the typical suburban home where residents enter through the garage, in the garage door handle. Or I would affix the flyer to the door with a piece of clear tape. Whatever it took to leave that literature where it would be read, that's what we would do. Then we would move on to the next house.

At first, we made it a point to avoid cutting across lawns. We were concerned about offending grass-worshipping suburbanites. It soon became obvious, however, that the name of the game in this exercise was volume. Every wasted step represented lost time. So, I spent the entire campaign marching across lawns and bounding over hedges, like a steeple-chaser.

Mike and I did the math. If we managed to hit a house every two minutes, we would average 30 houses an hour. With four hours walking every weeknight and six hours each weekend day, that was more than 900 houses a week we would walk to. Factor in bad weather and nights off for public appearances, and we figured we could hit perhaps 10,000 homes by election day. At an average of 1.5 votes per household unit, that meant we could personally connect with 15,000 of the district's 93,000 voters through this method. That 15,000 figure represented roughly 25 per cent of the 60,000 or so voters I expected to cast ballots in this race, based on the 1996 turnout figures.

Within a few weeks, after walking three or four hours every evening and as many as six hours each weekend day, both my knees were acting up. They'd been shredded many years earlier in high school football. I'd never gotten around to having the necessary surgery performed to remove excess scar tissue from the knee joints, and I certainly couldn't afford to be off my feet even a single day during this campaign. So, each morning I would brace the knees with stretch bandages, pulled tight across the joints. The last few months of the campaign, I was also taping my ankles. This was like high school football all over again, only now I was 54 years old.

Despite his reputation as a tireless door-to-door campaigner, Prentiss never got out on the streets until after Labor Day. The Democratic committee people in all four towns in the district were well aware of when and where candidates went door-to-door. They were surprised that Prentiss took so long to get busy. I wasn't. He hadn't had a real contest in four years, and he was a decade older than I was. I'd figured that Prentiss could no longer tolerate the summer heat. That was, in fact, one reason I began walking early in the race—because I could do it and I doubted that he could. Most afternoons, Mike and I walked drenched in sweat, periodically dousing ourselves from small plastic bottles of cologne. That effort scored points with people at their doors.

"Wow," one woman told me that first day walking, "it's pretty hot to be doing what you're doing."

"That's okay," I told her. "In October, it'll be cold, so it all evens out."

Most walking tours generated personal contact with voters in their doorways at two houses in three. I found myself recognized by not quite half the people to whom I spoke. Where candidates with enrollment edges tended to use voter rolls as road maps and knocked on the doors only of independents and voters enrolled in their own party, I couldn't afford that luxury—not with Democrats constituting only 25 per cent of the district's voters. So Mike and I walked to every door, regardless of the enrollment of the voters therein.

Even though I was well aware that stops at the doors of most Republican voters were a time-consuming waste of effort and energy, I still had to try.

Sandy Family, a successful financial advisor and, briefly, a neighbor of mine, had offered, before I announced my candidacy, to throw a fundraising event on my behalf. Now, I was calling on him.

"How do we do this?" he asked.

"Well, I'll write up a letter that you can send out to clients on your stationery inviting them to a fundraising cocktail party. We can hold the event in your office or in a rented room in some hotel. The campaign will handle the mailing and whatever costs are involved."

"Fax me the letter," Sandy suggested.

I wrote up the letter and faxed it to Sandy's office.

Thereafter, he refused to accept my calls or to return them. I never had the slightest clue as to what that was all about.

The first propaganda letter appeared June 26th.

A standard technique for any political campaign is the creation of a "message group." These are campaign workers who call in to radio talk shows, where virtually every listener is also a voter, to deliver the campaign's "message." Their names also appear at the bottom of letters to the editors of various newspapers—again, delivering the message to voters that the candidate wants delivered.

In reality, most of these letters are crafted by the campaign's wordsmiths and only signed by the purported author. In some cases, the supposed letter-writer simply gives the campaign permission to use his or her name on any letter the campaign wants to see printed. Anybody who believes letters to the editor relating to any campaign to be legitimate expressions of viewpoint by ordinary, concerned citizens is living in dreamland.

This letter appeared in a weekly, give-away newspaper that circulated in the Capitol and state office. The *Legislative Gazette* was produced by students in the State University of New York system and was designed to reach people with an interest in state government. This letter was signed by some guy in Latham I'd never heard of, although he clearly was one of Prentiss's campaign people.

"I am surprised," the letter read, "that former *Times Union* columnist and radio talk show host Dan Lynch is seeking the Civil Service Employees Union (CSEA) endorsement.

[Actually, the union's name was the Civil Service Employees *Association*, but in virtually every one of its written communications the Prentiss campaign could be counted upon to commit some boneheaded error.] Dan Lynch has been an outspoken critic of the need for village and town governments in New York and more than 50 per cent of CSEA's members work in local government units."

That was close to being true, actually. I'd done several columns on the need to streamline local government. For historical reasons, New York had nearly 3,500 units of local government—villages inside towns inside counties. New York had more than 800 separate school districts instead of administering education on the county level, as did low-cost states. New York was the most minutely governed major state in the nation. The Albany metro area, with fewer than a million residents, was governed by 770 separate taxing units. The half dozen or so states that had more units of local government were places like Nebraska—states with many tiny, far-flung farming communities. In the land of the five-man high school football team— Nebraska has 21 citizens per square mile—people needed that many local governments. Most New Yorkers—the Empire State has 385 citizens per square mile—didn't.

I'd explained this under questioning by the CSEA screening panel. I'm not talking about doing away with your jobs, I explained. The snow will fall regardless of artificial lines on some political map, and it'll still have to be plowed. I'm talking instead, I said, about doing away with the jobs of some of those thousands of small-town, small-time local politicians who are collecting needless public salaries and, later, fat, publicly supported pensions. New York, I pointed out to the CSEA screening panel, was an 8-5 Democratic state, but three out of four of its local elected officials were Republicans holding down offices in outdated, totally vestigial local governments. The current system worked to give New York the highest per capita local taxes in America—fully 70 per cent over the national average—and it essentially constituted welfare for local GOP politicians and their campaign workers in local government patronage positions.

The letter in the *Legislative Gazette* went on to quote from a couple of my columns—totally out of context, of course—and concluded by saying, "This is truly an astonishing campaign plank for a candidate seeking the endorsement of New York's largest union of local government employees. The question is whether the lure of a celebrity endorsement is worth risking the jobs of thousands of CSEA's members."

Mr. High Road was at it again.

In every spare moment I could squeeze out, I'd been on the phone, pressing Mike Burns and Tom Bayly to get that Wilson-Pakula Proclamation signed. By law, they had to meet formally and sign the thing together in the presence of a notary public. I even offered to pick up Burns at his ironworkers union office and drive him to Bayly's house. Given what I knew was grumbling opposition to my candidacy in some quarters of the Albany County Democratic machine—especially the tepid support of Jennings, who controlled Burns utterly—I fretted over Burns simply deciding not to sign the document. If he didn't, then I would be on the ballot lines of the other three political parties that had endorsed me, but not on the key line I needed to win this thing. Burns kept putting me off.

Finally, I got a call from Josh Ehrlich. He was an election lawyer who worked for the Democratic minority in the

New York State Senate. Bob Berry had recruited Ehrlich to guide the campaign through the thicket of legal minutiae that surrounded the petition process and ensure that those petitions stood up to court challenges. Meet me, Ehrlich said.

We got together at a diner in the district. He presented me with the signed Wilson-Pakula Proclamation for my own signature. Burns had come through after all. All lawyers in New York are automatically notaries. I signed. Josh witnessed. It was done. I was officially the Democratic Party's candidate for the New York Assembly in the 107th District.

Now, all I had to do was win.

9

A KNIFE IN THE BACK

"Journalism: A profession whose business it is to explain to others what it personally does not understand."—Lord Northcliffe

In a letter to Larry Rosenbaum, the leader of the Albany County Independence Party, Prentiss said he wanted the party leadership's permission to permit his name to appear on the party's ballot in the September primary election. Essentially, Prentiss wanted the party leadership's permission to challenge me in the Independence Party's primary. Prentiss was requesting that Rosenbaum issue him what the assemblyman's letter referred to as a "Wilson-Pecula." The proper name of this legal document was a "Wilson-Pakula Proclamation." No, Rosenbaum replied.

Thirty years in politics, and Prentiss still couldn't spell the name of one of the lawmakers who'd sponsored that crucial portion of the New York election code.

On my way home from an early morning appointment, with Vandenburgh's show coming through my car radio, I heard him chatting on the air with Fred Dicker of the *New York Post*, who had a one-hour program on WROW.

"I haven't seen Lynch lately," Vandenburgh was saying. "I wonder where he is. Some mail came into the station for him."

I was driving near the radio station, so I swung by there just as Vandenburgh was coming off the air and emerging from his studio. The mail he had for me consisted of a few letters from would-be volunteers who knew no other way to contact me. This conservative Republican talk show host told me, however, that he was being swamped by e-mails and blind faxes accusing him of serving as my on-air campaign manager. Apparently, Prentiss was trying to intimidate Vandenburgh just as he was trying to intimidate Channel 13. Vandenburgh, however, was not easily bullied into ignoring political news. Local politics was the mainstay of the news-talk radio station he ran.

"I want to hold a debate on my show between you and Prentiss," he told me.

"Fine. Just let me know the day and time, and I'll be here."

"Well, I'm not sure he'll do it. He debated on my show in his other campaigns, but he's not returning my calls to his office this time. I think he's afraid to debate you."

That was my supposition as well. Prentiss was widely viewed as a clumsy speaker and not at all quick on his feet. He would dodge every debate invitation, I was certain, fearful that his poor performance would cost him votes.

That meant that I would, at some point, have to come up with some mechanism for flushing the incumbent out of hiding.

Still struggling to get those few final names on my campaign committee, I called George Infante. He was a man of about 80, a retired senior New York State Police officer who'd served a few terms as Albany County sheriff. He was now serving as one of Albany County's 39 legislators. George didn't live in the district, but we'd always had a cordial relationship, and I liked him enormously. He hadn't responded to my request to have his name appear on the committee stationery. I wondered what his problem might be.

I can't do it, Infante told me. There are a few paragraphs in the Sons of Italy newsletter critical of a column you wrote. Which column, I asked? The Godfather column, Infante explained.

The column in question had appeared in early February. It had dealt with the sudden firing by the Pataki administration of several high-ranking patronage workers who'd obtained their jobs courtesy of Joe Bruno, the State Senate majority leader. It was unclear whether Pataki had ordered the firings himself or if the action had been taken by his chief political aide, a notoriously warlike woman named Zenia Mucha. What was clear, however, was that Bruno had been butting heads with the governor over several issues, most notably over whether New York City Mayor Rudy Giuliani should be the party's candidate against Hillary Clinton for the U.S. Senate. Bruno was for Giuliani. Pataki opposed him. Thus, the patronage appointees had been fired.

The firings also had given rise to speculation that Pataki, who was angling for the second spot on the GOP presidential ticket as George W. Bush's running mate, was trying to convince the State Senate Republicans to oust Bruno as their leader. The governor and then-U.S. Senator Al D'Amato had done precisely that to Bruno's predecessor, Ralph Marino. There was strong talk that Pataki was trying to replace Bruno with one of three other, more pliable senators—Tom Libous of Binghamton, Dean Skelos of Long Island or Nick Spano of Westchester County.

Bruno's press secretary, Marcia White, had downplayed the seriousness of the clash, trying to make the strife go away. In supporting Bruno in the dispute, I'd done a satirical piece on the purported assassination plot. The *Times Union* copy desk had put this headline on it—"And check the bed for horse heads." The column had read as follows:

> *A totally true news item:*
>
> *Without warning, the office of Gov. George E. Pataki fired a half dozen or so administration employees who'd obtained their jobs courtesy of State Senate Majority Leader Joe Bruno, a member of the governor's own party.*
>
> *For the record, the governor's office would say only that people come and go in government jobs. For the record, Senator Bruno's office would say only that the closest of family members can have their differences.*
>
> As usual, the drapes were tightly closed in Don Joe's dimly lit office. His consigliere, Marcia White, entered to find the Don behind his desk, deep in thought.
>
> "You sent for me, Don Joe?" the consigliere said.
>
> "Yes. It has come to my attention that some of our most highly valued soldiers now sleep with the fishes because of an unfortunate action by Don George 'The Hungarian' Pataki. I am much distressed by this. As you know, I am by nature a peaceful man. Why do you think The Hungarian has done such a thing?"
>
> "It might not have been him, Don Joe. All this blood-shed might have been the work of one or several of his

capos. It is widely suspected that The Hungarian is too weak a Don to control his people. We all know that The Hungarian is not attentive to his family's affairs. All too often, he's at home in Garrison watching 'The Sopranos.'"

"This is true," Don Joe replied, "but it is hard for me to conceive of a Don so uninvolved in his family's business that murder on such a scale could occur without his approval. The question is, what is The Hungarian after?"

"Apparently," the consigliere said, "The Hungarian seeks a seat on the national commission. Perhaps he feels the need to whack anyone who offers him anything but unqualified support in all matters. Consider, after all, how hard he worked against the interests of Don Rudy 'The Pussycat' Giuliani before pressure from you and the other Dons forced him to reconsider."

"But what might The Hungarian do next?" Don Joe wondered aloud.

"Well," said the consigliere, "he might be working secretly with some of your capos to have you whacked, too, Don Joe."

"The possibility of treachery has crossed my mind," Don Joe admitted. "I have reason to believe that The Hungarian has been meeting privately with some of my capos, possibly in an attempt to move against me. I recall with great vividness how The Hungarian and his late sponsor, the sainted Don Alfonse 'The Ethical Humanist' D'Amato, whacked my predecessor, Don Ralph Marino. Don Ralph's capos turned on him, and the garrote was around his neck before he knew it."

"Can we trust all our capos, Don Joe?"

"Surely not. But which of them might be in league with The Hungarian? That's the question."

"How can you determine which capo it is until it's too late?"

"Oh, I'll know," Don Joe assured his consigliere. "The one who offers to set up a meeting between The Hungarian and me, that'll be the one."

At which point Don Joe's phone rang. He answered to hear his secretary say, "Don Joe, Capos Skelos, Spano and Libous are here. They say they're trying to set up a meeting they would like you to attend."

Don Joe ran his hand slowly through his silvery hair. He gazed up at his consigliere, an expression of resignation on his face.

"Contact Don Shelly," he ordered. "And while you're at it, order some mattresses."

This column had annoyed a retired college professor named Jim Mancuso. He'd written a letter to the editor complaining about it, and I'd invited him on my radio program for a full hour to debate the issue with me. Mancuso had turned out to be a bright, highly opinionated guy, and the debate had been spirited. He'd steadfastly maintained that the column had constituted an anti-Italian slur. What really had him upset, it seemed, was HBO's immensely popular mob-oriented series, "The Sopranos." I have nothing to do with that series, I told him on the air, and this column was satire, not a slur. Mancuso had remained unconvinced, but I'd given him his say in front of many thousands of people.

Mancuso, George Infante told me, was extremely active in the Sons of Italy. Send me the newsletter, I asked George. No, he said. Annoyed now, I demanded, "Do you think I'm an anti-Italian bigot?" No, Infante said; he'd had no problem with the column personally, but he had to consider what other people were thinking. I was disappointed at how spineless George seemed to be over all this. Then set me up for a meeting with the group, I urged him. Infante said he would call the president of the local Sons of Italy chapter. I had my doubts, however, that he actually would do it.

The fact was that I hadn't heard even a peep out of any of the Italian-American community groups in the district, and I'd already attended several of their functions, shaking hands and chatting with hundreds of people. I was acutely aware that people with Italian surnames constituted more than one in four voters in the district and they tended to be Republicans. That was one reason I'd wanted George on my committee—along with such people as Mario Cuomo, Tony Catalfamo and Frank Commisso, the majority leader of the Albany County Legislature.

So, here was a little problem I'd found out about purely by accident—which, incidentally, is generally how you learn about problems in politics. Nobody, I was coming to realize, would ever stand up and say anything to my face.

Given my doubts about George Infante's willingness to set me up with a meeting with the Sons of Italy leadership, I then called Al Paolucci. Al was a Jack McEneny staffer and active in Italian-American community affairs. I briefed him on the situation and asked him to set up a meeting for me.

No problem, Al said.

Mike Mann and I were walking Election District 21 in Colonie, a collection of steep hills studded with fancy suburban homes. We were leaving a trail of sweat as we stomped up and down the hills in the summer swelter.

"You told me we'd be walking," Mike grumbled to me. "This is hiking."

"Remind me," I told him, "the next time I run for office, I should do it in Kansas."

At one house in this fairly ritzy neighborhood, we encountered a retired Republican judge and his wife. They knew Prentiss personally. They were voting for me. The next night, we walked another neighborhood in that same district, accompanied by a guy who lived there. His name was Carl Korn. He'd once worked for me at the *Times Union*. Carl now worked for the New York State United Teachers, the key teachers union in the state and the district.

As usual, we ignored the voter rolls—or, as they were referred to by the party organizations, the "walk sheets"—and went to every house. One guy was extraordinarily gracious. He smiled, took my flyer and wished me luck. We'd known when we'd knocked on his door that he was a lawyer for the Assembly Republicans. This guy's boss was John Faso, the Assembly GOP leader.

As we left the house, Carl Korn said, "Well, if Prentiss doesn't have a copy of your campaign literature by now, he'll have a piece of it tomorrow."

Carl was surprised at how well we were being received in what was generally a Republican neighborhood. By now, Mike and I had knocked on roughly 1,000 doors. Response had been almost universally favorable. Nobody had been rude. Many people had promised to vote for me. Anecdotally, we were looking pretty good in this race.

Which, without a poll, meant precisely nothing.

❖ ❖ ❖

At this early stage of the race, Bill Hammond of the *Gazette* was the only daily newspaper reporter writing anything about this campaign. Given what Carl Strock, the *Gazette*'s local columnist, had told me about his bosses asking him to bash me, I wasn't at all sure that Hammond's attentions represented good news. His story a few days later seemed a case in point.

Three in four voters in the district weren't Democrats, and neither was I, even though I was on the Democratic Party tickct, among others. Nonetheless, Hammond reported that I'd recently enrolled as a Democrat, which I had not done.

In a story headlined, "Lynch lines up top names for campaign," he reported that my campaign committee consisted of the state's most prominent Democrats. (Only U.S. Senator Daniel Patrick Moynihan was not among them—Moynihan having finally gotten back to me days after the deadline and after the campaign stationery already had been printed.) Hammond didn't bother to mention in that story that my campaign committee also included the leadership of the Independence Party and a number of union leaders.

Hammond quoted Prentiss as saying, "What's the news here? That's the leadership of the Democratic Party. I have the support of the Republican Party—starting with the governor on down."

The fact was that Prentiss had no campaign committee. That was because none of the state's prominent Republicans, with the exception of Faso, would have lent their names to his campaign fundraising efforts. The governor never endorsed him. Joe Bruno never endorsed him. Hammond, however, never asked these guys about that. He merely took what Prentiss told him and committed it to print, like a stenographer.

"We haven't produced a letterhead with the names on it," he quoted Prentiss as saying. "I don't think there's much point to it. . . . It's just so much window-dressing."

The *Gazette* editors also took another Prentiss statement in the story and pulled it out to display in bigger type under the headline in what's known in the newspaper trade as a "billboard quote." The billboard quote read:

> "It just shows [Lynch] is going to be beholden to the
> downstate, New York City liberal political bosses."
> —Robert Prentiss, Assemblyman, R-Colonie

Fred LeBrun, the *Times Union* columnist, was on the radio, telling WROW listeners as he filled in for one of the regular talk show hosts that he disapproved of my running for office. Journalists should never involve themselves in politics, LeBrun was saying; it's unseemly.

Hearing this as I drove to a campaign appearance, I contemplated calling in and pointing out that the only paying job John F. Kennedy ever held down, aside from military service, was as a journalist. He'd written a book on World War II and covered foreign affairs for some news service for a while. Then Kennedy got elected to Congress and was off and running in politics. For a long moment, I pondered making that call on my cell phone.

The hell with it, I decided finally.

Bob Berry finally had hired a hotel meeting room and scheduled the campaign's first fundraising event. Now, I needed to put together a mailing list. It was easy enough to get a list of the 2,000-plus lobbyists registered with state government. Grudgingly, the Legislature finally had made that information available to the public on-line. With me not yet a DACC "client," however, the lobbying community would be unlikely to show up in great numbers at any fundraiser for me. Without DACC in my corner after a DACC poll deemed me a viable candidate, I might be down with the electorate by 2-1 for all the lobbyists knew. And even lobbyists need to hoard their money. The names of faithful Democratic givers on the local level, therefore, were crucial. This would be the fundraiser that would raise the money for DACC's poll. Then, if I did well in that poll, the next fundraiser would raise money for the campaign itself.

I could have a volunteer—or, more appropriately, an entire squad of volunteers—dig through the financial filings of every Democratic politician in the Albany metro area. They were all on file with the State Board of Elections. That would be a monumental chore, however. It seemed to make more sense to ask Burns and Bayly for their fundraising lists, so I did.

Bayly said he would get his list to me. He never did. I later came to realize that probably was because he had no such list—or because the list he did have was so slim that it would have embarrassed him to supply me with it. His party was down 3-1 in enrollment in Saratoga County and held no county offices. Any money the Saratoga County Democratic Party raised came in mainly on the basis of political conviction, not the power to award patronage or local government contracts. Conviction tends not to be a lucrative source of funding for local political organizations.

The Albany Democratic organization, however, operated under no such handicap. It controlled government both on the county level and in the city. Surely, the Albany County Democrats owned a fat fundraising list. I asked for it. At Burns' instructions, I directed my request to Betty Momrow, the elderly woman who served as the county party's secretary.

Betty was utterly devoted to the Albany County Democratic organization. Past 80, she went to party headquarters every day and functioned as the organization's unpaid but ferociously dedicated office manager. She'd been the Colonie Democratic chair until Tony Catalfamo had defeated her for that leadership role. Betty was always polite to me, and she'd agreed to go on my committee after I'd hounded her on the topic. I was well aware, however, that she was no fan. I was Tony's candidate, not hers. Moreover, Jim Coyne, the disgraced former county executive who'd been sent to federal prison after the *Times Union*'s three years of reporting on corruption in the construction of the downtown arena, had been Betty's boy.

When I called to ask her for the fundraising list, Betty hemmed and hawed. Call Burns, I suggested, informing her that I was getting into my car and headed toward party headquarters on Colvin Avenue to get the thing from her. Once I picked up the list, I met Bob Berry for lunch and handed it to him.

"It was a bitch to get this thing," I told him.

"So," Bob Berry said, "what's the surprise?"

A few days later, I learned of another problem. Mayor Jennings wasn't up for election until the following year. Nonetheless, he'd scheduled a $400-a-head fundraiser to be held precisely two days before mine. That timing was certain to reduce the take at my own affair. Political contributors, like everybody else, have only so much money available at any given moment.

I couldn't help but suspect that Jennings might have scheduled this fundraiser at that precise time at the request of U.S. Representative John Sweeney, his close personal friend and a guy who surely was not pleased at the prospect of having me serving in public office in his district and possibly representing a threat down the road. Jennings had helped Sweeney before. He'd even sponsored a fundraiser for Sweeney two years earlier, openly opposing the Democratic party's candidate in that race. If Jennings had timed this event to conform with Sweeney's wishes, then the mayor of Albany was actively working against me, despite having lent his name to my campaign committee.

And despite having promised me that he would help me win this election.

I owed Donna a bagel.

Every day, I was out early and home late. My wife and I weren't seeing much of one another. So, one morning—before the day's frenzy began—I took her out for breakfast. The jaunt was partly business, though. We had to stop by Jan Lemon's house so Donna, who was an enrolled Democrat while I was not, could sign some candidates' petitions, including mine.

Jan Lemon's attitude toward my candidacy seemed to have undergone a distinct transformation. As her committee people carried my petitions around Clifton Park, she told me, they were getting highly positive responses from Democratic voters they asked to sign them. The committee people had touched base with hundreds of Democratic voters, she told me, and I seemed to be both well-known and highly thought of.

Maybe a few people in town had heard of me after all, Jan had concluded. She said that she was glad to have me as the candidate.

I was reading the papers, sipping coffee and listening to Vandenburgh's morning program on WROW. Phil Barrett, the Republican supervisor of Clifton Park, was being interviewed by phone. Out of the blue, Barrett said to Vandenburgh: "Did you know that Dan Lynch wants to consolidate all the volunteer fire companies in the district?"

Instantly, I grabbed the phone and called the show. By the time I got on, though, Barrett was off the air.

"I understand that Phil Barrett was just on your show telling lies about me," I told Vandenburgh and his listeners. "Just to set the record straight, what Barrett said about me wanting to consolidate all the volunteer fire companies bears no relationship to anything I've ever said or written. It's just the usual fiction. Barrett can call in again, if he likes, and try to support that lie. I would love to hear him do that."

For some reason, Barrett declined to call back.

The *Spotlight* newspapers ran a huge story on the Albany County Republican party. It was, the weeklies reported, enrolling its workers in the Independence Party in an attempt to elect Independence Party committee people who were actually GOP loyalists. The plan was to have the Republicans elected in the September primary election as Independence Party committee people and then to knock out Larry Rosenbaum and the other legitimately elected Independence Party leadership.

The motivation? To ensure that the Independence Party endorsed no more candidates backed by the Democrats—people like Dan Lynch, the story reported—and to wreak vengeance on Rosenbaum and company for failing to back Prentiss this time around.

"We're challenging them across the board," Albany County Republican Chairman Peter Kermani said in the *Spotlight* story.

There was only one problem. Doing what the Republicans were doing was an explicit violation of New York state election law. Kermani, a new county chairman, apparently hadn't understood that and had made the mistake of speaking freely to the *Spotlight* reporter. In the end, the Republicans backed off the plan. Not before they had Larry Rosenbaum sweating profusely, though.

Prentiss immediately held a press conference to assail Rosenbaum for the Independence Party's decision to deny Prentiss a Wilson-Pakula Proclamation. That meant that if Prentiss wanted to wage a primary fight against me on that line in September, he would have to do it as a write-in candidate. Prentiss was livid at the press conference. All three daily newspapers covered it, although the *Times Union* failed to contact me for my reaction to what Prentiss had to say. The extent to which my old employer was bending over backwards to appear unbiased in this race actually was doing me harm.

Hilariously, Prentiss took the occasion to call for term

limits. This guy had held down one public office or another for three decades. On his way out of the Albany County Legislature after 19 years of service to challenge Arnie Proskin for the Assembly, Prentiss had introduced a bill to limit county legislators' terms to eight years. Apparently, term limits hadn't struck him as a good idea until precisely that moment, when he was no longer personally affected.

Kevin Hogan of the *Record* called for my reaction to Prentiss's complaint about the Independence Party and his call for term limits. I pointed out that this was only one more example of the blatant hypocrisy that politicians engage in routinely. You'll notice, I told Hogan, that you don't see Prentiss demanding that the Conservative Party issue me a Wilson-Pakula so I can challenge him in the primary for that line. And, as for his call for term limits?

"If you look up the phrase 'professional politician' in the dictionary," I told Hogan, "you'll find Bob Prentiss's picture right next to it."

The deadline arrived and my petitions were submitted to the New York State Board of Elections. The party organizations and my volunteers had gathered 1,360 signatures on my behalf—three times what the law required. The sheer volume of names, Josh Ehrlich assured me, guaranteed that Prentiss wouldn't bother challenging my nominating petitions.

Quite definitely, my name would be on the ballot in November.

The following Sunday, I picked up all three local dailies, as was my custom. There was Prentiss on the front page of both the *Record* and *Gazette*, gathered with about 40 people in front of an abandoned house in Colonie. He was demanding that the bank that was foreclosing on the vacant property mow the lawn and clean up the lot.

This was strictly a local government matter. The state legislator for the district had no role whatever in this neighborhood issue. Moreover, despite the fact that the bank didn't have custody of the property, Prentiss had made it a point to attack the bank rather than the town government because town government in Colonie was controlled by the Republicans.

Although the *Times Union* ran a piece on it the following day, the story quickly died. Prentiss never again mentioned the issue—although, after all the attention he'd gotten on it, I'd expected him to set up a vigil on the lawn until it was mowed. I later learned why he'd dropped it. Bill Powers, the state Republican chairman, was a member of the bank's board. Prentiss, apparently, had failed to check the board's membership before beating up on the bank, and Powers had been less than thrilled.

Immediately, I called Bob Berry and made sure that the bank's executive committee received invitations to my fundraiser.

By law, candidates' fundraising committees must file periodically with the state board of elections a list of contributions and expenditures. Rose Egan, Donna's best friend, was the treasurer of the Committee to Elect Dan Lynch. She filed the report of our meager contributions and expenditures. That was, surely, examined in minute detail by Prentiss's campaign people. My team examined his filing, certainly.

We found some odd stuff. For one thing, I noticed that the Ironworkers Union had contributed $250 to the Prentiss campaign. Clearly, that was a ticket to some fundraising event. The problem with that was only that Mike Burns was the leader of the Ironworkers. What was his union doing donating to Republican candidates—particularly, this Republican candidate—while Burns was serving as chairman of the Albany County Democratic Party?

I called Burns and asked him about it directly. It always seemed to freak out politicians when I did a thing like that. Direct questions unnerved them. Well, Burns explained, I'm the union leader, but I don't have much to do with its political action operations. Burns said he would check into it and get back to me with a more precise explanation. He never did. It was right about then that I concluded that Mike Burns might not be the world's most trustworthy and honorable guy.

While my campaign had spent about $1,700 of the $3,163 we'd collected—a grand of our total collections having come in the form of a donation from my brother, Tim, and another as a $1,000 loan from an old friend of mine in Philadelphia, a lawyer named Allen Beckman—Prentiss had more than $48,000 on hand. About $32,000 of it was cash he'd personally lent his campaign committee. What was intriguing about that loan was a story that had run in the *Times Union* a few months earlier.

Prentiss owned two houses on the same street in

Colonie. One he lived in; the other he rented out. He was late in paying property taxes on both of them. In fact, he didn't pay the taxes at all until the *Times Union* called him and asked why not. Prentiss had explained to the *Times Union* reporter that he hadn't paid his property taxes because his state salary had been held up. That had happened because the Legislature had—for the 16th year in a row—failed to pass a budget by the statutory deadline, he said.

A few years earlier, in an attempt to mislead the voters that they really wanted to pass a timely budget—which they definitely did not want to do, since that would dry up political contributions—the lawmakers had created a law that required their own salaries to be docked after that statutory deadline. They couldn't get paid until a budget passed.

As a practical matter, that presented no hardship whatever to the legislators. All 211 of them could simply go to a bank and set up a line of credit. The banks knew the legislators were good for the money. After all, each lawmaker served a fixed term, and their salaries were set by law. Moreover, banks are always eager to offer help to people who exert control over state banking regulations.

The hole in Prentiss's story was that his salary hadn't been docked until April 1st. That was the statutory deadline for passing the budget. Meanwhile, his taxes had been due on January 1st. The *Times Union* reporter—and, presumably, most of the voters reading the story—hadn't put that together. So, Prentiss's excuse for failing to pay his property taxes in the community he represented in the Assembly was nothing more than sheer smoke.

What his financial filing to the State Board of Elections revealed was that, at the same time he'd decided not to pay his $3,500 in property taxes on time, Prentiss had been loaning his campaign $32,000. To me, that irresponsibility and the naked lie Prentiss had concocted to cover it up was a news story. I had it shopped around to various media outlets. In fact, I made it a point to mention it myself, in some detail, to Bill Hammond, the *Gazette*'s reporter covering the campaign, and to Carl Strock, the newspaper's local columnist. For some reason, neither *Gazette* employee seemed to think that duplicity on Prentiss's part was worth a story.

And, oddly, neither did anybody else in the Albany news media.

On the union front, both good news and bad.

Calls came in to me on the stances taken in the race by the regional political action committees of the two big state unions. The CSEA, the more important of the two, had backed me. Predictably, the regional PEF political action committee had supported Prentiss. The statewide PEF executive committee, however, could overturn that verdict. Meanwhile, somebody—I never found out who, for sure—had been kind enough to send me an envelope containing the names and home and office phone numbers of all the PEF state executive committee members.

Tom Bayly called to say that the Saratoga County AFL-CIO council, whose screener had interviewed both Prentiss and me on the same day, had decided to remain neutral in the race.

"That's not bad news," the Saratoga County Democratic chairman told me. "In this county, any time you can keep the unions from going with the Republicans you're doing okay."

"Which unions refused to support me, Tom?" I asked.

From the other end of the phone came a long silence. Then Tom said into the phone, "It was the Ironworkers. They sent three guys up from Albany to stand against you in the vote."

So, Mike Burns' union had derailed my endorsement by the Saratoga County AFL-CIO. That action seemed to make Burns' treachery pretty clear.

"Well, Tom," I said, "what am I supposed to make of that?"

My county chairman was silent for a long moment. Clearly, he was choosing his words with care. Then he said, "Well, some people, they give you their word and you can go to the bank with it. Other people? Well, with some of them their word doesn't mean a whole lot."

"Should I call Burns?"

"If he'll talk to you."

Mike Burns ducked me for 10 days. Three times a day, I called his office, his home and his cell phone, leaving messages all over. Finally, he got back to me. He had the same lame story he'd had with his union's contribution to Prentiss's campaign. Well, he said, I don't have much to do with the political action stuff in my union. I'll get back to you, though, and let you know what's going on. I knew how much that promise was worth the moment I heard it. Burns never got back to me with anything. Since he was Jennings' guy, I figured that was where the problem was. I didn't bother to try to contact the mayor. He would just refuse to return my calls. Clearly, Jennings was carrying out Sweeney's requests, and Burns was carrying out Jennings' wishes.

For the most part, though, the union people never promised anything they weren't willing to deliver. A classic example was Kevin Hicks, the balding, brawny, straight-shooting guy

who ran the Carpenters Union. Kevin told me that his union
was backing me. The carpenters, he assured me, would provide
me with manpower to put up my lawn signs in the weeks just
before election day. And they did, too. I also was looking good
with the Pipefitters Union. I gave a talk at their state convention at a resort on Lake George. Standing at the podium, I told
them a story.

"There was a guy named Pat," I said. "He came over
from Ireland and found work as a railroad laborer. At age 44,
with a wife and three kids, he dropped dead one day over breakfast. Not to worry, though. That railroad had an insurance policy for his family. If any man died while holding down a job as
a roughneck, his oldest son could take his place on the laboring
gang. Pat's only son was Tom, who was 14. The next day, Tom
picked up his father's 12-pound sledge and went to work laying
rail.

"Eventually, Tom got to be an engineer, one of the railroad's best. After he got his younger sisters married off, he got
married relatively late in life for those days and fathered six
kids. When he was 59, Tom was pulling his locomotive into the
yard in Buffalo one day when he dropped dead at the throttle.
But none of his six kids had to pick up a sledge to support the
family.

"That's because, after Tom went to work on that railroad, the workforce was unionized. By the time Tom died, the
employees all had life insurance that the union had gotten for
them. Because of that, each of Tom's six kids had a chance to
finish school.

"I know about this," I told the pipefitters, "because Tom
Lynch was my grandfather. And because I know what a positive difference the organized labor movement made in the life
of my family and countless others, you can trust me to be somebody who'll support the union movement in the New York State
Assembly."

The crowd applauded. Jimmy Hart, the union's political action director, leaned over to me I sat down.

He whispered in my ear, "We're with you, too."

10

FACING THE LIONS

"The hardest thing about any political campaign is how to win without proving that you are unworthy of winning."—Adlai Stevenson

Albany was a touch too small, and both New York and Boston were a bit too close, for a major league sports franchise to succeed in the Albany metro area. That's why the Saratoga Race Course was the biggest of deals locally. Open only half the summer, the track made the Albany area the center of the horse racing world every August. For people like me—utterly disinterested in which large, stupid animal could outrun the other large, stupid animals—the track was inconsequential. I preferred more genteel sporting events—boxing, for instance. Except during a political campaign, that was.

Open house at the Saratoga Race Course attracted many thousands of people. A fair percentage of them lived and, hopefully, voted in the 107th Assembly District. So, one afternoon in late July, Mike Mann, Donna and I were parading around the grounds at the track, sporting our campaign buttons, being seen, grinning and shaking hands.

It was a steamy day, and Donna and I were dog tired when we got home in the early evening. We found a message on our answering machine. A friend of mine who belonged to the Muslim Alliance had learned that I had not been invited to a dinner meeting of the group that evening while a number of other politicians had, including Bob Prentiss. Immediately, Donna and I jumped into more formal clothing. Then we went roaring off to crash the Muslim Alliance dinner.

This was a group of professional people, mostly immigrants with advanced degrees adjusting to life in America and to life in a democracy. Perhaps 75 of them were on hand this evening. We arrived on the scene as the meal was ending and the speeches beginning. Seated side-by-side along one wall of the dining room were the Breslin brothers—Albany County Executive, Mike, and Neil, the state senator. Jack McEneny and Prentiss were seated next to them. Pleading a scheduling conflict, a totally fictional appearance I said I had to make elsewhere, I talked the alliance into squeezing me in as the next speaker, after McEneny and before Prentiss.

For about five minutes, I spoke to the group about the crucial and positive impact immigrants have had on America—of their priceless contributions both to American commerce and American culture over the centuries. This country has grown strong, I said, through the contributions of strivers from other lands with big dreams and itchy feet. The nation has prospered by the addition of intrepid men and women willing to leave all they'd ever known to begin life anew in a huge, complex and often befuddling place. I spoke about how rapidly the 107th Assembly District had grown, about how much of that growth was in the Muslim community. I finished up with a few words about how vividly the growing Muslim community had added to the American mosaic and how delighted I was to be able to share this small moment with them.

Then I was out of there, and Prentiss was taking the microphone. As Donna and I slipped out the door, he was babbling something about the New York quarter with its image of the Statue of Liberty on its flip side. I later asked a few people who'd sat through his entire talk what he'd said. Nobody I'd asked had managed to figure out Prentiss's point about the quarter—although they did say that he'd quickly segued into his regular stump speech in which this utterly powerless member of the Assembly minority conference took personal credit for the passage of every positive piece of legislation passed during the previous two years.

As I'd spoken and moved out the door, I'd noticed Mike Breslin glowering at me. From his expression, you would have thought he'd just licked a piece of public plumbing. Neil later explained why.

"We had to spend the whole evening there," he said. "You got in, scored your points and got out. You didn't really have someplace else to go, did you?"

"Actually, I did," I assured him.

That someplace else was bed. I was exhausted that night. Neil ran as an incumbent in a district where he was invulnerable in a general election. He wasn't working up a sweat during that election season. I, on the other hand, was in an uphill battle against an incumbent with a heavy enrollment edge. I was working like a sled dog in the summer sun.

Unlike the Breslin brothers, I didn't have time to sit around.

The following day, I met McEneny for lunch at Albany's Gateway Diner. I wanted advice on how to handle these problems with Burns and Jennings.

Should I simply go public, I asked, with what these guys are doing? They're both supporting me publicly. Meanwhile, quite clearly, they're doing everything they can privately to defeat me and let a Republican win reelection. I knew some people, I told McEneny, who might view treachery at such a high level in the party as a news story.

Wait, he counseled. You have a fundraiser in a few days. See if Burns sends anybody to your fundraiser with some cash for your campaign. Don't go to war publicly, McEneny advised, unless there's no other way to win the election.

I remained unconvinced. Frankly, I felt like getting into a fight. This whole campaign was like punching smoke. It felt like nothing was happening—although, clearly, a good deal was going on behind my back. As I left the diner after that lunch, I stumbled into somebody I knew in the parking lot. The guy I'd bumped into was a shrewd, experienced Democratic Party operative who'd given me sage advice on several matters early in the campaign.

"How's the campaign going?" he asked.

I told him. Burns and Jennings seem to be flinging daggers at my back, I said, and I was considering ways to make as much noise as possible about it. I was already drafting the press release in my mind.

"Believe me, you don't want to do that," he warned.

"Why not? Most of the voters in the district are Republicans. I'll get points with them for taking these guys on. Besides, they're already doing everything they can to screw me. What can they do to me if I simply tell people the truth about all this?"

It was crucial for me to realize, the operative warned me, that the Albany County Democratic organization controlled the county board of elections, where the votes would be tallied on election night. Piss off the party leadership with a public declaration of war, he said, and I could lose this election whether I'd really won it or not.

"You'll have a tight race," the operative predicted. "If you win, your margin of victory will come out of Colonie, not the Saratoga County towns. If the party leadership wants you to lose, they can make that happen just by tampering with the absentee ballots in the board of elections in the dark of night."

"You're kidding," I said. "Isn't that a felony?"

"Sure it is," he agreed. "And who would prosecute them for vote fraud—Sol?"

Inwardly, I groaned at the very prospect of hanging my hopes on Sol Greenberg. The Albany County district attorney was the quintessential party hack. Pushing 80 now, Greenberg had refused steadfastly, throughout a lengthy and lackluster career in law enforcement, ever to prosecute a case of political corruption. It had been the feds who'd had to come in to nail Jim Coyne, after all. It had been Eliot Spitzer, the state's attorney general, who'd stepped up to the plate and gotten a guilty plea from Davis Etkin, the corrupt longtime head of the Capital District Off-Track Betting Corp. The kindest thing that could be said for Greenberg in both cases was that he'd been asleep.

As I pondered what I was being told, I recalled a column I'd done for the *Times Union* early in the year. The state had formally turned over to Greenberg the responsibility of probing possible criminal activity in a lobbying scandal. Greenberg had done nothing in the case. At the time, I'd written, "The politicians could be selling off the Capitol, block by block, and Sol would be the very last guy to notice."

"You have to remember," the party operative told me, "that a guy like you scares the hell out of these guys. What do they need with somebody like you in office? You've made your name standing up for the little guy. These guys stand up only for themselves and their rich friends."

So, there it was. The Albany County Democratic Party leadership had been willing to back me when they'd been fairly certain that I would lose. Now, watching this campaign unfold and fearing that I might actually pull this off, they were gleefully engaging in political treason and doing everything they could to sink my campaign. If I spoke out publicly about that treachery, they literally could steal victory from me in the board of elections. Also, the only conceivable protection available to keep that from happening was embodied in, of all people, Sol Greenberg. To top off everything, I'd written columns calling for Greenberg's resignation. I was professionally cordial to him whenever I bumped into him, but Greenberg obviously despised me.

So, I finally realized, this is what it really meant to be running with the machine.

As I got into my car to leave, I asked myself: How had I ever let myself get mixed up with people like this?

Mike Mann and I were banging on doors in Clifton Park, only a half mile or so from my house. At one house, a guy came to the door, took one look at me and bellowed, "Dan Lynch? No thanks!"

He slammed the door in our faces. Armed with my newly discovered insight into the breathtaking flexibility of political conviction, I turned to Mike, who was carrying his pen and notebook.

"Let's put him down as a maybe," I suggested.

Al Paolucci got back to me. The meeting with the Sons of Italy was set for the following evening, he said. It would be held in a second-floor meeting room at Albany's Italian-American Community Center—which, incidentally, also happened to house the best Italian restaurant in town, although I was never able to get there as often as I would have liked.

I thanked Al and considered how I should handle this. I could go in and apologize for my column. I could go in and simply pronounce myself hopelessly insensitive, then throw myself on the mercy of the Sons of Italy senior officers. I could be a phony. Politicians do that all the time. Many people, especially people in organized groups, enjoy bullying politicians and are prone to support politicians who cower before them.

No, I decided, I was not about to express agreement with Jim Mancuso's contention on my radio program that most people believe all Italian-Americans to be "goons and buffoons" involved in organized crime. That was nonsensical on its face. I would stand up firmly for free expression. I wasn't going to pander to this group. I was not about to whore myself into public office.

It simply wasn't worth it to me.

I spent the next morning at a screening session conducted by the League of Conservation Voters in the conference room of a downtown law firm. I thought there was a chance that this group might adopt neutrality in the race, since I'd written any number of columns attacking environmental extremism. The League, however, was a sensible group that seemed to shun extremism. Meanwhile, Prentiss ranked 125th out of the 150 members of the Assembly in his environmental voting record, so I figured I had at least a shot at this group's support—

which, in fact, I later got.

Later in the day, as I sat in my home office firing off fundraising letters, Bill Hammond of the *Gazette* called. Prentiss had sent a flunky to Hammond's desk in the Capitol to alert him to the meeting that evening with the Sons of Italy. I was going to get beaten up—figuratively, anyway—at that meeting, Hammond was told. It was then that I realized that at least some of the people at this event would be Prentiss plants— stalking horses for my opponent who had no intention of listening to anything I might have to say. They would be partisan operatives not in search of a solution but in search of the biggest problem they could manufacture.

I downplayed the issue as best I could to Hammond. "I speak to all sorts of groups," I told him. "I spoke just the other night to the Muslim Alliance. Frankly, I'll speak to anybody who'll have me."

Hammond said he was armed with a copy of the *Godfather* column and that he expected Prentiss to have that meeting room stacked. Well, I said, if it turns out to be stacked, then I'll handle it. I took the opportunity to remark on how odd it struck me that the *Gazette* considered this a story but exhibited no interest whatever in Prentiss loaning his campaign 32 grand at a time when the assemblyman was refusing to pay his property taxes on time.

Hammond didn't respond to the comment.

Mike Mann accompanied me to the meeting with the Sons of Italy. We also took along Jerry Vitagliano, our campaign photographer and the sort of warm, smiling, gregarious guy with a gift for disarming just about anybody he might meet.

After chasing around all day, making a number of campaign stops, I was uncharacteristically late for this meeting. Al Paolucci met us in the parking lot. He warned that some people were sitting around the meeting room, grumbling about my tardiness, and that a few of them clearly were loaded for bear. I should keep a careful eye on a physician named John Fiore, Al warned me. The day after the meeting, I checked on Fiore's voter registration. He was, no surprise, a Republican.

We climbed the stairs to the community center's boardroom. I found myself sitting at the head of a U-shaped table with a good two dozen people arrayed on either side of me. It was a distinguished group of middle-aged people or older— lawyers, physicians and other professionals. George Infante was on hand, although utterly silent throughout the meeting. I knew a few other people, too. Phil Calderone, the lawyer who served as Jerry Jennings' deputy mayor, was there. Given what seemed to be going on with Burns and Jennings, I expected trouble from Calderone, but it turned out to be fortunate for me that Calderone had attended. He behaved with restraint and politeness, although he had the same complaint that everybody else had—precisely what Mancuso's had been.

Everybody took the position that any literary reference to the *Godfather*, satirical or otherwise, reinforced negative stereotypes and constituted an anti-Italian slur. I replied to the group that I respected the intensity of their conviction, but I warned that they would not find me a typical politician eager to agree with everybody on every point. I pointed out that I'd put Mancuso on my radio program to criticize me and my column when I'd been under no obligation to do so. I added that I'd asked for this meeting when most candidates would have hidden from this group. I stressed that I was conducting a campaign of conscience, not a campaign based on my adoption of popular positions that pandered to whatever group I might be addressing.

The meeting lasted more than two hours. Most members of the group wanted to discuss the high level of anti-Italian discrimination they'd encountered over the years. I sympathized and pointed out that my own people, the Irish, had been the targets of discrimination as well. I told them about Prentiss's "Irish drunk" remark and added that I was saying nothing about it publicly. I didn't want the campaign conducted on that basis, I told the group.

In response to comments about bigots and the saturation of *Godfather* images in the popular media, I said I would take responsibility for my column but not for any other media portrayal of anything. I also said that I would not be held responsible for the attitudes of all the stupid people in the world. I pointed out that there existed some serious free expression issues in a debate like this. Some African-American groups wanted *Huckleberry Finn* pulled from library shelves because they objected to Mark Twain's portrayal of Jim, the slave character in the novel. I told them that I'd once received complaints about a line I'd used in a column to the effect that a particular battle in the state Capitol was creating more noise than the bomb that had been dropped on Hiroshima. It's virtually impossible, I explained, to write a newspaper column four days a week without somehow, sometimes, offending somebody in some fashion—unless, of course, you decide to say nothing in your column and to say it in the dullest fashion imaginable.

Well, the group said, that stuff is different. Not to the blacks and to Japanese-Americans, I pointed out.

A few people were openly nasty early on, as I'd anticipated. I thought it wise to take them on directly. A retired college professor named Phil DiNovo got so confrontational that I finally said to him, "I have the distinct impression that anything I might say you will instantly disagree with, regardless of the merits." At that point, DiNovo loosened up considerably. By the end of the meeting, he was actually friendly.

I made it a point not to be provoked into losing my temper. It became clear after a while that I was making a generally good impression by standing up, politely but firmly, to criticism of the column and to a few of the people around the table who seemed to be pressing for a nasty scene. About halfway through the meeting, I told the group about Hammond's call that afternoon and about the way Prentiss had been spreading the word that I would be sandbagged at this meeting. Some time after that, during the course of the gathering, a few people got up and left. One was Dr. Fiore. He'd said little before he departed. Apparently, he didn't like the way things were going.

Mike Mann was watching another guy, a lawyer. This guy said little, but what he did say included the word, "bigot." That was my opening to discuss my long and conspicuous record of standing up in print and over the air against bigotry and discrimination of all kinds. DiNovo, the retired college professor, asked me if I'd ever written anything complimentary about Italian-Americans. I pointed out that I'd often praised both Mario Cuomo and Joe Bruno in my column. I added that I'd done that, however, not because of their ethnicity but because of their actions. By the end of the meeting, everybody was gracious and cordial, even Mancuso.

"I just wanted you to see," he told me, "that I'm not the only person who feels this way."

I told him, "That was effectively communicated."

Mike Mann reported to me later that, as the lawyer who'd used the word "bigot" was leaving at the end of the meeting, he'd grumbled that he'd apparently been the only Republican in the room.

The next morning, I briefed Bob Berry on how the meeting had gone. Fine, he said, but don't think this is going away. Prentiss, he said, was sure to try to find some way to get mileage out of this dispute before election day. Berry was right. Hammond called me that afternoon. He'd spoken to Dr. Fiore—it was unclear to me precisely who had called whom— and was doing a story for the *Gazette* on the meeting, which Hammond hadn't attended. So, here was Prentiss now doing his best to paint me as an anti-Italian bigot. Hammond admitted to me in that telephone conversation that Prentiss was the guy feeding Hammond on this one. And here was the *Gazette*, predictably playing right along.

I urged Hammond to call Calderone to get his version of events, instead of simply relying on Dr. Fiore's recollections. The good doctor, I told Hammond, had left in the middle of the session. Don't you see what this is, I asked Hammond? Take a look at what Prentiss did with the charity groups, I said; take a look at what he pulled with Channel 13.

"This is scummy campaigning," I told Hammond. "Take a look at the Italian-American names on my committee. Take a look at the no names on his committee—because nobody wants to be associated with him. Don't be a part of this."

Hammond asked for a list of columns in which I'd stood up against bigotry. I went back three years in my files and found 57 columns I'd done on the topic. I faxed the list to Hammond along with this note:

> This is a vicious, totally dishonorable smear campaign. Prentiss is behind it. You knew that yesterday, and you know what role he's playing in this. Nobody with a public voice in this town has spoken louder than I have for ethnic and racial harmony. Nobody has taken more heat for that. You can check with the Colonie Police Department for records of the death threats I've

received for standing up on these issues.

    This is, quite simply, the vilest sort of political warfare . . . . [Prentiss] will do anything and everything but stand up to me, face to face, and deal with the issues in this election and with his record of abject failure as a lawmaker. Forget the phony, professional politician's grin; this is not a nice man.

    Hammond's story, complete with my head shot, ran on the *Gazette*'s local front page the next day. The headline read: "Lynch defends column."

    Hammond had never checked with the Colonie Police Department for information on the death threats. He'd called Joe Bruno for comment, however, and Bruno had refused to say a word. The State Senate Republican leader couldn't publicly defend me, but he pointedly refused to criticize me or to help Prentiss in any way in this smear attempt.

    Hammond quoted Mancuso as saying that nobody's mind had been changed at the meeting. Dr. Fiore was quoted as saying, "He said this was a satire. It wasn't meant to offend anyone. That's the weakest argument of them all."

    In response to my comment that Prentiss had manipulated the incident, his campaign manager, a Republican legislative employee named Bob Spearman, told Hammond that I suffered "from diarrhea of the mouth and constipation of thought."

    In describing the column, Hammond reported that Pataki had Italian roots. Actually, the governor was of Hungarian and Irish extraction. He'd had a grandmother named Agnes Lynch. Over lunch at the Republican National Convention in San Diego four years earlier, Pataki and I had discussed the possibility that we might be distant cousins.

In the *Gazette* story—and no other media outlet would touch this thing, by the way—Phil Calderone came through for me. He hadn't liked the column, he said, but he'd added, "I find Dan Lynch to be a very open-minded, fair individual. I don't believe he's bigoted in the least."

That quote appeared on the jump of the story—on its continuation on an inside page. I knew from readership surveys that fully half the people who read a jumped story never read the second half.

The *Gazette* had made Calderone's quote the story's very last paragraph.

The fundraiser was not exactly a rousing success.

We held it at the Desmond. Unfortunately, the date that Bob Berry had booked turned out to be opening day at the track, where everybody in Albany with any money would be instead of attending my fundraiser. Moreover, anybody at the track who might want to attend would have to miss the last race. Also, just as icing on the cake, the skies opened up in a tropical deluge about an hour before our cocktail party got underway.

This was a modestly priced affair, and most of the elected officials showed up—McEneny, the Breslins and a few others. A few lobbyists appeared. Once again, Jennings was conspicuously absent. Tom Bayly came in his wheelchair. Just to keep me off balance, apparently, Mike Burns appeared and bought a ticket. I now had collected a grand total of $250 from the Albany County Democratic Party.

Gazing out over the sparse crowd, I got up at the podium and muttered a few words as music blared from the hotel sound system, drowning me out. In the end, we'd collected a grand total of $5,000—precisely half that from a clergyman I'd known for a few years and who'd inherited a few bucks from his father. With all the phone calls and solicitation letters and now this affair, the Lynch campaign had all of $8,000 on hand— slightly more than half the price of the DACC poll. Also, we had debts.

Unlike most people who run for the Legislature, I hadn't been out there raising money for a solid year before I announced my candidacy. We held this fundraising cocktail party on July 27th. Four years earlier, Kevin Dailey had been able to give DACC its $15,000 in June.

And he'd still lost.

My old competitors at the *Gazette* weren't even making an effort to be subtle. They were really rocking and rolling on this one.

Now the paper was running an editorial cartoon. It showed an Irishman, a Frenchman and a Britisher standing on a sidewalk reading a newspaper. Across the front of the newspaper in the cartoon was a headline: "Lynch defends column." The Irishman was saying to his two buddies, "That's weird! All us Limeys, Frogs and Micks thought Lynch's *Godfather* column was very amusing."

"Oui!" the Frenchman was saying in response.

"Quite!" the Englishman was saying.

Apparently, this was Dan Lynch Day on the *Gazette*'s editorial page. The paper also ran an editorial, headlined "Dan

Lynch's conflict." It defended the *Godfather* column as, "funny, a well-written satire (as opposed to those unintentionally humorous pieces in which he went on about tough towns, neighborhoods and characters he has known)."

The editorial went on to say, however, that some people might accuse me of a conflict of interest for having supported state workers in my columns and then having decided to run for office.

"Now," the editorial said, "Lynch can doubtless point to a history of support for public employees, and could argue plausibly that he wrote about them this year because they were in the news. Those who know him as a man of integrity would discount any suggestion that he was tailoring what he wrote in his column so as to win support from labor unions with lots of members in the Assembly district where he intended to run. But most people, including most residents of the district, do not know Lynch personally, and so cannot be certain of his integrity."

It was an interesting approach. The editorial told readers that people who knew me personally would vouch for my integrity. Then it reminded readers that they didn't know me personally and hinted broadly that they should figure I was nobody to be trusted.

The editorial also faulted me for criticizing the style of campaign Prentiss was running.

"As a politician," the *Gazette* editorial said, "Lynch has demonstrated an overly thin skin, allowing his campaign against Assemblyman Bob Prentiss to degenerate into exchanges of personal abuse over matters of little moment, such as this fuss about 'Don George "The Hungarian" Pataki' and his associates."

Metroland, the Albany area's left-leaning, entertainment-oriented weekly newspaper, conducted a readers' poll. My daughter, Kelly, was one of the winners listed under the category, "Best Local Celebrity With Whom You'd Like To Have a One-Night Stand." It was enough to make any daddy proud.

Along with several other people, including the Dali Lama, I was listed under, "Best Person To Run The Capital Region After the Revolution."

Bob Prentiss made the list, too. He was voted by *Metroland* readers as one of the Albany area's top contenders for, "Best Village Idiot."

After that tepid fundraiser, we remained seven grand short of DACC's admission fee. There was only one way to deal with that—by begging, ferociously, shamelessly and relentlessly. So, that's what we did.

Donna and I called everybody we could think of—family, friends, lobbyists, union leaders. My wife, by the way, was turning out to be one kick-ass little fundraiser. Ultimately, after long, grinding days of intense personal humiliation, we came within striking distance of the DACC figure. Donna had even hit up her widowed mother for an $1,100 loan. I then loaned my campaign $2,500 from our dwindling savings account. We added it all up. Finally, we were there.

And we felt like throwing up.

We had a headquarters.

Bob Berry and Donna had been negotiating separately with the same commercial real estate company. They'd looked at two separate properties. The one eventually selected was in a storefront in a new shopping center in Clifton Park—2,700 feet of space strategically located between a breakfast joint, a terrific pizzeria and a first-class bar right next door. The shopping center also boasted a Chinese take-out place. Campaign headquarters didn't come any better than that.

Plus, the place was right off a superhighway exit, so volunteers could get there with ease. It had plenty of parking. Also, the place was only about a mile and a half from my home and only a few hundred yards from the post office branch where the campaign had its post office box.

Not that I was going to spend any time there personally. Candidates meet no voters at headquarters. They're too busy banging on doors, being stabbed in the back by people who'd promised to support them and being savaged by newspapers they used to compete against. Well, that's the way it works in some campaigns, at least.

We borrowed some office furniture. Jerry Vitagliano got out his carpenter's tools and built a few room dividers. Despite my worries, the Republican-controlled town government of Clifton Park gave us no problems on permits.

Shelly Silver's approved polling outfit was Kiley & Company, out of Boston. In the conference room of DACC's basement headquarters near the Capitol, we met with a Kiley & Company guy named Matt something. Mike Kane, DACC's deputy director, also was on hand. I was asked for my views on the issues in the race and what I wanted out of the poll.

This is a suburban district, I told Matt. Don't think upstate New York; think Long Island. The district needs better mass transit in the northern end, better infrastructure in the booming areas north of the Mohawk River, better home health care for the elderly, lower electricity rates to attract industry, tougher penalties for drunken drivers who kill, consolidation of local governments to lower property taxes. Tersely, I ran through the issues I thought most crucial to the communities I sought to represent.

Obviously, I said, I want the poll to tell me who's ahead. Also, I said, I wanted raw numbers on the perceived strengths and weaknesses of each candidate as well as detailed breakdowns, both by geography and demographic classification, of how voters felt on all that. I added that I wanted information on the popularity levels of the people who would be on the ballot with me—Al Gore, Neil Breslin and all the Republican candidates as well. With Hillary Clinton, I said, I could make a strong guess. That guess was that she was pure poison in my Assembly district. I wanted to know for sure, however. Hey, I pointed out, maybe Hillary would want to hang out with me. I urged also that Shelly Silver's name be included in the poll. Clearly, the Republicans were eager to link my name to this "downstate, liberal, political boss." How damaging could that linkage be, I wanted to know?

"As you go door-to-door," Matt asked me, "how are you handling questions about Hillary?"

"I'm saying that I support the Democratic ticket, but I'm

not doing back flips over it."

"Have you enrolled as a Democrat?" Mike Kane asked.

"No."

"Good," he said.

Kane said he expected my campaign to cost about $400,000—a figure that made my heart go pitty-pat. If I looked good in this poll, he added, and DACC took on this race, then DACC would handle all strategy and media. I would have to raise money for housekeeping items—signs, bumper stickers, headquarters rent, etc. As we talked, John Longo dropped into the meeting. So did Ron Canestrari, the assemblyman from suburban Albany who co-chaired DACC with another assemblyman from Long Island.

I handed over the check to Kiley & Company. DACC would fax me poll results the moment the numbers were in. The poll would be conducted over four days with results based on a sample of 400 voters.

Isn't that a little light, I asked? I'd been involved in polling as the *Times Union*'s managing editor. The newspaper's pollsters had never used a sample smaller than 800.

"We've done a lot of this," Kane assured me. "This'll be a good poll; don't worry about it."

At this point, though, I was worrying about everything.

11

TROUBLED WATERS

"It's dangerous for a candidate to say things that people might remember."—Eugene McCarthy

T he union breakfasts were held once a month at the restaurant at the Albany municipal golf course. Generally, as many as 40 union officials were on hand, each of whom had received a letter from me requesting an interview with the union's political action committee.

Only one union, the Operating Engineers, had granted me such an interview. A few other unions already had endorsed me without the formality of an interview. Most of the union leaders, however, had failed to respond to my letters. They would wait until the fall, to see which way the wind was blowing in my campaign. I was, after all, a novice politician running against an incumbent with an enrollment advantage. DACC hadn't signed on to my campaign. There was no need to rush on this, the union bosses figured.

Most unions tended to endorse candidates or to oppose them on the whim of their top officials. Moreover, most union members trusted their presidents or business agents to back the candidate who would do those members the most good in office. Backing helpful politicians was, after all, part of the leadership job to which these people had been elected. So, it made sense for me to show up at these affairs, to schmooze with the union leaders and to let these people get to know me personally. Most of these union bosses knew me only through my columns or broadcast appearances, and they relied heavily on the judgments of politicians they already knew—some of whom, it seemed, weren't exactly knocking themselves out on my behalf.

Victor Stewart worked on the staff of an Ironworkers local in New York City. He'd started out as a newspaper reporter and had quickly become active in the newsroom union. When I'd come to Albany as managing editor 21 years before I ran for the Assembly, one of my first acts had been to take the newsroom union leadership out to dinner. We'd gone to an Italian restaurant where I'd plied them with veal, pasta and booze and saw to it that we got to know one another. Victor and I had always gotten along reasonably well. I hadn't seen much of him since he'd left the paper and gone to work fulltime in the union movement. At that first union breakfast, he approached me.

"Your opponent is a scumbag," said Victor Stewart, who happened to live in the 107th Assembly District.

"I've figured that out by now," I said, "but that didn't keep you bastards in the Ironworkers from endorsing him."

"That's true," he admitted.

I'd made it a point to attend this breakfast to see Mike Burns. He'd been dodging my phone calls, but I'd known that he would have to attend this gathering. I was going to sit him down and talk to him if I had to grab the county chairman by the lapels and wrestle him to the ground to accomplish that chore. After coming up with DACC's $15,000 polling fee, my campaign was totally tapped out. Tom Bayly, the Saratoga

County Democratic chairman, had donated $5,000 to my campaign. It was virtually every dime the Saratoga County party had, and I knew how painful it had been for Tom to part with that cash. Now, the question was, what was Burns going to do? He had roughly $70,000 in the Albany County committee's bank account. Was the Albany County machine going to support my campaign or not?

Burns spotted me at the breakfast. He knew what I wanted and figured that he couldn't escape me gracefully—which, incidentally, he couldn't. So, after the breakfast ended, we sat down, off in a corner of the restaurant. Burns was fiercely apologetic for ducking my phone calls and about his union opposing me. He said he was 59, was retiring from the union the following spring and that he no longer had much to say about the union's political positions. He seemed genuinely embarrassed.

"You can make it up to me, Mike," I told him. "I need $5,000 from the Albany County Democratic Committee. Make it a loan, if you like, but I need it after meeting DACC's figure. Remember, after all, I did raise the DACC money in just eight weeks, and I had to do it during the petitioning process. That's one reason my fundraiser wasn't such a smashing success. The timing was unavoidably horrible. That part isn't your fault, I know, but I need this help regardless—at least until I can get another fundraiser set for next month."

Burns gazed at the table top, silent for a long moment.

"I'll let you know," he told me. "I have to check with Jerry."

The previous day, Donna had found a $150 donation from Jennings in our campaign post office box. We didn't know what to make of it. Was Jennings now my friend once again? If so, I just hoped that burst of good feeling lasted long enough for me to squeeze that five grand out of Mike Burns.

That day in April, in his State Senate office—when I'd told Neil Breslin that I was very close to running and asked for his support—I'd asked him if I could put a "Lynch for Assembly" sign in the window of his highly visible campaign headquarters on Central Avenue. Sure, he'd told me.

Mary Gilson, the director of volunteers for my campaign, bumped into Neil Breslin at a political function. Are you ready to have that sign go up, she asked him?

"No," Neil Breslin told her.

One of my dearest and oldest friends was an editor at the *Philadelphia Inquirer*, Terry Bitman. We tended to communicate mostly by phone and mail. He'd asked me how the campaign was unfolding. Early one morning, I knocked out a note to him that read, in part:

> I've learned a few things about politics during the past six weeks—stuff you really wouldn't expect after spending decades of life in a real business with a real chain of command.
>
> 1. There's no such thing as a political boss. Except for a few paid staff people and some patronage workers, everybody in politics is a volunteer or an independently elected official. That means that nobody is in charge of anything. It's all chaos.

2. Nobody keeps his word. The idea that a politician's word is his bond is sheer bullshit. People promise and promise, then they either don't deliver or they don't return your calls. Quite literally, you can't trust anybody.

3. The egos are out of control. Elected officials suck up shamelessly to the press, but they tend to be real putzes toward everybody else they deal with.

4. Nobody is straightforward with you. You find out who your enemies are more or less by accident. If somebody has a problem with you, he never comes to you and says, "I have a problem." Once you hear there's a problem with somebody, you have to seek out that person and confront him. Generally, that freaks them out, and they fall immediately into line. And, as you might imagine, my columns over the years have pissed off a good many people.

The fact was that there were good and honorable people in politics—people you could trust and whose word you could count on. Jack McEneny was one of them. So was Mike Conners, the Albany County comptroller. Tom Bayly, the Saratoga County Democratic chairman, was as decent a man as I'd ever met. There were others, too.

All badly outnumbered, however.

I'd just finished a brief talk before the Albany Building Trades Council. The meeting had taken place at Albany's Labor

Temple. That was a big, brick building just off a superhighway housing a collection of union offices and a cavernous meeting hall.

"This is a presidential year," I told the union leaders. "That means a generally heavy turnout, and it means that this election is less likely to be affected by the efforts of pressure groups on either side. This an election in which, to a greater degree than in an off-year, the people will decide the outcome."

What I was saying was that I wanted their backing but that, if they opposed me, they might find me in office anyway. Once I got outside and into my car, I called Bob Berry to see if anything was going on that I should know about. He had news from the swamp that was the New York State Board of Elections, where Josh Ehrlich was doing battle on my behalf and running up legal bills for my flat-busted campaign. Prentiss was challenging my petitions. He was doing that not because he expected to win but because he knew from my financial filings that I had little in the way of cash. Prentiss was hassling me on legalities because he wanted to drain off as much of my money as he could manage. So, since we were spending the money already, we'd challenged his petitions, too.

Good news and bad news, Bob Berry told me. The good news was that the State Board of Elections had invalidated Prentiss's petitions to wage a write-in campaign against me in the Independence Party primary. The bad news was that the board had thrown out my petitions for the Liberal Party line. The witness to those petitions had screwed up in some technical way. Josh thought we could get it straightened out, but the costs were mounting.

Also, Berry told me, the Green Party had fielded a candidate in the race—some woman named Kimberly Audi-Desorbo. Nobody had ever heard of her. She'd needed only a few signatures to get on the November ballot on that party line.

The Greens were a brand new political party, and they had only few members in my district.

I was surprised at that. I knew Mark Dunlea, the local leader of the Greens. I'd been helpful in getting his party on the ballot in the first place. Under New York law, a political party can automatically get on the ballot for the next four years if its candidate for governor gets 50,000 votes. Two years earlier, the Greens had run as their gubernatorial candidate a cranky, cigar-chomping old actor named Al Lewis, who'd once played Grandpa Munster on television. I'd given Al a fair amount of publicity in my column and on my radio program, trying to help the Greens get their 50,000 votes, which they'd managed to do.

It wasn't that I'd agreed with them on the issues or thought that Al Lewis should be elected governor—although that would have been great news for the Albany press corps. Al had promised to wear his vampire outfit to his inauguration. No, I'd pushed Lewis's candidacy simply because that I felt the process of a minor party getting on the ballot was too restrictive and anti-democratic.

I hadn't wanted the Green Party line in my race. The party was so far left that it made the Liberals seem like middle-of-the-roaders, and I'd felt that I couldn't fairly represent the party membership's extreme viewpoint in the Assembly. I'd thought, though, that Dunlea would have figured he owed me a little something and would have declined to put up anybody against me.

As it turned out, we later learned, Kimberly Audi-Desorbo wasn't really a Green. She was enrolled in the party, all right, but signatures on her nominating petitions had been rounded up by enrolled Republicans. She never campaigned, never responded to a single questionnaire, never answered to a single reporter's query. She was strictly a stalking horse, and she apparently had gone through the trouble of getting on that ballot for one reason and one reason only.   Somebody, it seemed, had asked her to.

To siphon votes away from me.

Donna had been working hard to get me the endorsement of the New York State United Teachers. She belonged to that union, and we both knew that its backing could be crucial. NYSUT had played a large role two years before in engineering Chuck Schumer's defeat of Al D'Amato in the U.S. Senate race.

I'd written the NYSUT local presidents in the district. I'd lobbied the union's top state officials. Donna had done much the same, nagging NYSUT people incessantly on my behalf. The problem was that NYSUT tended, virtually always, to support incumbents.   Unlike the national teacher's union, party membership was incidental to the biggest New York teachers union. Backing winners counted for more.

The phone call came in early August. It was one of the presidents of the NYSUT locals in the district. The union was staying neutral in the race. It was the best they could do. Donna was disappointed. I was relieved.

Prentiss would be the only incumbent in the Assembly that NYSUT wouldn't support in that year's elections.

Bill Hammond of the *Gazette* was on the phone again.

I'd figured out by now that no phone call from that newspaper was good news, but the *Gazette* was the only daily newspaper in the district paying any attention to this race. After New York Mayor Rudy Giuliani had dropped out of the U.S. Senate contest, his campaign derailed by an attack of prostate cancer and by Giuilani's sudden decision to ditch his wife in favor of his girlfriend, the race between Hillary Clinton and a downstate congressman named Rick Lazio got big attention in every paper every day. Meanwhile, contests further down the ballot were being roundly ignored by every news outlet but the *Gazette*, which seemed to exhibit a unique fascination with my contest with Prentiss.

Hammond was doing a story on whether the positions I'd taken in my columns over the years could hurt me in this election. Had I ever written anything that worried me, he wanted to know? No, I told him—although I had little doubt by now that those positions would be wildly misrepresented in Prentiss's campaign literature. I told Hammond about the phone call to Vandenburgh's radio program by Phil Barrett, the Clifton Park town supervisor, who'd managed to come up with that loony assertion that I wanted to kill all the volunteer fire companies—and then, of course, had refused to call back to the show and defend that lie once I'd gone on the air and called him on it.

I took the opportunity to tell Hammond that I'd always made a point in my column of giving readers the best possible version of the truth—as opposed to Prentiss, who routinely took credit for legislative measures to which he'd had no connection whatever.

I spent more time talking to Hammond than I would have liked. When I'd begun this campaign, given my background, I'd felt a special obligation to be responsive to reporters. I'd learned from earlier stories, however, that being fully responsive provided reporters with too much material. They invariably chose to use the weakest of my quotes, not the strong ones, and I was developing an appreciation for why so many politicians refused to talk to reporters at all. Instead, they would limit their remarks to prepared, written statements to ensure that they were quoted only on what they wanted to say and in precisely the form in which they wanted to say it.

After three decades in journalism, I didn't want to do that. I wanted desperately to be able to trust the reporters' sense of fairness and their professional skill at recognizing which quotes had value and which did not.

I suspected by this point, though, that I would have to abandon that strategy before election day rolled around and behave with reporters precisely the way real politicians behaved. Like it or not, I figured that I eventually would have to adopt their tactics in dealing with the media.

It was 92 degrees, and Mike Mann and I were walking, sweating, and walking and sweating some more in Colonie's Latham section.

"Isn't it pretty hot to be doing what you're doing?" a woman asked from her doorway.

"Oh," I told her, "It's not so bad. It's no hotter than downtown Nairobi."

Burns had not gotten back to me with word on my request for the $5,000 loan. I called him. Meet me at party headquarters on Saturday morning, he suggested. Sure thing, I replied. On Saturday morning, I went to Colvin Avenue and sat there. Burns never showed. I left messages on his voice mail. He didn't return them.

Tony Catalfamo, the Colonie Democratic chairman, gave me a call. This guy called me, he told me. He wants to talk to you; here's the number.

The caller turned out to be a man named John Myers. He was a substitute teacher who lobbied for a group called the Coalition for Safer Schools. It was a group, he informed me, that lobbied for laws protecting gay adolescents from harassment in school. He said that he and another guy, a lawyer, had gone to see Prentiss to ask for the assemblyman's support on a particular bill. Not until I'm reelected, Prentiss had told them.

Then, incredibly, the lobbyist from the Coalition for Safer Schools told me that Prentiss had treated both men to a lengthy recitation of all the fun he'd had as a Marine in the 1950s going out in San Francisco on Saturday nights to beat up on "queers." The lobbyist wanted me to know about this.

I said to him, "What do you expect me to do with a thing like this? If it happened at all, it happened 45 years ago. Look, I'm not out to denigrate Prentiss, to humiliate him or to attack him. I just want to beat him in November. I'll fight back vigorously when I'm unfairly attacked, but I'm trying to run a positive campaign."

I mentioned the conversation to Bob Berry. He was extremely interested. He said he wanted to talk to Myers.

"Okay," I said, "go ahead, but let's not get carried away. First of all, what do you do with a thing like this? Second, news reports that Prentiss used to beat up gays might even help him in this district. What we really need to do is get some money together, get the headquarters up and running, get the volunteers organized and get some advertising put together."

We never did do anything with that story, although Myers had struck me as willing to take part in a press conference. I wanted to win the election, all right.

I didn't want to win that way, though.

Not the best news I'd ever received.

With Labor Day approaching—and with what I knew would be unmitigated frenzy after that, day and night, every day of the week—Donna and I squeezed out a few days to sneak off to our little summer cottage in the Finger Lakes, four hours west of Albany. That would be long enough to take a few deep breaths, participate in a modest fundraising event with people in New York's wine industry—a distressingly Republican industry, by the way—and to receive our poll results from DACC.

That morning in mid-August, I was sipping coffee and watching poll numbers roll in on the old fax I had at the cottage. As I'd suspected, George W. Bush was running ahead of Al Gore in the 107th Assembly District, 46 per cent to 37. Rick Lazio was whomping Hillary Clinton, 56 per cent to 39 per cent. Hillary had a 51 per cent unfavorable rating in the district.

Shelly Silver was running a 42 per cent negative. Not one of these people was anybody with whom I wanted to be publicly associated in this campaign.

The key numbers were these: Prentiss stood at 51 per cent, precisely the percentage of voters in the district who called themselves conservatives. I stood at 37 per cent. Not quite 13 per cent of the voters were undecided. I'd expected to be at rough parity with Prentiss. I'd heard rumors of a GOP poll, taken just after I'd announced my candidacy, that actually had put me ahead.

When Kevin Dailey had run against Prentiss four years earlier, losing by only a whisker in November of 1996, 69 per cent of the voters in the prosperous 107th Assembly District had felt that things were "basically heading in the right direction." Response to that key question generally was a reliable index of how difficult it would be to dislodge any incumbent. The 107th was the fastest growing of all the state's 150 Assembly Districts. The northern end of the district was booming with expensive new houses sprouting up in what had been forests and farmers' fields. In the four years since Dailey's run against Prentiss, the district had changed markedly, and not in the favor of any challenger. Now, fully 79 per cent of the district's voters felt that everything was just ducky.

Much of what I was seeing in these numbers seemed fraught with illogic. While only 37 per cent of the voters were able to volunteer Prentiss's name as their assemblyman, fully 59 per cent reported having a favorable impression of him once they were told who he was. His negative rating was 17 per cent. Forty-four per cent favored his reelection against any opponent. More than two in three voters over 50 felt that way.

Meanwhile, 15 per cent of the district had listened to my radio program. A total of 68 per cent of the voters had read my column, and 50 per cent had agreed with my positions most of the time. Only 18 per cent had disagreed with me regularly. The other 32 per cent couldn't recall whether they'd agreed or disagreed with what I'd had to say. Nonetheless, I had a total positive rating of only 33 per cent and a total negative of 18.

Moreover, fully 40 per cent of the voters reported that they didn't know enough about me, positive or negative, to form an opinion as to whether I should be their assemblyman. And, meanwhile, only slightly more than a third of them could identify their assemblyman by name?

I asked the DACC people about that later. How could a guy who'd had so little impact on the voters in six years in office enjoy such strong reelection numbers? Well, he's the incumbent, I was told. Even though most people don't know who the hell he is, they make the presumption that if he's already in office then he must have something on the ball. Even after 30-some years of dealing with this stuff as a journalist, this was the first time I'd fully appreciated the true power of incumbency. It's a power based, as much as anything, on the complacency of the voters—and on their really breathtaking ignorance of who their representatives are.

My key chore in this race, the DACC people told me later, was in making the transition in the voters' minds from local news media figure to public official. In Kiley & Company's more detailed, final report, the company noted, "Although Lynch enters the race with a much higher level of visibility that most first-time candidates, we still need to do more to establish his candidacy in voters' minds. Prentiss has been in office for six years now, and most voters have at least some familiarity with him. And while the electorate knows Dan Lynch the journalist, we need to introduce them quickly to Dan Lynch the Assembly candidate."

I also had to make inroads with male voters, where

Prentiss held a 51 to 38 per cent advantage. I was perceived as more independent than Prentiss by a hefty margin of 49 to 22 per cent and, by a margin of 35 to 29 per cent, voters thought me more likely to stand up for my beliefs. Prentiss, however, was viewed as more effective than me in fighting crime and drugs and in bringing jobs to the district.

Most disturbing, three in four Republican voters would never vote for any candidate who wasn't running on the Republican line. Fully one-third of the 25 per cent of the district's voters who were Democrats would move off their party's line to vote for the candidate rather than the party. Republicans were far less likely to do that. I couldn't figure that out.

Later in the campaign, I met U.S. Senator Chuck Schumer for a cup of coffee near the Albany Airport. Schumer, who was four years younger than I was, had been a professional politician for more than 25 years. He'd gotten elected to the Assembly from Brooklyn just after his graduation from Harvard Law School. His mother had been so disturbed at his decision to go into politics instead of applying to one of the Wall Street law firms that she'd gone around the neighborhood urging people to vote against her son. After a few terms in the Assembly, Schumer had been elected to Congress and, two years earlier, had knocked off U.S. Senator Al D'Amato, a three-term incumbent.

"Explain something to me," I urged Schumer. "When I look at the difference in sheer quality between the people the Democrats put in their safe seats in the Assembly—bright, conscientious guys like McEneny, Tonko and Canestrari—and then look at who the Republicans put in their safe seats—hopeless boneheads like Prentiss—the difference is just startling. In every category—intellect, command of the issues, in simple personal style—the Democratic officeholders are conspicuously better people. Yet my poll showed that the Republicans in my district are much more likely to be party-line voters than the Democrats."

"Every poll shows that," Schumer said.

"Why, though? These are the better-educated voters. They make more money. Theoretically, at least, they're better informed. Why should they be more likely to vote for the party than for the candidate?"

"Look," Chuck Schumer explained, "most Republican voters hate government to begin with. All they want from government is that it should cost them as little money as possible. They figure that government isn't going to do anything for them, and they don't care if it does anything for anybody else. They're not really concerned about who holds public office as long as it's not us. Their goal as voters is to keep Democrats out, period."

The DACC poll differed from the sort of public opinion polls I'd dealt with so often in the newspaper business. Those polls had merely been a snapshot in time—a measurement of public sentiment at a given moment. The DACC poll did that, but it also was a marketing road map. The poll measured how that sentiment might change if I transmitted certain messages to the voters.

For example, it asked respondents if they would be more or less likely to vote for me if they knew certain things about me. The poll said: "Lynch supports the rights of law-abiding gun owners but says we have to do more to keep guns out of the hands of kids. Bob Prentiss has accepted campaign contributions from the NRA, and consistently voted against even moderate gun control measures." Three in five voters responded that, armed with that information, they were likely to vote for me over Prentiss.

The poll got similar responses on environmental issues and after the transmission of the message that I would be an independent voice for the district devoted to solutions rather than "partisan bickering." At the end of giving the respondents those messages, the pollsters again asked them who they would vote for. The new totals? Lynch 49 per cent, Prentiss 38 per cent.

In other words—despite the enrollment disadvantage, despite the opposition of the Albany County Democratic Party leadership, despite the complacency and essential conservatism of the voters in New York's107th Assembly District—I could turn around voter sentiment in the next 11 weeks and win this race.

If everything went just right, that was.

12

SOUND AND FURY

*"If I hadn't been President of the United States,
I probably would have ended up as a piano player in a
bawdy house."*—Harry S. Truman

The two voices came into my ear as hollow, disembodied echoes over the phone in my summer cottage in the Finger Lakes. One belonged to John Longo, in his DACC office back in Albany. The other was Bob Berry's voice, coming in from his vacation home in Boca Raton, Florida, where he'd retreated for a few days to tend to some private business.

DACC would take me on as a client, Longo was saying in that conference call. DACC would handle the media portion of the campaign, coming up with $200,000 in services. For my part, I would have to raise $100,000 for the campaign's operating expenses. My head was spinning at those numbers. That meant attracting more than 1,000 contributors to my $99-a-head fundraising cocktail parties during the next 11 weeks. Or, it meant somehow provoking immense generosity on the part of the unions and lobbyists and individual contributors, who were limited under New York state election law to total individual contributions of $3,100 each. Either that, or it meant robbing a bank.

"The poll," Longo was telling me, "shows you as not a normal candidate. It shows you as widely known and generally well thought of. It shows you as somebody perceived of as honest and untainted by the political system. It shows Prentiss weaker in some areas, both geographically and demographically, than he should be as a three-term incumbent with an enrollment edge. And it shows that your positions on issues, properly communicated, can move voters."

His sole concern about the poll results, Longo said, was that after each candidate's sales pitch was delivered to the voters I still didn't reach 50 per cent. However, that final tally had 13 per cent undecided, and the undecideds in any election tend to go overwhelmingly to the challenger.

"If that happens this time," Longo said, "you should win, but it'll be tight. This is a competitive race. You can figure that Prentiss has these same polling numbers, and he has to fear for his life."

What intrigued me about those poll numbers, as I studied them over and over again on the deck of my cottage, was the stunning presumption of trust accorded incumbent politicians by the voters. The poll's "cross-tabs"—the minute slicing and dicing the pollsters had performed on the sample, detailing their views by demographic group—were even more revealing. I'd known that the audience for my talk radio program had been 2-1 male, middle-aged and relatively prosperous. That's the national profile of the talk radio audience. My ratings had been good, however, so I'd presumed that—despite the ingrained conservatism of that audience and my moderate stands on most issues—most of my WROW audience would be with me in this race. That presumption had been dead wrong.

Prentiss had a 59 per cent favorable with my radio audience and a 23 per cent negative. I had only a 49 per cent favorable and an 18 per cent negative. And that radio audience, while only 15 per cent of the electorate, consisted of the voters who knew me and my thinking most intimately. They'd been listening to me prattle on for an hour a day for nearly three years.

With readers of my column, who constituted a much larger segment of the voting public, the numbers were more congenial. Before my message was delivered, I had 45 per cent of them, compared to Prentiss's 43 per cent, with 12 per cent undecided. Once the radio audience was exposed to my sales pitch, the poll showed, I would win them, too, by 49 to 43 per cent.

I had my doubts, however. I wasn't surprised by my steady 17 and 18 per cent negative ratings with both audiences. Those were the hard-core right-wingers in the district, who not only would disagree with most of my middle-of-the-road positions but who also despised anybody even remotely associated with what their philosophical spokesman, Rush Limbaugh, kept merrily reviling as the "liberal, left-wing, mainstream media." I'd understood from the start that, given the enrollment of the district, I was going into this gunfight with a .22-cal target pistol while Prentiss would be armed with an AK-47. My one consolation was that I was a vastly better shot. I spoke better, enjoyed a stronger grasp of the issues and had figured—correctly, as the poll showed—that most people would view me as somebody they could trust.

Still, if I couldn't get a majority of my column and radio audiences up front, when they'd already had such heavy exposure to my views and thoughts, then could I really be so confident of winning those groups in November after a few direct mail pieces and some one-minute radio ads? That's what I found most sobering about those poll results—no, not just sobering, downright worrisome. Don't sweat it, Longo assured me. They simply don't think of you yet as an Assembly candidate. Our media campaign will help you make that transition, he said.

I remained startled, though—and disappointed, too—that those so many people who'd read and heard my words so regularly still needed to be sold on my ability to do the job of a state legislator. I'd hoped that I would be able to win this race on the basis of my reputation and avoid hitting up so many people for cash.

Clearly, though, I was now forced to shake the money tree with enormous vigor.

It was sun-splashed Sunday afternoon. Armed with the list of home addresses and phone numbers that somebody had sent me anonymously in the mail, I was sitting in the side yard of the cottage, on my wireless phone, calling around the state to the homes of members of the PEF statewide executive committee.

"I'm Dan Lynch," I was saying. "I'm the Democratic Party's candidate in the 107th Assembly District, in suburban Albany. You should already have received a letter from me. I'm looking for your support in overturning the regional PAC's decision and in getting PEF's backing in this election."

There were 100 or so of these people who needed to be called, wheedled and cajoled. It was difficult to persuade the members of the statewide executive committee to overturn a local political action committee's decision, and it was crucial that I make this sales pitch anyway. Personal phone calls from the candidate tended to be persuasive, especially on weekends. It demonstrated to these people that I took their union seriously and that I would be likely to adopt the same attitude in the Assembly.

I'd been making these calls for three days, beginning on Friday night. The response had been favorable, but I knew better than to take that seriously. I was well aware that every noncommittal response equated to a no. At the end of that day, I did the math, totaling up the yeses, the relatively few overt nos and the distressingly high, "We'll have to see," responses. The executive committee would meet the following week.

This would be close.

I drove back home, more than four hours, in a pounding rainstorm. When I got into the house in Clifton Park, I immediately dived for the newspapers that had built up during my absence. Both my opponent and the press had been busy during the few days I'd been out of town.

Thanks to Josh Ehrlich's shrewd lawyering, I'd won back my place on the Liberal Party line. Meanwhile, Prentiss had filed papers with the State Board of Elections announcing that he would be challenging my place on the Working Families line in the September 12th primary via a write-in campaign. Now, both the *Record* and *Gazette* had stories on an independent political party that Prentiss was trying to form that could get his name on the ballot on still another line. He already had the Republican line and the Conservative Party line. Under New York law, he could get his name on another line, too, if he got enough signatures on nominating petitions.

He was calling his new, independent political party the "No Home Heat Tax Party." It was his way of communicating to voters that he was in favor of doing away with state taxes on electricity and natural gas, the price of which was predicted to rise dramatically that winter. I was for that, too, by the way, but I also understood that the real problem with energy costs in New York wasn't the taxes, which averaged less than three cents on the dollar. It was the rates themselves, which had been inadequately regulated in New York for decades. I paid 14 cents per kilowatt hour for electricity at both my houses in New York. My brother, Tim, paid a bit more than half that rate to power his home in Maryland.

In another *Gazette* piece, Prentiss was railing against the Democratic majority in the Assembly for refusing to send out two Prentiss mailings at taxpayer expense. Using his franking privilege, he'd sent out two mailings in June, bragging about his utterly fictional role in passing a few pro-education bills. This time, though, his staff had screwed up and delivered these mailings too late for the Assembly mailroom staff to process them and get them out before the deadline.

The *Gazette* piece explained, "Assembly rules prohibit members from using government resources to distribute newsletters and brochures to their constituents within 60 days of a general election or 30 days of a primary election. The idea behind this moratorium—which does not apply in the Republican-controlled Senate—is to avoid giving incumbent lawmakers a taxpayer-financed advantage in their re-election campaigns."

Prentiss was alleging that he'd delivered the mailings to the staff two days before the deadline and that they hadn't tried hard enough. This was a plot by the Democratic majority, he was charging—which, I thought as I read the story, might very well have been the case. If so, then this was just a tiny bit of payback for Prentiss's vile threats to the charity groups.

Bill Hammond of the *Gazette* also had dug through the latest round of financial filings and had a story informing readers that I'd spent 15 grand on a poll by DACC's pollster.

"DACC," Hammond wrote, "which is controlled by Assembly Speaker Sheldon Silver, D-Manhattan, collects millions each year from interest groups and lobbyists with business before the Legislature."

Somehow, I'd figured that the *Gazette*—under the guidance of the Prentiss campaign—would take every opportunity to link my name with Shelly's, and this clearly was just the beginning of establishing that linkage. It wasn't until the final paragraph of his story that Hammond bothered to mention that I had precisely $1,400 in cash in my campaign bank account while Prentiss was sitting on $48,500. Also, Hammond never mentioned that Prentiss was a client of the Republican Assembly Campaign Committee, RACC, controlled by Assembly Republican boss John Faso. RACC, of course, was sitting on a half million bucks from those same "interest groups and lobbyists with business before the Legislature."

I decided that I'd had it with this stuff. I called Tom Woodman, the *Gazette*'s managing editor and a guy I knew slightly. I was polite about it, but I said I was discerning a conspicuous double standard in the newspaper's coverage of this race, and I hoped the *Gazette* would examine its performance more carefully. Oh, no, Woodman assured me. We're doing everything we can to be fair in this.

Before the day was out, Hammond was on the phone with me, furious that I'd called his boss. Why didn't you call me directly, he demanded?

"Because" I explained, "the last time I asked you why all your coverage focuses on me and none on Prentiss—especially in connection with the 32 grand he loaned his campaign while he was refusing to pay his property taxes—you didn't even answer the question. All you've done is to look at the columns I've written and at my campaign finances. Have you even looked at this guy's voting record? Have you even asked if he has polled?"

Well, Hammond said, it's still early in the campaign. I've been planning a story on his voting record, he assured me. Hammond said he would look into polls taken on Prentiss's behalf. He would be fair in his coverage, Hammond assured me.

"That's all I ask," I told him.

I then offered to fax him copies of Prentiss's tax-supported mailings in which Prentiss had claimed authorship of bills in which his only contribution had been his vote. Hammond said he thought that might be a story.

Paul Rickard was on the phone. He was furious. I'd lost the Public Employees Federation.

Prentiss had won the union's endorsement by about nine of the 100 or so votes on the state executive committee. The Long Island delegation, represented in the Assembly almost exclusively by Republicans, had voted against me as a block. I saw John Faso's fingerprints all over that.

The Assembly Republican leader had lost two seats in 1998, during his first year as the Assembly's GOP leader. If he lost two more seats this year, then he would be out as Republican leader and he could kiss goodbye to his dreams of running for state comptroller. He had two races that worried him this year—Prentiss's seat and the seat of another incumbent, a single-termer, in suburban Buffalo. Faso was personally involving himself in each race.

Now the breakdown among the public employee unions was me with two—the Civil Service Employees Association and the National Education Association. Prentiss had one— PEF. The New York United Teachers were neutral. So, too, thanks to the treachery of Mike Burns' Ironworkers, were the AFL-CIO councils in both Albany and Saratoga Counties. My next crucial chore was to win the backing of the New York State AFL-CIO Council, which was holding its statewide convention the following week in Manhattan.

Where I most definitely would have to show up.

Walking door-to-door in the summer swelter.

A woman came to the door in Latham, her face flushed and expression grim. In her right hand, she brandished a long, gleaming chef's knife.

"This is not a good time," she hissed at me.

Mike Mann took down the address. We speculated that a few months later the cops would find her husband's corpse buried under the flower beds behind the house.

We were meeting in the conference room of DACC's basement suite of offices near the Capitol. Crowded around the table with me were Donna, Bob Berry and Mary Gilson. On

DACC's side were Longo, Ron Canestrari and a short guy in his early 30s whom I was meeting for the first time. This was Neil Fisher. He would be DACC's coordinator for my campaign.

Longo handed me a proposed budget for my campaign. It ran several pages. DACC would contribute $200,000 in services, according to the budget. My contribution now had risen to $200,000, not the $100,000 figure Longo had given me during our conference call. I felt my mouth go dry.

"Is that okay with you?" Longo wanted to know.

"Oh, sure," I gasped out.

Once more, Longo went over the poll findings. The district has changed in the past four years, he said, and not for the better. Prentiss also had been in office for two additional terms. And, Longo added, the power of incumbency is awesome, even for dopes like Bob Prentiss.

"Voters have to make the journey to view you as a legislator rather than as a media figure," he said. "That's what this campaign is all about."

They produced samples of campaign literature the organization had produced for other campaigns. Essentially, DACC had a formula for this stuff and simply plugged in the new candidate's photo and language in the text specific to that race. Their stuff was slick and professional. The first mailing, they said, would be a black-and-white introductory brochure, targeted to specific demographic groups in the district. It would tell them who I was and why they should vote for me. DACC needed a selection of family photos for that, and they needed them right away. They also needed a photo shoot with me.

This can be done, Longo assured me, despite the essential difficulty of the district. Everything, however, would have to go just perfectly, he said.

What disturbed me about that assessment was that, so far, not everything had gone perfectly, had it?

Walking door-to-door.

Everybody was being quite nice to us. They recognized me from my column. One elderly couple we caught in their garage had listened faithfully to my radio show every day. They were at least as impressed to meet Mike Mann, whom I introduced as my show's producer, as they were with meeting me in person.

At one comfortable, suburban house in Clifton Park, a guy opened his front door just a crack. Through the two-inch gap between the door and the frame, he peered out at me and Mike, presenting us with only a suspicious, profoundly spooky, Norman Bates-style eyeball.

"Hi," I began brightly, "I'm Dan Lynch, and—"

"—Just give me the literature," the eyeball instructed.

"Uh, okay. Here it is. My phone number is on the bottom, if you have any questions."

Wordlessly, the eyeball closed the door.

Well, I thought when I saw her come in, now we'll see if Prentiss's intimidation tactic worked.

Antoinette Biordi was a young reporter for Channel 13. She was a pretty, dark-haired woman not long out of college and working the low seniority shifts at the television station. I'd met her some months earlier, before I'd retired from the *Times Union* and been persuaded to make this mad leap into politics. As a newspaper columnist and broadcast political commentator, I'd gone to Channel 13 one morning to sit in front of a fixed camera in the corner of the newsroom to serve as a talking head on some news program on MSNBC. Antionette had been working that morning, and we'd said hello.

That evening, Mike Mann and I had been banging on doors in Colonie. We'd cut walking short to attend an informational session at a firehouse sponsored by the U.S. Army Corps of Engineers. Roughly 50 people were present.

The issue: what the Corps was or was not doing to remove radioactive soil from a defunct manufacturing facility not far away. NL Industries had left a mess when it had shut down the site. The neighborhood was terrified, and the Corps had scheduled this session in a vain attempt to allay their fears. Prentiss had made a huge amount of noise on this issue, doing everything he could to attract attention with it and scare people in the neighborhood along the way. He'd organized a petition drive to insist that all the radioactive soil be removed immediately.

The reality, however, was that the Corps had a schedule of soil removal that was occurring over a period of several years, and they weren't about to alter that schedule dramatically just because the local assemblyman was howling about it. The federal government maintained that the stuff was safely contained. I wanted to see the New York State Health Department conduct an epidemiological study in the neighborhood just to see if the continued presence of this stuff in a densely populated neighborhood posed any real health hazard. I also wanted to grill the Army Corps of Engineers people to see what I could learn about their detailed view of any potential dangers. I had a few of the Corps' officials off to one side of the firehouse meeting room when Antoinette came in with her camera crew.

"Hi, Dan," she said. "What are you doing here?"

I smiled and shrugged. "Getting some information, just like everybody else."

Antoinette was reporting for the 11 o'clock news. She began grabbing residents of the neighborhood and putting them in front of her camera to describe the depth of their terror on all this. She never came near me, however. I then watched with interest as Prentiss entered, in a suit and tie and ready to go on television. Antoinette accommodated him. She shoved her mike in front of his face, and the camera zeroed in on Prentiss, babbling away on the immense—and, the Corps people had assured me, largely imaginary—dangers of this fully contained radioactive soil.

Then, as Antoinette's camera operator packed up the gear, I debated going over to her and pointing out that we were in the middle of a political campaign and that there were two Assembly candidates in this room, not just one. But Al Paolucci was in the room, and he took the opportunity to grab her and point that out to her. Antoinette cleared out of the place just a moment later with only one candidate on tape.

"Well," I told Mike Mann, "it worked. All those letters and those e-mails to Channel 13? They did the job, apparently—unless, of course, she was simply running tape to look good and had no plans to use Prentiss on the air."

That night I made it a point to watch Channel 13 at 11. Prentiss was there, all right, for a good 45 seconds in the middle of the story. The next day, I placed a call to Paul Conti, the news director. He was out of the office for a day, so I placed a second call to Steve Baboulis, the station's general manager. I told him the story. He didn't seem too thrilled to listen to my complaint. Neither did he seem overly disturbed about Prentiss getting air time while I'd been ignored.

"Reporters can do pretty much what they want, can't they?" Baboulis said.

"Yeah," I agreed, "as long as they're fair about it. This one wasn't—not even close."

Baboulis said he would have Conti look into the matter. As soon as I got off the phone with Baboulis, Bill Hammond from the *Gazette* called. Okay, he demanded, what is it, precisely, that you object to in the taxpayer-financed mailings that Prentiss sent out?

The fact that they're crammed with lies, I explained.

The Legislature had voted for an increase in the Tuition Assistance Program—widely known in New York as TAP—from $4,125 to $5,000 a year. Prentiss had then charged the taxpayers to send out a mailing headlined, "Assemblyman Prentiss fought and won the battle to raise the maximum TAP award."

No, he hadn't, I pointed out to Hammond. All he'd done had been to cast a vote on that measure—along with 149 other members of the Assembly. Nothing Prentiss sponsored ever got out of committee, I stressed. He could claim about as much responsibility for the TAP increase as he could for the construction of the George Washington Bridge.

"That's lying," I told Hammond. "What he's doing is engaging in taxpayer-funded consumer fraud."

Then, amazingly, Hammond asked, "How is that different from what Bill Clinton does? Doesn't he lie all the time, too?"

I waited a long moment before responding. I wanted to make certain that I said nothing intemperate. Then, very slowly, I said, "Bill, you should understand that I'm not running against Bill Clinton. I'm running against Bob Prentiss, remember?"

I could hardly wait to see that story.

I called Mike Burns and informed him that Tom Bayly
and the financially strapped Saratoga County Democratic Party
had contributed $5,000 to my campaign.

"What's the Albany County party going to do?" I asked.

"I'll get back to you," Burns promised.

I then called Jennings. Neither guy got back to me.

Hammond's story ran in the *Gazette* a few days later. It
wasn't bad. Shelly Silver's name was never mentioned, and the
piece fairly outlined my objections to the Prentiss mailing. The
story included some response from Bob Spearman, Prentiss's
campaign manager. Spearman basically admitted that the mailing was a lie and did his best to downplay it.

"He's raising a tempest in a teapot," Hammond quoted
Spearman as saying. "This is done all the time by these guys,
trumpeting things they voted on. . . .

"Every guy who voted for [expanding TAP] is going to
say he helped on this. If they do [exaggerate], then there are at
least 50 other guys doing the same thing."

The problem was that Prentiss wasn't saying that he'd
"helped." He was saying that he'd "fought and won the battle."

Meanwhile, just to balance out that story, apparently, the
Gazette ran a letter to the editor from some guy I'd never heard

of. The same letter ran later in the campaign in one of the weeklies. The letter was headlined, "Dem voters stuck with Hillary, Lynch." The thing was basically gibberish.

It read, in part, "First, state Democratic Party leaders bypass several qualified New York Democrats to handpick Hillary Rodham Clinton. . . . Then, to rub salt in the wound, Clifton Park and Colonie Democratic Party leaders prostitute their political souls to encourage former *Times Union* columnist Dan Lynch [who has the name recognition party leaders won't have to buy] in his bid for the state Assembly, notwithstanding the fact that the years of columns written by Mr. Lynch would lead any unbiased observer to conclude that his viewpoints are solidly Republican."

Thank God, I thought, for all those "unbiased observers" in this solidly Republican Assembly district.

I'd spent a long time with Hammond while he interviewed me on the issue of whether the stands I'd taken over the years in my newspaper columns would help or hurt me in this campaign. His story on what I'd said over the years in my column turned out to be nothing short of a monster. It started out over four columns on the *Sunday Gazette* metro front, jumped inside and ran more than 70 column inches—a monumental story for the *Gazette* on any topic, let alone on a single state Assembly race. I felt positively honored by all that attention.

"As a newspaper columnist," Hammond wrote, "Lynch was professionally obliged to report the truth as he saw it, without worrying too much who he offended. Candidates for public office, however, are usually more cautious in their public statements—especially on issues that might turn off large numbers of voters."

"My position is a little different than that of a politician," Lynch said in a recent interview. "I have not been running around for the past 20 years taking the temperature of the group I'm in front of and telling them what they want to hear. . . ."

"I have no doubt some of the opinions are disagreed with, but my public life evolved in the vigorous clash of important ideas. That's what politics is supposed to be about."

Lynch insisted he would not change his outspoken ways, saying his campaign is "about being straight with people. . . ."

"The fact is, I'm not a conventional politician and will not be a conventional legislator," he said.

Hammond had studied 1,300 of my *Times Union* columns and reported in this story that "Lynch's politics are difficult to pigeonhole." He pointed out that I'd taken some positions supported by the Democrats and some supported by Republicans and that I'd been relentlessly critical of extremists on both the far left and far right. The only problem I had with the story was Hammond's implication that I'd somehow been "hypocritical" in criticizing the Legislature and then deciding to run for office in that same body. He did give me the chance, though, to say that "there is no contradiction in wanting to join a group he so bitterly derided.

"'There are a lot of fine people in the Legislature,' he said. 'There are also people who are not so fine. . . . The difficulty is, the people who are not so fine end up setting the tone of the institution.'"

In all, I had no problem with the story—and, frankly, I'd expected to. What I did have a problem with was the fact that the issue in this campaign—as defined by my old competitors at the *Gazette*, at least—was what I'd had to say in print or over the air and not the voting record of the three-term incumbent. That's why, after I read that huge piece in the *Gazette*, I left Hammond a voice mail message. From my perspective, I told him, the story had been fine.

"I do have one suggestion, though," I said in that voice mail message. "Now that you've done 70 inches on my record in my columns, I think the fair thing to do with Prentiss would be to devote 70 inches to his voting record—and not just his record for this past session but to his record during the first year of the term he's serving out and his voting record in past terms. What you'll find is that, despite his public claims, this guy has voted relentlessly as a hard right-winger. You'll find that he has voted against choice and against devoting more resources to higher education. You'll find that despite his claim in his mailings, he had voted time and again against the interests of ordinary people and, instead, voted in the interests of the big, monied corporate operations that finance RACC and Prentiss's campaigns. So, thanks for being fair on my record, but please pay an equal amount of attention to my opponent's record as well."

Bob Berry was out of the campaign.

I was solidly on the ballot on four lines. We had a September fundraiser scheduled. DACC was on fully on board in what these hardened political pros considered a competitive race, offering advertising support and management guidance. Mike Mann was in place as walking boss, press secretary—and as my personal father confessor, listening to me bitch as we stomped around the district, going door-to-door.

Berry had done his job, and now he had a business to run. I thanked him for all the help he'd given me. He wished me luck. Labor Day was coming up. We were poised to move into our headquarters.

At long last, we were moving into the home stretch of this campaign.

13

ROUGH AND TUMBLE

"Don't worry about polls, but if you do, don't admit it."
—Rosalynn Carter

❖ ❖ ❖

Paul Conti, Channel 13's news director, got back me to on my complaint over the Antionette Biordi incident. He apologized.

"That isn't policy," Conti told me. "She probably behaved that way because she sees all the harassing letters and e-mails that come into the station about our supposed pro-Lynch bias. It won't happen again."

Which, in fact, it did not. Prentiss's campaign of intimidation against that television station had achieved its goal. None of the TV stations were doing much on any of the local contests. After that incident, however, Channel 13 essentially ignored the race in the 107th Assembly District until months later, on election night.

After the votes had been counted.

❖ ❖ ❖

Ed Donnelly was the state AFL-CIO's chief lobbyist in
Albany. Word had reached me that he'd been badmouthing me
to some union leaders. Supposedly, he was upset over a column
I'd done five years earlier. And, of course, Donnelly never had
made any attempt to speak to me directly about his complaint.

The piece in question had dealt with a huge battle
between the Pataki Administration and the Democrats over the
towering cost of Workers Compensation in New York. At the
time, the rates had been the highest in America—just like the
cost of everything else in the Empire State. To measure the
impact of the high cost of Workers Comp in New York, I'd compared the employers' costs between a factory in Albany that
manufactured specialized dental appliances and its only competitor, an outfit in Chicago. The difference in premiums had
been the equivalent of three jobs that the Albany concern could-
n't afford to create.

These costs have to come down, I'd written. I'd also
reported that the unions were blaming the sky-high costs on the
state board that set insurance rates. It was organized labor's
position that the board was pandering to the insurance companies, I'd reported. I'd gotten that information during a phone
call to—guess who?—Ed Donnelly, who'd been lobbying the
Legislature on the unions' position.

When Donna and I arrived on a Sunday night at
Manhattan's Sheraton Tower for the New York State AFL-CIO
convention, I called Donnelly in his room and made a date to
meet him the following morning in the lobby. I'd spoken with
Donnelly on the phone but had never actually laid eyes on him.
The following morning, I was approached in the hotel lobby by
a short, stocky, white-haired guy. We stepped off to one side.

"I'm told that you have a problem with the AFL-CIO
supporting me," I said. "What is that problem, precisely?"

I don't like that column you wrote five years ago, he

said. You didn't represent my point of view.

From my inside suitcoat pocket, I produced a photocopy of the column. The paragraphs containing Donnelly's viewpoint on the issue were circled in red ink. I held it out in front of him and pointed to those paragraphs. He didn't bother to look at them.

"That's the point of view you presented to me at the time," I told him. "Is there something wrong with this? Are you saying that I misrepresented you?"

"No, I'm saying it wasn't good enough."

I said, "Okay, Ed, now let me be sure that I understand what you're saying. It doesn't really matter that I included your side, does it?"

"Nope," Donnelly said.

"And it doesn't matter what Prentiss's voting record is on labor issues, right?"

"Nope."

"So, any conversation with you is just a waste of time, right?"

"Right."

I folded up the photocopy and put it back in my pocket. "Have a nice day, Ed."

This was serious. Although I'd managed to earn the backing of some unions already, no more would come on board if the state AFL-CIO endorsed Prentiss. And the ones who were on board with me might not provide any more help. It was abundantly clear now that Donnelly, a key staffer for the state AFL-CIO, had been working against me, and working hard. It also was clear from his manner that he felt pretty pleased with the outcome of his efforts. This guy apparently figured that he'd managed to get my opponent the state AFL-CIO endorsement. That was why he'd permitted himself to gloat a bit during our brief conversation.

He was gloating a bit too early in the game, however. When he was messing with me, he was also messing with my wife, and he had no idea what he was getting into there. I ran down Donna, who was elsewhere in the hotel, schmoozing with union leaders. She'd already dug out the news that state AFL-CIO president Denis Hughes was going to recommend Prentiss's endorsement to his executive committee that day at lunch. Then the executive committee's recommendation would be offered to the full convention the following day. We had only a few hours until the luncheon meeting. We had to work quickly.

Donna got on the phone to Neil Fisher at DACC. She explained the crisis and asked that Prentiss's voting record for all his six years in office be faxed to us at the hotel. Then we lined up the support of Danny Donohue, the state president of the Civil Service Employees Association. At 265,000 members, his union's membership was the state's largest. CSEA had more than 10 per cent of the state AFL-CIO's 2.5 million members. And CSEA, which had backed Prentiss two years earlier, was backing me in this race. Danny knew me, and he also knew Donna. He lived in Clifton Park. Donna had taught his son in high school. Danny would lead the charge for us at this executive committee luncheon.

When the fax arrived from DACC, I realized that Donnelly's criticisms of my column of five years earlier had been sheer smoke. Prentiss had been a co-sponsor of the Workers Comp reform bill that Ed Donnelly had been lobbying against five years earlier—the one I'd dealt with in my column. And Donnelly was working for Prentiss and against me?

Whatever was really bothering Ed Donnelly, I decided, this wasn't it. Yes, John Faso had seen to it that each of his incumbents had voted 100 per cent for organized labor's agenda in that legislative session, but Donnelly's opposition seemed to be based on some other concern—maybe on something else I'd written that had offended him on a personal level that he was unwilling to discuss openly. Whatever it was—and, after 1,300 columns, it could have been anything, frankly—I never did figure it out. Now we were too busy to worry about it.

Donna took Prentiss's voting record for 1995 and a copy of the bill he'd co-sponsored and had two dozen copies made of everything. These were placed in Danny Donohue's hands to be distributed at the luncheon before the vote was taken. As it turned out, he didn't use them. Danny counted noses at lunch and figured that he couldn't get me the endorsement no matter what he did, but he could get neutrality. That would leave local unions free to endorse either candidate.

Denis Hughes did recommend an endorsement for Prentiss, but the moment he sensed a disturbance in the force, he went down at the first punch. The executive committee voted for neutrality in the race for the 107th.

Donna and I weren't in New York the following day for the convention's full floor vote. We had to be back in Clifton Park for a friend's funeral. Prentiss apparently had gotten the word that things hadn't worked out for him in the AFL-CIO executive committee. People loyal to him tried to make a floor fight of it the next day, but neither his side nor mine could get two-thirds of the votes of the 1,100 delegates, so the executive committee's vote for neutrality was upheld.

That made Bob Prentiss the only incumbent assemblyman in New York with a 100 per cent pro-labor voting record in that legislative session not to be endorsed by the state AFL-CIO.

And my campaign had dodged a large-bore bullet.

Amazingly, after many days, Jerry Jennings returned one of the many calls I'd made to him. I suspected he'd heard that Bob Berry had left my campaign after DACC had come on board. Just in case the mayor hadn't heard that, I told him.

"What can I do to help?" Jennings asked immediately.

Did I want money from Mike Burns? Did I want more union support? Both would be nice, I said. Don't sweat it, the mayor assured me. Things were looking up.

My daughter, Kelly, got a post card at Channel 13. It was neatly typed and signed simply, "LCT."

It read, "Kelly, friendly advice. Be very, very careful about every political word you read. People are taping your every story, hoping to use it to publicly embarrass Dan and his campaign.

"You should think of relinquishing your anchoring role from Labor Day to Election Day."

Going door-to-door, Mike Mann and I were now handing out a slick palm card produced in the DACC print shop. DACC also had given us boxes of Lynch campaign post cards to mail to people with whom we spoke in their doorways,

Lynch in the Oval Office with President Nixon, 1972.
Philadelphia Daily News photo

Lynch on the campaign trail with Hubert Humphrey in 1972.
Philadelphia Inquirer photo

Lynch, far right, in the White House Cabinet Room with President Reagan and Hearst Corp. editors and executives.
Official White House photo

The candidate addresses a depressingly sparse crowd at the campaign's first fundraising cocktail party. Donna Lynch is at left.

After incumbent Assemblyman Bob Prentiss began ducking debates with Lynch, Cardboard Bob was introduced to afternoon commuters at one of the 107th Assembly District's busiest intersections.

Eight months before his death, Tom Bayly, chairman of the Saratoga County Democratic Committee, attends Lynch's first fundraiser in his wheelchair.

Hillary Clinton waves to the party faithful at the Albany machine's annual fundraising picnic. Next to Mrs. Clinton from left to right are Albany County Democratic Chairman Mike Burns, Albany County Executive Mike Breslin, State Senator Neil Breslin and Assemblyman Paul Tonko. By design, Lynch is completely out of the camera's lens.

Albany Mayor Jerry Jennings addresses the crowd at the Democratic machine's fundraising picnic. Behind Jennings at right are Assemblyman Ron Canestrari and countyDemocratic chairman Mike Burns.

Assemblyman Jack McEneny, surrogate court judge candidate Kate Doyle, Dan Lynch and Donna Lynch (far right) at the Democratic picnic.

Lynch lingers after the meeting with the Sons of Italy for further discussion of the "Godfather column."

Lynch and Prentiss shake hands at the start of the WMHT debate.
Gary Carter is the moderator.
Michael P. Farrell/Albany Times Union photo

Mike Mann and Lynch, doing "The Wave"
beneath a blazing summer sun.

At campaign headquarters, Lynch collects literature and lawn signs from
Jeanine Gomez, one of the DACC operatives working on the campaign.

Lynch is interviewed on election day by WNYT-TV 13,
Albany's NBC affiliate.

The candidate explains the election returns to his daughter, Kelly, on election night at campaign headquarters. Ken Champagne of the Independence Party is in the background.

Lynch being interviewed at campaign headquarters on election night.

thanking them for their polite receptions and asking for their support in November. The palm cards had replaced my self-designed campaign flyer containing the phone number of my home office. A woman who'd received one of those flyers at her home called me one morning.

She'd been attending a craft fair, she told me, and Prentiss had been on hand asking people to sign his petition to do away with the home heat tax. She'd been angered when she'd read in the newspaper later that what she'd really signed had not been a petition to do away with the tax but, instead, a petition to put Prentiss's name on the November ballot on his No Home Heat Tax independent party line. That had struck the woman as fraud, she told me, and she wanted me to know about it. By the time I'd received the fourth such call, I decided to do something about it.

I could call the *Times Union*. The problem was that my old newspaper simply wasn't covering this campaign. I could call the *Gazette*, but I was reasonably certain that would result in a story somehow accusing me of dirty campaigning. So, I called Kevin Hogan of the *Record*.

You might look into this, I suggested. I'm getting phone calls from people telling me that Prentiss presented this petition to get another ballot line as something else entirely. To be fair about it—and I understood by now how demented a concept that seemed to most people in politics—I refused to give Hogan the names of the people who'd called me. Just look at the petitions, I suggested, and make a few random calls to some of the 3,000 people who'd signed them. Ask them if Prentiss had properly explained to them that they were signing a petition to get him another ballot line instead of a petition to do away with the tax.

Hogan did that. His story ended up on page one of the *Record*.

> They thought they were signing a petition opposing
> a state energy tax. Instead, they were giving their bless-
> ing for a new political party created by a state politician
> seeking re-election.
>
> Assemblyman Robert Prentiss insists he told people
> when they signed his minor party nominating petitions
> that it was intended to give him a new line on November's
> ballot. But some of those who signed the petitions dis-
> agree with that claim, and feel as they were deceived by
> the Colonie Republican.

In the story, Prentiss vehemently denied misleading anybody. Five of the 15 people Hogan contacted, however, told him that Prentiss had sold them on signing by telling them that the petition was a way for them to oppose the tax.

"Nothing was said about a party," Hogan quoted one woman as saying. He quoted another as saying, "I'm not happy to hear that what I signed was not what I thought it was. I thought the signature was to promote reducing taxes. I don't recall him mentioning anything about creating a new political party."

Hogan quoted me as saying, "I do think this is a question of basic honesty. If you run for office, you need to tell people the truth. In this case and many other cases, he just hasn't been honest with people."

Prentiss was quoted in response as saying, "All this name calling is an act of desperation by a desperate politician who is bankrupt on issues and who is floating a loan on personalities."

I couldn't quite figure out what Mr. High Road had been trying to convey with "floating a loan on personalities," but phrase-making was not among my opponent's talents. After the *Record* story appeared, the *Times Union* still refused to cover the campaign, but the *Gazette* did its own piece on the topic.

Bill Hammond called eight of the people who'd signed Prentiss's petitions and got the same story from half of them—that they hadn't been told that they were actually signing a nominating petition. Prentiss denied any wrongdoing, and Hammond told readers that "Lynch, who has previously accused Prentiss of engaging in deceptive campaign tactics, was not immediately available for comment." That mystified me, since Hammond had all my phone numbers, including the number of the cell phone Mike Mann carried on his belt at all times. Hammond's story also included this paragraph:

> The petition forms, if read carefully, make it clear
> that they are intended to nominate Prentiss as the candi-
> date of the "No Home Heat Tax" party. Prentiss's name
> and the office he is seeking are printed in large type.

The *Gazette* story ran deep inside the paper's local section. Its basic thrust was that if Prentiss had misled people about the petitions it was no big deal—and that anybody who'd permitted himself or herself to be misled had pretty much deserved to be defrauded.

After the *Record* story appeared, I was asked by WROW talk show host Joe Lirosi to come on his show by phone and talk about the incident. I did 15 low-key minutes on Lirosi's program, after which Prentiss came on with his defense. When he left the air, Lirosi began taking phone calls. The first half dozen clearly were from people in Prentiss's message group, calling to bash me.

And, of course, to bash my daughter.

Bill Hammond called. He was getting around to reporting on Prentiss's voting record. What was there about his
record that troubled me, Hammond wanted to know? Which
particular votes did I have problems with?

"Have you looked at his voting record?" I inquired.

Well, Hammond said, voting records could be difficult
to figure out. I took that to mean that he hadn't looked at it. I
told him I would get back to him. I called Neil Fisher at DACC
and asked him to dig out the material for me, which he did in a
few hours. I then returned Hammond's call and unloaded the
material on him in voluminous detail.

Again, I could hardly wait to see this story.

WROW was conducting a poll on its Web site.

The question asked was, "Will Bob Prentiss beat Dan
Lynch in the race for the New York State Assembly?"

Thirty one per cent of the 80 respondents said yes.
Sixty nine per cent said no.

On Labor Day weekend, accompanied by Mike Mann
and Cynthia Pooler, I started doing "The Wave."

Since so much of campaigning for office consists simply of being seen by the voters—especially if you're somebody
they're likely to recognize on sight—I knew that I would now
be devoting some time during morning and evening rush hours

to merely standing at busy intersections with volunteers. The volunteers would display "Lynch for the Assembly" signs. I would stand next to them as cars flowed by and wave and grin at motorists. They would either ignore me, honk and give me a thumbs up sign or give me the finger.

I felt like a total horse's ass, but this was necessary, so I forced myself to do it, day after day, before going out to bang on strangers' doors at dinnertime, which I was also forcing myself to do. It was either that or work the phones, trying to shake down traditional Democratic Party contributors for money, and we were working on the money problem anyway.

We had a fundraiser coming up at an American Legion post in Colonie. We'd mailed out literally thousands of invitations. You could attend as a friend for $35, as a sponsor for $65 or as a benefactor for $99. That last figure was selected for ease of reporting contributions to the state board of elections. Any contribution of $100 or more meant that a name had to be listed next to it, and trimming a buck off that figure saved the effort of typing in name after name after name when the filing came due. That seemed to happen every two weeks or so. Rose Egan, our campaign treasurer, would put the filing together with Donna's help on the computer in our family room.

Not that we were averse to anybody giving more. If you didn't want to be a friend, sponsor or benefactor, you could attend as an "other" and kick in more than $99. I, personally, was praying for a good many "others" to attend this thing.

That $200,000 figure DACC had given me to raise was keeping me awake nights.

On a chilly and drizzly Monday on Labor Day weekend, Mike Mann and I were at a Labor Day union picnic. A first-class musical group, the Solidarity Singers, was regaling the crowd under the picnic pavilion with old, leftist labor movement songs. I was introduced to the crowd from the microphone. Then I made my way around the group, shaking hands and grabbing individual labor leaders. My message was simple and to the point—no more bullshit, guys, I need some money, and I need it now. I felt like a loan shark's enforcer.

Later in the day, I put together the campaign's first issues-oriented press release and fired it off via fax to every news outlet in town. I was promising that, if elected, I would push for an expansion of New York's Elderly Pharmaceutical Insurance Program (EPIC) to aid the elderly in paying for prescription drugs.

"Medications are better than ever," I quoted myself as saying in that release, "but they're also more costly than ever. For too many elderly New Yorkers, the choice is paying for food and shelter and heat or for medicine. State government is awash in tax dollars these days. We're in a position to provide older New Yorkers with more help in paying for medications that keep them alive and functional, and we need to do it."

The issue had come to my attention when I'd still been writing columns. I'd found myself in a pharmacy line behind an elderly woman who'd been picking up some pills.

"You have to take these twice a day," the pharmacist had told her, "once in the morning and once in the evening. You take them with food."

The old lady had said, "I can take only one a day, though, can't I?"

The pharmacist had rolled her eyes and replied, "Ma'am, they won't work unless you take them twice a day, as directed. They won't work if you take just one a day, understand?"

The old woman had nodded dumbly, taken her pills and shuffled off in silence. Both the pharmacist and I knew that she wouldn't take two pills a day.. She couldn't afford it. That incident was one of the factors that had prompted me to run for office in the first place. I knew that if I could get into the Assembly and play a real role in getting that program expanded, it would make all the insanity of this campaign worthwhile.

The press release got some attention. The *Record* called for details. So did the weekly *Spotlight* newspapers. Fred Dicker of the *New York Post* asked me to appear on his daily show on WROW, which I did. I took the occasion to challenge Prentiss to a debate. He'd hemmed and hawed on the topic during his appearance on Lirosi's program the previous week.

The *Record* also came out with an editorial on the race, assailing Prentiss for his flam-flam of the citizenry with the petitions for his "No Home Heat Tax" party and for the general scumminess of the way he was campaigning. He was running scared, the editorial said, and was not distinguishing himself in the process.

"This year," the editorial said, "Prentiss is facing the only real competition he's had in his lengthy career. . . . Prentiss says he is proud of his record of service, so why not run on that rather than wallowing in the mud?" The editorial went on to observe that, "Prentiss is running the serious risk of losing backers if he betrays the trust he had built up while serving his constituents. Our advice? Run on your record, not on your fears."

The *Times Union* and *Gazette* ignored the press release. Hammond did call me, however, to ask me questions about my campaign's latest financial filing. It was his view, apparently, that voters were vastly more interested in who was giving me money than in what I might do if I won the election. Why did the Saratoga County Democratic Committee give you $5,000, he asked. Because I'm the endorsed Democratic candidate for the 107th Assembly District, I explained. What's DACC doing on your behalf, he asked? Offering advice and guidance, I said. If you want more detail, ask them. (I was well aware that nobody at DACC would take any reporter's calls.) I also asked him when, if ever, he was going to ask Prentiss about the $2,900 that RACC had contributed to his campaign? That was also in the financial filings.

The tone of the questioning made it clear to me that Hammond was trying to put together some sort of story that portrayed me as the creature of Shelly Silver. At the same time, he seemed to have no interest whatever in any story that might paint Prentiss as RACC's creature, financing his campaign on corporate, pro-gun and anti-choice contributions.

Later in the day, he called me back. Had I fired Bob Berry, Hammond demanded? No, I explained, Berry had been with me only through the petitioning process. He had a private business to run, and he had personal business to attend to as well. We'd parted friends, I said. And, I requested, please do me a favor; don't bother the guy. He's not involved with the campaign any more.

Less than an hour later, Berry called. Hammond had called him to ask if he'd been fired—as Hammond had told Berry he'd been assured was the case by "a Republican source." I had a pretty good idea who that "Republican source" might be. No, Berry had told him. He said that his role had been reduced at his own request because of business concerns. Berry was angry over the question. He was worried about his reputation—and understandably so.

I immediately called Hammond. What the hell is this, I demanded? Well, he said, I'm not doing a story on this. He said he'd merely wanted to see if Berry's story would be the same as mine.

"Really," I said. "Look, I want to be as open with reporters as possible. . . . At this point, though, I don't see much point in being open with you any more."

"I did nothing wrong," Hammond insisted.

"From my perspective you did. And, from now on, if I have a complaint about you I might not make it merely to you."

Not that I believed that any complaints about Hammond would make much difference. The *Gazette* had made it clear where that newspaper was going in this race. The weekly *Spotlight* newspapers also seemed to have staked out their ground. As a matter of editorial policy—irresponsible editorial policy, as far as I was concerned—neither newspaper endorsed political candidates. Newspapers that refuse to endorse, however, find other ways to make their point to the readers. They simply disguise their endorsements as news stories.

The *Spotlight* story and editorial that week made that point perfectly. The story on Prentiss's petitions never mentioned that two reporters for two daily newspapers had called the signers and reported independently on their complaints. Instead, the *Spotlight* story made it seem as if I'd made the charges that Prentiss had conned people into signing, which I'd specifically avoided doing. I'd merely responded to questions from reporters who'd done the actual reporting. The *Spotlight* editorial was even worse.

"The flap over Assemblyman Bob Prentiss' petitions establishing the creation of a 'No Home Heat Tax' party line seems silly, both in terms of the flap and the petition," the editorial read. "The implication that Prentiss snookered people into signing something they didn't know they were signing seems shaky. Sometimes people do not know or read carefully what they are signing, and thus aren't clear about finer details. In such a situation, motives aren't questionable."

I complained to the weekly. They could say anything

they wanted to say in an editorial, and I wouldn't say a word. The news story, however, had been written by a kid reporter whose skills were decidedly unimpressive. The story was flat-out inaccurate, and the newspaper flatly refused to run a correction on it. Write a letter to the editor, they told me.

Which I did.

I put out another press release on a bill I promised to introduce that would provide incentives to encourage health care professionals to work in nursing homes, where the labor shortage was critical. The key element of the proposal was offering student loan forgiveness and tax credits for people who would agree to work in nursing homes for specified periods of time. I put out a separate release on my endorsement by the New York State Parole Officers Association, which liked my criminal justice proposals.

The *Record* put the nursing home release on its metro front. WROW made the release an item on the station's twice hourly news broadcast.

As near as I could determine, none of the other 20 news outlets to which the releases were faxed used either item.

I was at a retirement dinner for a labor leader at the Desmond. The place was mobbed. Mayor Jennings was there. So was Congressman Sweeney. They embraced warmly. That warmth, I figured, bore some relationship to my inability to shake loose money from certain unions that were friendly to Jennings.

Sweeney said to me, "You don't look like you've lost much weight going door-to-door."

"Well, you're not a good judge of weight, John," I responded. "That's because, for every pound of fat you've put on over the years, you've lost a pound of hair."

Sweeney and Jennings both laughed. Then Jennings nudged Sweeney in the ribs.

"Good thing he's not writing any more, isn't it?" the mayor said.

The mayor had that right.

Bill Hammond of the *Gazette* had called me on primary day to ask me about my response to a Faso-Prentiss press conference in which my opponent and the Assembly Republican leader had put forth a tax relief proposal. Hammond also asked me about my nursing home proposal. The following day, however, the *Gazette* carried nothing on my proposal and, instead, ran a story on the Faso-Prentiss proposal.

Hammond also informed me that he'd received a blind fax, clearly from the Prentiss campaign, filled with some fairly vicious stuff about me. Hammond had no intention of printing any of it, he said. Please fax it to me, I requested. He did. Yes, the stuff was extremely vicious.

The thing bore the title, "THE POLITICAL INSIDER REPORT." It billed itself as, "All the news that's fit to print, but won't be printed." This was "Volume 1, Issue 1" of the "tip sheet edition." It displayed my campaign head shot, apparently lifted from my palm card, and announced that my fundraiser had been canceled, which was completely untrue. It also carried a story headlined, "Lynch campaign in disarray. Campaign spokesman quits after Lynch refuses to heed his advice."

The text of the story was more of the same. It read:

> Campaign insiders have confirmed reports that high priced Lynch spokesman and advisor, Bob Berry, has quit the campaign. Sources close to the campaign have said that Berry was totally disgusted with Lynch's campaign style calling him arrogant and devoid of any issues.
>
> Unconfirmed reports suggest that Lynch would not listen to any advice. Campaign officials have been urging Lynch to get out on the campaign trail, knock on doors, come up with some issues, and stop running down his opponent in one of the most negative campaigns in recent memory.
>
> Other sources have suggested that the final straw was the recently completed poll results. Some are saying that the poll gave Lynch very high negatives. Those polled had a very unfavorable opinion of him. The number one response was that Lynch was a liberal elitist who could care less about his constituents and just needs a job after being let go by the *Times Union*.
>
> Others suggest that the rats may be getting off the sinking ship because Lynch couldn't close his opponents (sic) 10 point lead suggesting that Sheldon Silver may pull or reduce funding making the campaign even weaker. Lynch did not return phone calls for comment. It seems that he has retired to his Finger Lakes vacation property and is consulting a wine bottle for advice.

> People are saying that he just couldn't relate with the
> common folks and the voters.

At the very bottom, in tiny type, the fax read, "For amusement only."

In 30-plus years in the newspaper business, I'd never seen anything quite like this. I couldn't imagine its purpose. It was inconceivable that anybody in the news media would actually print it, although I later learned that it had been faxed to every news outlet in the Albany area. I also learned, late in the election, that its primary purpose was to enrage me. It was a profoundly lame attempt to provoke me into erupting into some sort of fit before the television cameras.

I merely filed it away. Somehow, before election day, I would find a way to use this trash to my advantage. I also immediately sent a letter to Prentiss challenging him to a series of two-hour debates. Let's do four of them, I suggested, one in each town in the district and with no moderator—just Prentiss and me on stage talking things over before the voters. I also put out a press release on the invitation. I knew Prentiss would never accept it.

Not unless I could shame him into it.

On Tuesday, September 15th, I won my first election.

The Working Families Party had precisely 35 members among the 93,000 voters in the 107th Assembly District. As the party's endorsed candidate, my name was automatically on the primary election ballot. Prentiss, however, had filed notice with the state board of elections that he intended to oppose me in the primary as a write-in candidate. I'd responded, the week before primary day, by sending a letter to every member of the party and then had followed up with a personal phone call asking each person to vote for me and to reject any entreaty by Prentiss or his agents to write in his name.

On primary night, Donna and I were at Working Family Party headquarters—a cramped Albany storefront—checking election results via computer. I ended up with seven votes. One voter wrote in Prentiss's name, thus denying me my shutout.

Now, I supposed, I was officially a politician.

14

PITCHED BATTLE

*"I won't say the papers misquote me, but I sometimes wonder where
Christianity would be today if those reporters had been
Matthew, Mark, Luke and John."*—Barry Goldwater

The second fundraising cocktail party did a bit better
than the first.

We attracted about 150 people to the event in the
American Legion Hall. Rose Egan and Mary Gilson sat at a
table near the door and collected the money. I spent my time
buzzing around the meeting room, shaking hands and kissing
cheeks, both fore and aft. Again, most of the elected officials
showed up—McEneny, Canestrari, Tonko and the Breslins—
including the Democratic mayors of two cities in the Albany
metro area, Mark Pattison of Troy and Ken Klotz of Saratoga
Springs. The event was staged by a friend of mine, a jovial
radio personality named Joe Condon. I gave a 10-minute talk
that Donna later told me was the best she'd ever heard me deliver. I had no recollection of what I'd said.

Some of the labor bosses showed, but only one or two
of the ones loyal to Jennings and, again, not the mayor himself.
The Pipefitters union local president, Tony Potenza, showed up

with a much-needed check for $1,000. The Teamsters leader, John Bulgaro, said his union would come through down the road.

"Well, fine, John," I said, "but remember that the road in question goes right off a cliff in only another seven weeks, on election day."

What mystified me was the scarcity of lobbyists. We'd managed to raise a few grand. Now that DACC was on board, however, I'd expected the lobbying community to begin supporting my events, but only a few lobbyists had appeared at this one. By now I'd raised just short of $30,000, more than half of which had gone for the poll. DACC had promised to help me raise more, but I'd seen no sign of that assistance in this turnout.

Joe Parisi was a college professor who did a Sunday afternoon talk show on WROW. He invited me on. I eagerly accepted. I did a full hour on the program, delivered my message and took calls.

One caller came on the air to say that I clearly was a bright guy with good command of the issues, but that I kept talking about investments by government and not tax cuts. How and where would I cut? I ran down my list—energy taxes, targeted sales tax cuts, targeted income tax credits. The purpose of a tax code, I explained, was twofold—to raise money to operate the government and to encourage people to take actions that benefit society. I then focused on the need to consolidate services on the local level and to reduce the highest property taxes in America.

"If you do the math in your head," I told him, "you'll find that every year you pay about two-and-a-half per cent of the full market value of your home in property taxes. The national average is one-and-a-half per cent. That's part of what makes electricity costs in this state the highest in America—the towering property tax on generating facilities. The combination of high electricity costs and high property taxes has the effect of driving manufacturing jobs right out of New York. Manufacturers can't make goods that they can price competitively on the national market."

I spent a good minute explaining to this guy, and the other listeners as well, the economic costs of this situation—the reduction in percentage terms of relatively high-paying manufacturing jobs in the state's employment mix, the increase in lower-paying service and retail jobs. Finally, the caller broke in.

"You're just Sheldon Silver's flunky," he snarled, and hung up.

The caller had been a Prentiss plant. When he hadn't been able to trip me up on tax cuts, he'd reverted to the old standby tactic of trying to tie my name to Shelly's. This, apparently, was going to be Prentiss's entire campaign theme.

The *Spotlight* papers ran my letter. I was enthralled. After all those years of saying publicly whatever I wanted in my column, on my radio program and in television appearances, this is what I'd now been reduced to—thrills and chills when a weekly newspaper printed one of my letters to the editor.

I pointed out that the *Spotlight* story had simply been

wrong—that the reporting on the "No Home Heat Tax" party petitions had been done by Hammond and Hogan and that I hadn't supplied either reporter with a single name, so it was ludicrous to suggest that I'd cooked up the objections of people who'd been scammed into signing.

I wrote, "Your editorial on this issue claimed that this fraudulent action was no big deal—that people have a duty to know what they're signing. That's fine as far as it goes. But is any politician who misleads people—and, in this case, thousands of them, apparently—worthy of a defense by any newspaper for committing such a blatant act of deception?

"Or is it that the truth just doesn't matter any more?"

Prentiss wasn't biting on my invitation to debate.

All three daily newspapers were on this story. Bob Spearman, Prentiss's campaign manager, told the *Gazette* that Prentiss would debate only if the invitation came from a neutral organization, such as the League of Women Voters. Spearman then told the *Record* that the Prentiss campaign was considering accepting my invitation.

"I am absolutely convinced there will be debates," Spearman said in the *Record*. "I just don't know when and where."

Prentiss told the *Times Union* flat out, however, that he wouldn't do it.

"Where's the control to come from?" Prentiss demanded. "I wouldn't care to submit to any format for debate that isn't a debate at all."

The fact was, he wouldn't care to submit to any debate

at all, regardless of format. I would have to find a way to stampede him into it. I had a plan, though.

Walking door-to-door in Colonie with Mike Mann and a crew of volunteers.

We were going up and down both sides of the street. I rang a doorbell at a typical suburban split-level. The door flew open. Standing before me in a glorious state of total undress was a pretty woman about 40, her arms flung open wide. She took one look at me, her eyes bugging out with horror, and leaped behind the door.

"I take it you were expecting somebody else," I said.

From her hiding place, she popped out her head and said sheepishly, "Yes. He just called and said he would be right over."

I held out my palm card. From behind the door, her hand snaked out and grabbed it.

"Have a nice evening," I said.

We were meeting in DACC's basement offices, in the glass-walled conference room. Neil Fisher and John Longo sat across the table from me, inspecting a copy of the poison fax that the Prentiss campaign had sent to all the news operations in town. They were aghast at the thing.

"This is real desperation stuff," Longo told me. He

speculated that Prentiss had poll numbers that he didn't like. He said, "So much of what you get in polls depends on how the questions are asked. Whatever Prentiss has seems to be worrying him, though, and he's getting worried early."

They handed me the campaign plan they'd worked out. Going over this document was the purpose of this meeting. The plan consisted of a schedule of mailings to targeted groups of voters throughout the district and a schedule of radio and television ads. It called for two more polls. The plan was crammed with numbers detailing which costs DACC would bear and which my campaign would pick up. DACC would pick up printing and most mailing costs, for example, but the money to pay for the broadcast time would come from my portion of the campaign budget.

"Are you okay with this?" Longo wanted to know.

"Sure," I said. "Looks fine. Only one question. Under this plan, I have to raise a ton of money. The lobbying community didn't show up to any substantial degree at my fundraiser the other night. Do you know why not?"

"We didn't give them the signal," Longo explained.

Throwing a fundraiser is a massive amount of work—finding a suitable place to hold the event, printing up invitations, putting together a mailing list, stuffing five thousand envelopes. My wife, Mary Gilson and a squad of volunteers had busted their buns to put this thing together. The postage alone had run my campaign more than 1,500 bucks. DACC had known that we were throwing this event. Yet, with only seven weeks to go, DACC had failed to give the signal to the lobbyists that I'd been deemed a viable candidate with a good chance of winning this thing?

"Why not?" I asked Longo quietly.

"We wanted to get this plan put together first and make sure that we're all on the same page."

"We are," I said, even more quietly than before.

Appraising my facial expression, Longo suggested that I call the speaker. I did. I caught him in his car later that afternoon as he was about to enter the Queens-Midtown Tunnel. Longo had already reached him, Shelly told me.

"We're fully with you," the speaker assured me. "The signal will go out to the lobbyists. And, Dan, please charge more money for the next fundraiser."

"Believe me, looking at the numbers in this campaign plan, I'll have people re-mortgaging their homes."

Then Shelly asked me, "Are you planning to do a book on this campaign?"

"Who knows?" I told him. "I am keeping a few notes, though."

Campaign headquarters was coming together nicely.

We now had all our permits for the storefront. Jerry Vitagliano had erected walls and put down carpeting in the reception area. We'd plastered the walls with "Dan Lynch for the Assembly" signs—both the blue and white ones that Bob Berry had printed up and the green and white ones that my cousin Peggy in Elmira had come up with for my announcement so many weeks earlier. I took the rest of Peggy's signs, stapled them to gardening stakes and had them posted around Clifton Park as lawn signs. They were cardboard, and they wouldn't hold up under wet weather until election day, but they would do until I managed to raise the money for real lawn signs.

Rolling along the Northway one morning, the superhighway near my house and campaign headquarters, I spotted a vehicle coming toward me in the opposite lane. It was the huge, smoke-belching Jeep Wagoneer I'd bought extremely used for my son, Kevin, to drive in high school. I was fairly certain that, as a new driver, Kevin would hit something sooner or later, and I wanted whatever he might hit to be smaller than he was. He had managed, actually, to hit a tree at low speed at one point in the Jeep. The tree had lost.

That old Jeep had cost me $750. I'd spent weeks rebuilding the body for him before having the truck painted a gleaming black, bumpers and all. Painstakingly, I'd knelt in the driveway, sculpted every fender and body panel with fiberglass and sanded it smooth, hour after hour. After Kevin had left home for college, I'd sold the monster gas guzzler for $1,250. It was strange to see that old Jeep roll by, six years after I'd unloaded it.

For a single, brief, fleeting moment, I found myself reminded of real life.

Another blind, poison fax had been fired off by the Prentiss camp. A reporter got me a copy of it.

This one was headlined, "LYNCH PLEADS FOR DEBATES." The subhead read, "DOESN'T FEEL THAT ANYONE IS NOTICING HIM AND THROWS TEMPER TANTRUM."

The text proclaimed that, "Liberal Democrat candidate and media darling, Dan Lynch, is whining about having a debate. Lynch says that he would welcome a debate on his daughter's television station, WNYT, knowing he would be treated with kid gloves."

The screed went on to claim that my polls showed me well behind Prentiss and that the incumbent would debate only if I produced poll results that showed me at 15 per cent.

"This is the nationally accepted position by the reknowned (sic) debate commission and is widely respected as the standard for debates," the "Political Insider Report" proclaimed.

Apparently, Prentiss did have poll results he didn't care for and was trying to goad me into releasing my own poll numbers. Under New York law, any candidate who released part of a poll was obligated to release all of it. Lobbyists had pushed through this provision in the election code years earlier. They'd grown weary of legislative candidates hitting them up for money by selling themselves as ahead in the polls and then, after coughing up the contributions, discovering that the candidate in question was ahead only with one-eyed voters of Turkish extraction under four feet tall. Meanwhile, everybody else in the electorate planned to vote for the candidate's opponent.

I filed away that poison fax, too. I later got a call from Dev Tobin, the managing editor of the weekly *Spotlight* newspapers. He told me that a somewhat different version of the poison faxes was coming into his office. The ones the *Spotlight* were receiving were billed as "The Drudge Report." That apparently was an effort to convince the weekly's editors that the material had been taken from West Coast gonzo reporter Matt Drudge's Web site and deserved to be printed. Drudge, of course, wasn't exactly knocking himself out covering a state Assembly race in upstate New York.

It was Tobin's suspicion that this stuff was the work of Clifton Park Republican Chairman Mike Lisuzzo, the guy who'd delivered Prentiss's threats to the charity groups.

WROW's news director, Mike Carey, harbored the same suspicion. Each had received faxes from Lisuzzo in the past, and the portion of the poison faxes that listed the date and time they had been sent appeared in a typeface identical to the same material on Lisuzzo's signed press releases. Also, the writing in the poison faxes was bad enough, and the punctuation poor enough, to qualify as Lisuzzo's amateurish scribblings.

I never did find out precisely who was composing this stuff and sending it out. It really made no difference. Clearly, only one person could be held responsible for all these slanders—Assemblyman Robert G. Prentiss.

Mr. High Road.

Good news. I'd been endorsed by the building trades council—thanks to the efforts of Tony Potenza of the pipefitters and, especially, Kevin Hicks of the carpenters—and I'd also gotten the backing of the Communications Workers of America local in Albany.

I immediately called the Teamsters and said I wanted five grand from them. What the hell? Maybe I would get lucky. I didn't, though. The Teamsters put me off again.

The Civil Service Employees Association was a different matter entirely. Danny Donohue had tried to get away from simply offering candidates money. What CSEA offered was expertise and people. We met one morning at our new headquarters with Adam Acquario, the political action official for the union's Albany region. CSEA would handle our entire phone operation, a service that would save me what DACC had estimated would cost $40,000 if I were forced to hire a commercial phone solicitation group.

Using computerized phones and armed with a CD-ROM disk from DACC based on the poll results, CSEA would call members of my prime voter demographic group at the rate of 1,000 calls per hour. The CSEA volunteers, augmented by volunteers from my own campaign, would deliver my sales pitch and then call those same voters as election day approached to urge them to get out and vote.

I'd been a political reporter for the *Philadelphia Inquirer* in the early 1970s, and I understood phone banks. I'd learned the phone bank system, however, before the advent of computers and their myriad applications in the political process. A thousand calls per hour? I was amazed.

"A few things have changed since those days," Adam Acquario told me.

"I guess," I said.

Bill Hammond of the *Gazette* and a reporter for one of the weeklies called me separately. Prentiss had just staged a press conference at the Clifton Park Town Hall. Flanked by the chief executives of local government in the Saratoga County portion of his district, Prentiss had pronounced me an enemy of the people bent on destroying the fabric of civic life in the 107th Assembly District.

"My opponent would disband local governments," he proclaimed, "and force citizens to travel miles to regional government centers to bring their concerns to bureaucrats who just don't have the same interest in the community that our local officials do." Prentiss also quoted—accurately, for a change—

from one of my columns in which I'd criticized politicians who
held elective office in these overlapping local jurisdictions as
"clinging to their publicly supported jobs like wolves clinging
to the throat of a bleeding deer."

With Prentiss had been Phil Barrett, supervisor of
Clifton Park; Dave Meager, supervisor of the Town of Malta;
my old friend Butch Lilac, supervisor of the town of Stillwater;
the mayor of the village of Stillwater, which was located inside
the town's borders, and the mayor of Round Lake, a village
totally contained within the town of Malta—all Republicans,
naturally. Butch Lilac seemed to have settled in comfortably
with his new friends.

I pointed out to Hammond that, as an assemblyman, I
would have no power to disband anything, nor had I ever said I
would try to do that. I pointed out, however, that these five
local officials Prentiss had gathered to back him cost the 53,000
or so residents of the communities they presided over roughly a
quarter of a million dollars annually in salaries and health and
pension benefits. Plus, they all had town or village councils
loaded with other ravenous hacks pulling down similar benefits
at taxpayer expense. Do you see now why I've called this a system of welfare for small-town Republican politicians, I asked
him? Then I went on the offensive.

"Let me get this straight," I said to Hammond. "I've
now issued three press releases on positive, innovative programs I'll sponsor and push for if I get elected, and your newspaper has printed precisely nothing on them. But you plan to
do a story on this Prentiss publicity stunt in which he makes
phony accusations against me?"

You're right, Hammond admitted. He blamed his editor
for having ordered him to make the phone call to me.

I issued a statement. I was now devoted to staying on
message and saying only what I wanted to say. I would keep

conversations with reporters to a minimum. They simply couldn't be trusted to use the right quotes.

The statement read,

> Once again, Prentiss is struggling desperately to fool the voters by distorting my ideas and lying about what I've said. I've never, for example, called for the abolition of all New York's villages or its volunteer fire companies. . . . In 30 years on the public payroll, Prentiss has been useless in keeping down local taxes, useless in preventing business from moving out of this state and useless in preventing seniors from being driven from their homes and into nursing care. I'm not a politician, and most people understand that getting clueless, status-quo professional pols like Prentiss off the public payroll right now is the New York taxpayer's only chance for salvation.

Ultimately, though, nobody ended up using the story—not the *Gazette* and not the weekly.

Back from doing The Wave for morning rush hour commuters, I was in my home office, plowing through the local newspapers. I had WROW going on the radio. Paul Vandenburgh was out of town. Subbing for him on his morning show were the afternoon hosts on WROW, Joe Lirosi and Jaime Roberts. They were talking about the energy crisis. Prentiss had his message group on the job, calling the program as though they were ordinary listeners and touting him and his call for an end to state taxes on energy. I got fed up with it and called in myself.

I'm for cutting the tax, too, I said over the air, but that won't solve the problem. Killing the state energy tax would save each household an average of only $35 a year. The problem, I said, is that through industry-friendly regulation our energy rates in this state are totally out of sight, and the Legislature really has to crack down on the regulators.

I wasn't off the phone 30 seconds when Prentiss himself was calling in to WROW. Lynch is wrong, he said; killing the tax would save each household $70 a year. Jaime and Joe pressed him a bit, and he began babbling, just like always.

Clearly, Longo was right. Prentiss seemed freaked over this campaign, and he was reacting to my every public utterance.

The weekly edition of the *Spotlight* was out with still one more inaccurate story.

Under a headline reading, "Prentiss, Lynch will debate," the weekly quoted Prentiss as saying that he would "meet Lynch in unmoderated debates October 23 at Newtonville United Methodist Church, and at a date to be determined with the Colonie Jaycees, West Albany Neighborhood Association, the Southern Saratoga County Chamber of Commerce, the Clifton Park Sportsmen's Club and the League of Women Voters."

It was sheer nonsense. The events at the Methodist Church and the chamber of commerce were candidates nights. Both Prentiss and I had been invited to speak briefly and to take questions from the floor. In no way could these events be described as debates.

As for the other sessions? Prentiss simply had made them up. I'd received invitations from only one of those groups, the League of Women Voters. And that was for a candidates night held outside the district and on the same night as the event at the Methodist Church, which was in the heart of the district.

In short, Prentiss was lying through his teeth, and the *Spotlight* hadn't even checked with me to see if any of those appearances actually had been scheduled.

That edition of the weekly got even better, though. It dealt with the poison faxes and attributed them to "a supporter" of Prentiss's. "Prentiss, a former reporter," the editorial said, "knows that these anonymous slurs will inevitably hurt his campaign in the eyes of the local media and has called upon the derogatory faxer to stop. Let's hope the sneaky faxer is listening. . . ."

Reporting on that story had been woefully inept, and the editorial was simply a joke. First, Prentiss had worked for some little newspaper somewhere for about 20 minutes nearly four decades earlier. Second, the editorial seemed designed to absolve him of any responsibility for what the newspaper acknowledged were "sophomoric slurs."

And newspaper columnists and editorial writers complained so bitterly about candidates raising money to get out their messages accurately. I knew all about that.

Because I'd been one of them.

When I arrived at our campaign headquarters for our grand opening party, about 100 friends and volunteers were on hand. Also on hand, courtesy of Donna, was a bagpiper playing, "Danny Boy." We had a terrific party that went well into the night.

Already, I found myself deeply and genuinely touched by the efforts of the volunteers. I'd worked in large organizations all my life, and I'd had big groups of people working for me before. They'd done that, however, because they'd been paid to do it. These volunteers were people giving up their time and—many of them, working like dogs—solely out of personal loyalty, because they believed in me. When I was able to take the time to reflect on that, I began to grasp why so many politicians refuse to retire, refuse to make way for younger people, refuse to step out of the limelight.

In my case, I'd been in the limelight for most of my adult life, and I didn't particularly enjoy it any more. I was in this race not for the Assembly salary or the attention, but because I hoped I could do some good in office. The faith these volunteers had in me—and the efforts they made on my behalf—filled me, quite literally, with a sense of awe.

The following day, for the first time in my life, I marched in a parade. Donna and I marched, waving and smiling, with the Communications Workers of America in Albany's Labor Day Parade. We spent that drizzly afternoon at the Altamont Fairgrounds at the Irish Arts Festival, drinking stout, shaking hands and having an absolutely wonderful time. The day after that, the *Gazette* finally ran Bill Hammond's story on Prentiss's voting record. Like his story on the content of my columns over the years, it ran 70 column inches. It began:

ALBANY—When it comes to getting things done as a member of the state Assembly, Robert Prentiss of Colonie faces a serious handicap.

He's a Republican.

Any bill with his name on it has virtually no chance of passage in the Democrat-dominated Assembly— let alone becoming the law of New York state. And no matter what Prentiss says, or how he votes, the bills that Democrats bring to the floor almost invariably pass.

From my perspective, Hammond couldn't have written a better lead. The problem was, John Longo assured me, that voters—especially Republican voters—paid no attention whatever to the stark reality that Republicans in the Assembly could accomplish precisely nothing. DACC had polled on this issue over and over and had tested its effectiveness in campaign after campaign over the years. As Chuck Schumer had told me that day over coffee, Republican voters didn't want their representatives accomplishing anything in office. They figured that electing somebody who could and would do nothing in the Assembly would end up saving them money in taxes.

Longo later offered me the assessment that Hammond's lead had been "off-message." That was the favorite phrase of the DACC operatives—as though I'd had some control over what Hammond would lead his story with. Mike Mann also was always urging me to be less critical of Prentiss. He warned that I didn't want people to start to dislike me because I was "kicking the old dog." Since Mike was an Assembly employee, I knew that was coming from DACC. I merely pointed out to Mike, knowing it would get back to the DACC people, that Prentiss had begun this race in our poll with better than 50 per cent and that I hadn't gotten above 50 per cent even after the sales pitch had been delivered to the poll sample.

"I have to take votes away from this guy, Mike," I explained. "I have to give people reasons not just to vote for me but, also, to vote against him. And, the fact is, those reasons are there. I'm not saying a thing about him that's not completely truthful."

Hammond's story reported that Prentiss's voting record had been hostile to choice on abortion, on civil rights protection for gays, gun control and to tightening environmental regulation. It pointed out that Prentiss's labor record in the current session of the Legislature stood in contrast to that generally right-wing pattern. Hammond told the readers that Prentiss had voted against the first aid to education bill that had come before him that year and had voted instead for a later bill, which contained $1 million less in aid for the schools in the 107th Assembly District.

"I wouldn't have done that," he quoted me as saying.

Hammond also gave me the chance to point out that Prentiss, who bragged so loudly about being a tax-cutter, had voted for nearly a billion dollars in local sales tax increases during his six years in the Assembly. The story added, "But Prentiss said he has consistently opposed such measures, and suggested that he might have been accidentally recorded in the affirmative because he was absent from the chamber during some votes."

Near the end of the story, Prentiss acknowledged that he was accomplishing little in his job. But, he added, "You can't get anything done in the majority either. Unless you support Shelly Silver's liberal, New York City agenda . . . your influence is the same whether you're in the Republican minority or the Democratic majority. . . . My opponent would be pressured to support policies that would be great for New York City and the cronies down there, but would be bad for upstate. Sheldon

Silver would have another very willing vote whenever he needs one."

It was more smoke. The fact was that I'd already had that conversation separately with Shelly and with Denny Farrell, one of the Democratic majority's top people. Farrell was the Manhattan Democratic leader, the boss of what had once been called Tammany Hall.

"You know I won't be with you on a lot of things," I told both guys.

They'd both said pretty much the same thing: Don't sweat it. We have a majority of almost 2-1. Do what you want. What they were telling me was this:

We don't need your vote.

I went to headquarters one morning carrying a large scrap of cardboard from a packing case, a big envelope, a thick, black marking pen filled with waterproof ink and a box cutter. Mary Gilson glanced up from her desk as I came through the door.

"What's that?" she asked me.

"Just watch," I said.

I placed the cardboard on the floor and drew a cartoon figure on it. It was the form of a man in a suit and tie. The figure was about four feet high with a large head, totally out of proportion to the body. I then cut out the image with the box cutter and opened the envelope. Inside was a photo of Prentiss's face, a full head shot blown up to slightly larger than life size. I glued it to the cardboard head. Below that, I affixed to the cartoon figure's chest the other piece of paper I had in that envelope—a sign with big, black, block letters that read: "THIS MAN IS TERRIFIED TO DEBATE." I held the finished product up for Mary's inspection.

"Meet Cardboard Bob," I told her.

Mary Gilson studied Cardboard Bob appraisingly.

"Cute," she said.

15

THE IVORY TOWER

*"I am a man of fixed and unbending principles—
the first of which is to be flexible at all times."*—Everett Dirksen

❖   ❖   ❖

Walking in Colonie.

Mike and I had begun this grinding, time-consuming, door-to-door stuff in hot, muggy, summer swelter. Now, in late September, the sun sank below the horizon by about 7 p.m., and we wore light jackets as we stalked the suburban lanes, circles and courts in search of votes. We knocked on doors daily from about 4 until 8, and we now carried pocket flashlights for that final hour on the street—unless, of course, we took an hour or so to do The Wave at some busy intersection somewhere in the district. Or, unless there was a speech to give—or some potential contributor's pocket to be shamelessly picked.

For me, shame was strictly a thing of the past when it came to raising money. I made no promises, neither stated nor implied, in exchange for campaign cash, but I solicited it vigorously. At one house we visited, John Bulgaro answered the door. He ran the Albany area Teamsters Union.

"Hey, John," I said. "Good to see you. I'd like you to meet my friend, Mike Mann. He's a third-degree black belt in karate. He's here to break your kneecaps unless you give me a big contribution."

Bulgaro smiled nervously. Here I was at his doorstep, and he wasn't certain I was kidding, apparently.

Mike and I had walked to many thousands of doors by now, moving through the DACC list of election districts with speed and steadfast resolve. As we'd worked our way through the list of swing districts in the order of their productivity, we were now hitting election districts with more reliable party voters. In the 107th Assembly District, that tended to mean Republican voters. People were polite, for the most part, but it was clear that I was a tougher sell to voters in these increasingly GOP neighborhoods.

Most evenings we had volunteers with us. The most devoted of these was one of Tony Catalfamo's committeemen—an affable, energetic, Albany County employee named Tim Lane. Tim walked countless miles with us, night after night, although he was always baffled by our refusal to use walk sheets. Tim complained about our insistence on hitting every house, regardless of the owner's party enrollment. Committee people are trained to win elections by maximizing turnout by voters of their party. With three in four houses in this district occupied by voters who weren't Democrats, I couldn't work that way. I was trying both to maximize Democratic turnout and to earn Republican and independent votes at the same time. Given the enrollment disadvantage, I had no other choice.

Moving along a quiet suburban street as darkness fell, Mike and I rang the bell of a neat ranch house. A kid of 10 or so came to the door.

"Hi," I said to him. "Is anybody at home old enough to vote?"

"I'll get my grandfather," the kid said, zipping away from the door.

A moment later, an older man appeared in the doorway. I began my rap.

"Forget it," he said, obviously recognizing me. "I'm with the other party."

"And that's how you make decisions?" I asked him.

"Yes," he told me, "it is."

I wished him a good evening and moved on. Here was a candidate for the Assembly, standing right on this bozo's doorstep. Meanwhile, he didn't have a question and wasn't interested in reading a single word of campaign literature that would let him what that candidate stood for. If you've ever wondered how so many fools, fakes, phonies and outright crooks end up in public office, that guy in that doorway provided one powerful explanation for why that happens.

I had a call from a young reporter at the *Times Union* named Mike Fricano. Not long out of college, he'd joined the newsroom staff less than a year before I'd retired. Since I'd spent my time as a columnist on the street or in the Capitol, not in the newspaper office, I'd never exchanged a word with him face-to-face. He wanted to talk about the debate issue.

The *Spotlight* story, I told Fricano, had been total fiction. Prentiss had agreed to no debates. I asked him: "Is the *Times Union* now covering this campaign?"

"Well," Mike Fricano told me, "we've been real disorganized in election coverage."

"I've noticed," I told him.

The *Gazette* ran an editorial on news coverage of the Hillary Clinton-Rick Lazio campaign for the U.S. Senate. It was headlined, "Celebrity journalism." The editorial complained about the way reporters cover campaigns.

"Reporters seem to be interested primarily in campaign tactics and strategy, polling and image doctoring, 'unscripted moments' and emotional insights," the editorial intoned, "and very little in the substance of what Lazio and Clinton have said. If, say, Lazio announces a new education policy, it gets cursory coverage but is quickly ignored in favor of what the media seem to regard as the real story, the continuing psychodrama."

Meanwhile, in that same newspaper, Bill Hammond was printing another story on my campaign finances. The Committee to Elect Dan Lynch had raised $35,100 and had spent or owed $41,000. I fired off a fax to Bill Hammond that included the editorial from his own newspaper. It read:

> Bill—
>
> I'm confused about a few things. Why is a routine financial filing news but my endorsement by the state's leading environmental group and other key organizations is not? Why is every position paper issued in this campaign ignored? And why does the *Gazette* run an editorial like this one when it covers this campaign in precisely the fashion the editorial complains about?
>
> What am I missing here?

When Hammond failed to respond, I mailed a copy of the fax to Tom Woodman, the *Gazette*'s managing editor. I included a note that read:

Dear Tom:

In a state of utter bafflement, I faxed off the enclosed yesterday morning to Bill Hammond. Having heard nothing in response, I'm now sending it to you. I don't get this at all.

I didn't hear back from Woodman, either. It wasn't necessary, I supposed.

Where the *Gazette* was concerned, I figured I already knew the answer to that question.

Jan Lemon's Clifton Park committee people were beginning to go door-to-door distributing campaign literature for the party's candidates. Jan was the Saratoga County coordinator for the Hillary Clinton campaign. Hillary, she predicted, would get 50 per cent of the voters in this 3-1 Republican county.

At DACC's instructions, my campaign people dragged their feet in getting Jan our literature. DACC did not want my stuff going out with Hillary Clinton's. Hillary, I was assured, was not an anchor I needed hung around my neck at this precise point in the campaign.

Prentiss and Faso threw another press conference at the Capitol on the need to abolish another tax associated with energy—the energy transmission tax. Neil Fisher from DACC was all worked up about it. He called me on my cell phone as I was walking door-to-door to inform me that this was a tax imposed administratively by the Pataki Administration. The tax, he said, was scheduled to phase out of existence in three years anyway.

Essentially, Faso and Prentiss were grandstanding about killing a tax that already was scheduled for death. The tax also amounted to a whopping total of one percent of the average homeowner's monthly heating bill. Also, Neil told me, the tax affected businesses, not consumers.

I had a few questions for Neil, in case some reporter called for my reaction. How much did the tax bring in to state coffers annually? What was its rate? How was the tax collected? What would it cost the state to kill it outright rather than let it continue to phase out? Neil didn't know. It turned out to make no particular difference because no news outlet ran any story on the Faso-Prentiss press conference.

The *Record* did do an editorial, though, on what a dirty campaign season this was turning out to be. Most of the piece dealt with the Clinton-Lazio race, but the battle in the 107th Assembly District got some attention, too.

"Bob Prentiss attacks opponent Dan Lynch on everything except issues that concern voters, even creating a bogus political party by questionable means to get another line on the ballot," the *Record* editorial said.

That morning, Paul Vandenburgh was on WROW, reading the editorial to his audience. It was clear by now that Prentiss would not accept the radio station's invitation to participate in a debate. Prentiss, Vandenburgh was saying, apparently didn't want to win this election.

As I was listening, I was sending out a general press advisory on my home office fax notifying news outlets of my newest campaign worker.

Cardboard Bob.

A squad of volunteers was gathered with me at one of the district's busiest intersections—which just happened to be the corner that contained the *Times Union* building. Rose Egan was there, and Al Paolucci and Jerry Vitagliano and Mary Gilson, a young guy named Luke Canfora from Jack McEneny's office and some Colonie Democratic committee people. And, of course, my wife, Donna. We had "Dan Lynch for the Assembly" signs to wave at cars during rush hour. And, of course, we had Cardboard Bob at the curb for his maiden appearance before the public.

Thousands of cars rolled by during that afternoon rush hour. Cardboard Bob was the unqualified star of the show. Driver after driver broke up at seeing the cardboard cutout with its sign, "THIS MAN IS TERRIFIED TO DEBATE." By cell phone, I ended up on Joe Lirosi's show on WROW to bang on the real Bob during drive-time for ducking debates and to urge Prentiss to crawl out from under the bushes and face the voters. Photographers showed from both the *Times Union* and the *Record*, although—predictably—none from the *Gazette*. No television cameras showed either.

We got a decent ride from this stunt. The *Record* ended up running a color photo low on page one. The *Times Union* ran a brief story. Just as important, many thousands of voters in the district had seen the cardboard figure and gotten the message that Prentiss was hiding from me. Cardboard Bob also was going out with me and Jerry V. the following morning to do The Wave for morning commuters in Clifton Park. The heat was now on Prentiss concerning this debate business. He could lie about it all he wanted, but those lies now would subject him to ridicule and contempt rather than provide him shelter.

That evening, we had walking to do in Colonie. Luke and I and a few of the committee people walked a neighborhood less than half a mile from where we'd done The Wave with Cardboard Bob. We came across a couple of older guys who made it clear that they would never vote for anybody other than a Republican—including Jesus Christ, whom they suspected might have been a little on the liberal side, anyway. We also stumbled into what seemed quite clearly to be a drug deal. A few shady looking guys—one dressed all in black, bearded and heavily tattooed, and completely out of character in this suburban neighborhood—were standing guard outside a house, beside an expensive four-wheel-drive truck, also black.

"Don't knock on that door," the man in black told me and Luke threateningly. "The people in there, they don't want to be disturbed."

Briefly, I considered calling the cops on my cell phone, but whatever was going on inside that house would require a search warrant before the cops could act, and neither my suspicions nor theirs would be sufficient to obtain one.

"Have a nice evening," I urged the dealers as we moved on to the next house.

Now things were getting stranger than ever in the Albany County machine.

At nearly 80, District Attorney Sol Greenberg suddenly announced he was retiring. It either was an idea that hadn't occurred to him before the September 12th primary election or a scam cooked up by Mayor Jennings and Mike Burns to put a Greenberg successor into office without a primary fight. I figured I knew which one it was.

Under New York law, the county committee now could simply name a candidate and Democratic voters would have nothing to say in a primary election about that candidate's identity. Moreover, in that 2-1 Democratic county, the primary was the entire election. No conventional Republican candidate would have a chance in November.

This action provoked the predictable riot in the Albany County Democratic Party structure between the pro- and anti-Jennings forces. In the end, the party bosses selected Assistant District Attorney Paul Clyne as its candidate for D.A. Clyne was a capable courtroom prosecutor and the son of a late judge who'd been a key player in the O'Connell-Corning regime. The Republicans responded by selecting the guy who would have been Clyne's chief rival for the Democratic Party nomination, had a primary election been permitted. The county GOP leadership signed a Wilson-Pakula Proclamation to permit Assistant District Attorney Paul DerOhannesian, a Democrat and also a good guy in the courtroom, to run as the Republican candidate in the general election.

Then, out of the blue, a leftish lawyer named Mark Mischler ended up as a candidate on the Working Families line. Now there was a three-way fight for the Albany County D.A.'s seat in November, with DerOhannesian trying to win with the votes of Republicans and liberals against Clyne and the Democratic Albany County Democratic party machine. And, meanwhile, DerOhannesian also had to contend with this third candidate who would siphon off left-wing votes.

It was the usual down-and-dirty stuff you could expect from the Albany machine, and its effect on my campaign was not encouraging. The Clinton-Lazio race was getting heavy news coverage while local candidates were scrambling for media attention. Now, here was another hot local race to compete with mine for broadcast time and ink and the attention of the Colonie Democratic organization. Also, the Albany County machine could be counted on to throw a ton of money in Clyne's direction, further reducing my chances of squeezing even a dime out of Mike Burns. None of this was good news for my campaign.

Also, I was asked by dissidents in the Albany machine to endorse DerOhannesian. He's the reform guy, it was pointed out to me. You're not a Democrat, even though you're on the Democratic ticket. This would demonstrate your independence from the machine. Also, it was pointed out, you have to despise the way this was done, don't you?

All of which were fair arguments, and I considered them. In the end, though, I decided that I had a duty to stay out of it. I was backed by the Working Families Party, which had not backed DerOhannesian. Also, I was the candidate of the Democratic Party, which had backed Clyne. Maybe Jennings and Burns didn't figure they owed me anything, despite their promises to me before I'd announced. I felt, though, that accepting the Democratic Party's nomination had placed certain obligations on me, and I was unwilling to take any action that could publicly embarrass either Tony Catalfamo or Tom Bayly, both of whom had behaved fairly toward me, and with honor.

So, in the end, I stayed the hell out of the whole mess.

Walking in Colonie.

The guy was in his front yard. As I came up his driveway, he recognized me.

"I'm voting for you," he said as I handed him my palm card.

"You're a shrewd judge of character," I told him.

In the guy's back yard, tied to a stake in the lawn, was a striking, snow-white German shepherd. It was my firm policy, in every doorway where I found one, to compliment people on their kids or pets.

"That's a gorgeous dog," I said to the guy—and it was, too.

"That's Snow," he said. "Come and see him."

We walked around the side of the house. The white German shepherd glared at me warily.

"Go ahead, pet him," the guy told me. "He's just a little shy."

The shepherd cowered as I bent down. I permitted him to sniff my hand, redolent of the golden retriever I had back home. Then I stroked the animal's head. The dog remained motionless.

"Great dog," I said, standing up again.

Which was when the white German shepherd came flying off the ground—90 pounds of bone, muscle and teeth headed straight for my throat. I reacted instinctively, leaning back and out of the way as the fangs clicked together only inches from my jugular. The guy grabbed the rope and pulled the big dog back to the ground.

"Bad Snow!" he yelled. "Bad dog!"

Then the guy turned to me. "Sorry, he hardly ever does that."

Before newspapers make endorsements in political campaigns, they invite the candidates in for question-and-answer sessions with the paper's editorial board. I'd been part of those sessions at the *Times Union* for more than two decades, literally hundreds of them. Now, accompanied by Mike Mann and the ever-present Cardboard Bob, I found myself sitting at the end of the table in that familiar conference room, and my old colleagues were grilling me with great glee.

Who did I like in the D.A.'s race, I was asked? I support the Democratic ticket, I replied, but I very much like the fact that the voters have a choice in this contest. If elected, would I vote for Shelly for Assembly speaker? Let's see if he actually runs again and who's up against him, I said, adding that Shelly had been a capable, effective speaker who'd been given a bad rap by the Republicans and by some members of his own party. Without saying so directly, because I knew the DACC people would go wild if I openly supported Shelly's re-election as speaker in this conservative Republican district, I was saying that I would be with him if I got the chance and if he needed me.

My message to this group was simple and totally honest. I was the "un-politician," I said. Like outgoing U.S. Senator Daniel Patrick Moynihan, I said, my interest in office would be government, not politics. I had no interest in involving myself in party affairs and no interest whatever in seeking higher office. I said that I'd tried in the beginning of the race to raise only the money I needed but that the lack of news coverage on the contest had made clear to me that I had to be more aggressive on that score, despite my distaste for fundraising, because I now realized that I would have to advertise.

I told the *Times Union* editorial board that the newspaper—and, to be fair, every other news outlet as well—had failed to cover the difference between the reality of Prentiss's voting record and his false and inflated claims in his direct-mail pieces. I ran through the initiatives I would push for if elected. My favorite was a student aid proposal that would forgive student loans over a 10-year period if those students stayed in New York after graduation and became taxpayers in the Empire State.

How long would you serve if you win this thing, I was asked? Two terms, I said—three, tops. Actually, I planned to serve only one two-year term. I'd made up my mind by that point that I would never go through another political campaign—not with all the lying, duplicity, back-stabbing and stunning media incompetence that suffering through this process had revealed to me. I wanted only to get into the Assembly for two years, push for my proposals and then get out. I had books to write and golf to play.

How did I like being on the other side of this process?

"Well," I told my former colleagues at the *Times Union*, "it has been enlightening."

I had Jennings on the phone. I need the Albany County Democratic Committee to come through with some money, I told him. Reporters are going to start asking me about the party's rather obvious lack of support, and if there has ever been a candidate who can't lie to a reporter it's me.

It wasn't a threat—well, not exactly, anyway. I wasn't saying that I would throw a press conference to denounce the treachery to which I'd been subjected. I was way too worried about what might happen inside the Albany County Board of Elections on election night were I to do that. I was, however, putting the mayor on notice that, if asked about this, I would tell the truth about it, and vote fraud in the board of elections be damned.

Jennings said he would get back to me. To my shock, he did. The mayor would transfer $1,000 from his own bulging campaign committee bank account to mine, he pledged, and Burns also would kick in a grand from the Albany Party coffers. That would be precisely one-fifth of what Tom Bayly had given me. When Neil Breslin had run for the State Senate for the first time four years earlier, the Albany County machine had given his campaign $15,000.

I thanked the mayor for his help. I would believe it, however, only when I had the checks in my hand.

Later in the day, as Mike and I walked the streets, banging on doors, Shelly Silver called me on my cell phone. How's it going, he wanted to know?

"Somebody has to lean on Jennings and lean hard," I told him. "You have a big investment in me, Shelly. I'm trying hard to do my part, but I need help. As best I can figure, John Sweeney's influence with Jennings seems to be keeping me from getting the local backing I need."

"I'm here for you, Dan," the Assembly speaker assured me.

From the news coverage, it was clear that Prentiss had not been amused by Cardboard Bob.

"Bush league," he'd complained to the *Times Union*.

Nonetheless, Gary Carter from WMHT-Channel 17, the Albany area's public television station, was now calling to inform me that Prentiss had agreed to debate me on the station. It would be a brief debate, only a half hour, late in October. It would be held in WMHT's studios on a Friday morning and aired at 6 p.m. Saturday, going up against college football. Not an ideal venue, certainly, but better than nothing.

Unlike the flesh-and-blood leadership of the Albany County machine, Cardboard Bob seemed to be coming through for me.

Mike Lisuzzo, the Clifton Park GOP boss, had a letter to the editor in the *Spotlight* in response to my letter to the editor in response to the *Spotlight* story and editorial. In a display of hypocrisy simply breathtaking in its sheer splendor, Lisuzzo was accusing me of "mudslinging."

Jan Lemon agreed to lend her name to a letter in response to Lisuzzo's latest outburst. I wrote it myself. It began:

> I'm still laughing at the letter to the editor from Michael Lisuzzo, the chairman of the Clifton Park Republican Committee. He complains that Dan Lynch's letter to the editor, which accurately described Bob Prentiss's "deception" in creating his phony independent political party for the November ballot, constituted "mudslinging." Mr. Lisuzzo is the acknowledged global champion of political mudslinging. If mudslinging were an Olympic event, Lisuzzo would have brought home a gold medal from Sydney.

For the rest of the campaign, five full weeks, Lisuzzo laid fairly low. Shortly after the letter bearing Jan Lemon's name appeared in the *Spotlight*, however, two more anonymous, poison faxes were fired off to news media organizations. They contained precisely the sort of punctuation errors that had been so conspicuous in Lisuzzo's signed press releases. These faxes were ineptly disguised as press releases from my campaign. Emblazoned over my photo was the legend, "I'm terrified that I'll lose." Each also bore the message, "FOR IMMEDIATE RELEASE. CONTACT; MEDIA RELATIONS FIRMS THE TROY RECORD & WNYT-13."

The first fake press release read:

> CLIFTON PARK, N.Y.—Dan Lynch is launching into his campaign strategy for the final weeks of the very quiet campaign for the Assembly. Lynch is desperately trying to attract attention to himself.
>
> The new strategy, designed to get media attention, is to stand around street corners waving at constituents. Alongside Mr. Lynch is the campaign's secret weapon, a cardboard cutout of Dan's opponent, Assemblyman Bob Prentiss.
>
> Lynch said, "I got this idea from visiting my wife's class on government. The kids really had some great ideas. One student said he saw the cutout idea on Saturday morning cartoons and it really made a big impression on him."
>
> The campaign is really getting into high gear. Dan Lynch will no longer be sleeping 14 hours a day and spending his mornings sipping coffee and typing press releases. He has made the commitment to go out and look at people.
>
> Dan said, "I'm terrified of actually having to talk with the voters because I have no ideas. If I hang around street

corners it will at least look like I'm doing something even though most candidates wait until the last few days to do this."

The people seem to be responding. "They are beeping their horns at me," said Lynch. "Some even mutter 'get the hell out of the road you idiot.' I think they like me." concluded Lynch.

Other motorists are saying things that are really pleasing the campaign. Dan said, "I heard one guy scream 'You can bet I'll remember your name, Lynch, when I go to the polls.' I really couldn't hear what else he said because the car horns were so loud due to the traffic jams I guess I was causing."

Dan continued "I also found that holding up a cup with a sign saying WILL WORK FOR FOOD helped attract much needed campaign contributions. One nice lady said she would pay me to rake leaves for her."

The second "press release" was even more bizarre. It was a phony campaign schedule for me. It had me saying that I would be standing "at the corners of 1st Street and Main Street in Jersey City, New Jersey."

It then added that I was "spending 75% of his time outside of the Assembly District because 75% of his campaig (sic) contributions are from out of the district & from out of state."

The fake press release closed with, "Attn: Troy *Record*; you know what the deal is. Send a photographer and write an article on this for me. Your next Pro-Lynch editorial isn't scheduled until next week. Could you please do two pro-Lynch articles per week now that the election is getting closer?? Thanks."

The *Spotlight* newspaper reacted to this latest spewing of slime with a totally incomprehensible editorial that managed to mention Richard Jewell, the security guard who'd been false-ly accused in the Olympic bombing in Atlanta; Wen Ho Lee, a California scientist accused of espionage, and Matt Drudge.

  Somehow, though, the *Spotlight*'s editors couldn't bring themselves to criticize Prentiss for any of this.

  The day I'd gone before the *Times Union* editorial board, I'd been taken aside afterward by Jeff Cohen, the news-paper's editor.

  You've now seen this process from both sides, he said —both as a journalist and as a candidate. From your new perspective, Cohen asked, what do you perceive as the short-comings of the ways elections are covered? I told him I would drop him a note outlining my thoughts on that topic. A few days later, in a note labeled, "NOT FOR PUBLICATION," I did just that.

   You asked me the other day how I would go about covering this campaign were I not personally involved. I found the question intriguing for several reasons:

   1. Working on the other side for the past few months, I've developed a far sharper grasp of the tech-niques employed by politicians to persuade voters. The press plays a much smaller role in the process than it should. The press, in fact, is almost incidental to the entire electoral process. Its almost total lack of attentive-ness has made the press virtually irrelevant in informing the voters who the candidates are and what they really stand for.

2.   I've also been startled at the lack of press attention to some of the stark untruths promulgated by politicians in campaign literature. I've seen it most vividly in
my own race, but the scope of the lying across the board
is nothing less than breathtaking. The politicians do this
because they *can* do it—because they know that the press
simply isn't paying attention and that they can lie to the
voters with complete impunity. Locally, at least, nobody
in the press serves as a truth monitor.

I could give you example after example. To make
the point, though, I'll focus on only a few illustrations.

Politicians communicate with voters mainly through
mailings and handouts. Print and broadcast advertising
plays a role in bigger races toward the end of the election
process, but the press plays almost no role. Television
essentially ignores local politics. So does radio. And
newspapers generally respond to gimmicks—i.e.,
Cardboard Bob—or dismiss most races with a cursory
wrap-up story somewhere before election day.

What I'm enclosing here is my primary mechanism
for communicating with voters—my palm card. This is
what's handed out in door-to-door campaigning and at
commuter stops by me and by teams of volunteers. Its
basic message is that I'm not a politician, that I'll fight for
the interests of ordinary people in the Assembly just as I
tried to fight for them in my column. That'll also be the
central message of my mailings, which will begin this
week. It happens to be the truth. I tried to make clear in
Friday's editorial board meeting what sort of assemblyman I'll be if I win this thing. Nobody will own me. I
ended up with the nomination because a reform-oriented
wing of the Democratic Party sought me out and recruited me, and nobody else had the guts to take me on in a
primary fight. As a result, many people in the regular

Democratic organization really don't want me to win. They're acutely aware that I'm not one of them and never will be.

I'm also enclosing a few of Prentiss's mailings. He has mailed since June, the early stuff being sent out at public expense as part of his franking privilege. This stuff is crammed with half-truths and outright lies, and the people paid for it.

I went on to describe the contrast between Prentiss's right-wing voting record and the way he presented himself in his campaign literature. The differences between the truth and the moderate image Prentiss was trying to present of himself, I wrote, were extreme.

Nobody in the general public knows this stuff. Nobody in the general public really understands how incumbents have voted as opposed to the way they portray themselves in their mailings and handouts. And Prentiss is far and away the most shameless liar in the local legislative delegation. . . .

But back to your question. How would I cover the campaign if I weren't in it up to my eyeballs and if I didn't have a personal stake in its outcome?

The first thing I would do would be to demand to see the candidate's mailings and literature. Then I would compare the claims in the literature to the candidate's voting record and with his or her standing with the various pressure groups. That standard should be the basic test of whether the candidate is anybody the voters should trust. I also would take an intense look at the candidate's financial supporters and at his or her voting record. The pressure groups back or oppose people because their primary chore is getting legislation passed or killed. They don't care about personalities or basic competence. They care about how state money is spent and how intensely the state regulates them. . . .

What has surprised me has been the staggering magnitude of the lying he has done in his campaign literature and the almost total lack of attention or concern about it on the part of any news outlet. Part of that is because reporters don't understand how candidates sell themselves, door to door, voter by voter. Part of it is a shortage of staff, space and time. But a huge part of it seems to be the utter paucity of interest the media display about the basic integrity—or lack thereof—of people running for office. It's sad, and it's scary, and it explains why so many inept, untrustworthy people end up in the Legislature.

16

THE FIRST CASUALTY

"Government doesn't solve problems; it subsidizes them."
—Ronald Reagan

With slightly more than a month to go until election day, the Lynch for Assembly campaign finally was going public with a few items the public deserved to know about.

I put together a letter to Prentiss calling on him to abandon the sleazy conduct represented by the poison faxes and the other vile tactics he'd employed all through the campaign—beginning with the attacks on my daughter, Kelly, and the threats to the charity groups.

"This is a formal request," I wrote in that letter, "for you to put a stop to the disreputable tactics that have marked your campaign from the moment I announced my candidacy in May. The conduct of your campaign has been reprehensible. It has been documented in several newspapers, time and again, yet still you insist on behaving in such a shameful fashion. . . . As a professional politician for three long decades, you've now amply demonstrated that you know how to play dirty. You've employed tactics that sully and demean the democratic process, Now, finally, show a little class, and knock it off."

If, as I'd been told by somebody close to the Prentiss campaign, those attacks had been designed to infuriate me, they'd failed to accomplish that goal. They were so scummy and childish that they tended more to inspire amazement and puzzled revulsion than outrage. They also constituted a weapon I could use on behalf of my campaign. It was now time to beat the old faker like a gong with this seamy stuff.

I faxed the letter and a press release concerning it to Neil Fisher at DACC. Our deal was that they would put out nothing I hadn't signed off on, and I would do the same. Prentiss surely had the same deal with RACC, which meant that Faso and/or his agents probably had known about these faxes, too. Faso certainly had known about them after the first newspaper stories on them. Fisher clearly was nervous about the letter and press release. DACC wanted me to emphasize my independence from the conventional political structure and my record in my column for standing up for ordinary people. This letter was "off-message," he was saying.

"Neil," I told him, "the message is that I'm willing to fight the unprincipled professional politicians on behalf of the little guy. Well, this is fighting. That's right on message. Also, remember that, tactically, I must take votes away from this guy. The poll showed us that. We both know that he's behind this stuff. There's no out-of-control, renegade band of Prentiss campaign workers cranking out this crap. This is all approved. This letter is the truth, and I'm going after him with it."

At Fisher's request, I re-worked the press release, toning it down and adding a few self-serving platitudes. I dug in, though, when he advised that Prentiss should be called upon to "repudiate" the attacks rather than "abandon" them. No, I said. Those words have radically different meanings. Using "repudiate" instead of "abandon" would only make it easier for Prentiss to deny personal responsibility, which he surely would do anyway.

The next day, armed with a bundle of envelopes containing copies of the letter, my press release and copies of all those vicious faxes, I was cruising to the Capitol to appear on Fred Dicker's show on WROW. He did his one-hour program every morning from the *New York Post*'s office just outside the main Capitol pressroom. As I drove, listening to Vandenburgh's final hour on the station, I heard "Mark from Latham" call in. He berated Vandenburgh for allegedly cheerleading for my campaign.

"You're just a Prentiss shill," Vandenburgh roared at the guy. "He has you call in because he doesn't have the guts to call in himself."

The Prentiss intimidation tactics, I noted, didn't seem to be working with everybody in the Albany media.

At the Capitol, I sat in Dicker's office, before the microphone, and went through the interview. I was low-key on Prentiss, focusing on the positive programs I wanted to push in the Assembly. Everything was right on-message, Mike Mann assured me later by phone—which told me that DACC had approved of what I'd said on the air.

Immediately after Dicker's program—accompanied by Bill Hammond of the *Gazette*, Kevin Hogan of the *Record* and precisely nobody from the *Times Union*—I walked across State Street to the Legislative Office Building, went to Prentiss's fifth floor suite of offices and dropped off the letter. Most legislative offices were closed in deference to the election season. I'd hoped that Prentiss's office would be closed, too. I'd envisioned newspaper photos of me taping the letter to his door. Two people turned out to be in there, however—a secretary and Peter Potter, Prentiss's administrative assistant. Both were dressed casually, indicating to me that they'd been called in on short notice after WROW had reported during Vandenburgh's show that morning that I would be dropping off this letter later in the day.

Potter refused to accept the letter. Take it to our campaign headquarters out on Central Avenue, he instructed me; this is, after all, a government office. I dropped the envelope on the secretary's desk.

"This letter has been hand delivered by a constituent," I told him. "Please be sure that the assemblyman gets it."

Afterwards, on the steps of the LOB under gray skies on State Street, I stopped for questions from Hogan and Hammond. In his questioning, Hammond struck me as eager to defend Prentiss.

"Those blind faxes haven't really hurt your campaign, have they?" Hammond asked me. "After all, nobody has printed them, have they?"

"This is about character," I explained to Hammond. "It's about what kind of guy would put this stuff out and whether a guy who would do that is anybody voters should trust. . . . If he's in command of his campaign, then shame on him. If he's not in command of his campaign, then shame on him."

The coverage came out pretty much as I'd anticipated. The *Times Union* ran nothing. I later called Cohen and asked why not. He said he didn't know. Both the *Gazette* and *Record*, however, gave the story decent play. As Prentiss had denied any knowledge of the threats to the charity groups, he now denied any connection with the faxes.

"He's become hysterical," Prentiss told the *Record*. "He's making up fantasy issues."

By the time Hammond had gotten to him, Prentiss had come up with a totally different spin on the story. He speculated to the *Gazette* that I was sending out these faxes myself, to generate voter sympathy for my campaign. The *Record* also reported, however, that something similar had occurred in Prentiss's 1994 campaign against a Clifton Park lawyer named Kevin Luibrand. The stunt then had consisted of anonymous flyers distributed to Clifton Park mailboxes smearing Luibrand with various lies. This sort of thing, apparently, was old hat to Mr. High Road.

Neil Fisher gave me DACC's official verdict on the coverage. It was a wash, he said. Prentiss and I had come off simply as two politicians sniping at one another.

I issued a press release on a program I would introduce in the Assembly to bolster recruitment for volunteer fire companies. The new law would give volunteer firefighters college tuition credits comparable to those offered to members of the state's National Guard and a five per cent reduction in local property taxes, rising to 10 per cent after five years service, all at the option of the local government. It also would permit volunteer firefighters and emergency health care workers to shield up to $1,150 a year in income from state taxes in a tax-deferred fund to be collected beginning at age 55.

No news outlet ran a word on it.

The *Record* published an editorial urging Prentiss to take part in a legitimate debate. The editorial said, "Prentiss is a candidate who enjoys a huge enrollment advantage. His apparent willingness to sit on his status as as incumbent is inexcusable. It is time, Mr. Prentiss, to do the right thing and defend your record in a public debate. It's the American way."

I responded by sending a letter to Prentiss saying that I would debate him any time, any place. He could pick his own moderator, I wrote—anybody on the planet he liked, up to and including Rush Limbaugh or David Duke. Then I put out a press release on it.

Also, out of the blue, I got a phone call from Mike Fricano of the *Times Union*. He was working on a story, he said, that Prentiss had embellished on his career as a Marine in Korea. Did I want to beat on him over it?

"No," I said. "There certainly was nothing special about the time I spent in an Air Force uniform. I have nothing to say."

The following day, the *Times Union* ran a B-1 piece on Prentiss's war record, which turned out to be a little less impressive that he'd portrayed it as being. He liked to brag about being "a Korean War veteran" in his campaign literature. As it turned out, he'd been sent to Korea fully nine months after the cease-fire had been signed. He'd never fired a shot nor had anybody ever fired one at him. What a surprise, I thought.

The *Times Union* story said, "Prentiss stands by his description of himself as a war veteran, saying he enlisted while the war was still on and intended to go overseas to fight. He said the campaign literature is not misleading."

God was tempting me, and He never seemed to do it with beautiful women throwing themselves at my feet, for some reason. I could make this a two-day story by going after Prentiss—or by having the party people find some veterans to do it for me. No, I decided finally. In the grand, cosmic scheme of lies Prentiss was spinning in this campaign, this one was really nothing special. And I would not become one of these people, no matter what. I would not do business the way the professional politicians did business. Instead, I immediately fired off a letter to the editor of the *Times Union* and a press release about that letter to every other news media outlet in town. I wrote,

> I have no criticism of Assemb. Robert G. Prentiss describing himself as a Korean War veteran in his campaign literature even though your story of today reports that he never set foot in Korea until nine months after the cease-fire. My own military service during the Vietnam era was no more than routine. I served about a year on active duty and five years on reserve duty working stateside on a military newspaper.
>
> I have plenty of complaints about Prentiss's performance and his legislative record, which is why I'm running against him. The fact remains, however, that he served his country faithfully. He is to be commended for that.

My lawns signs had come in. They were blue with white lettering, and we had 1,000 of them. They were put out around the district by the Carpenters Union guys and by the party organization people in all four towns, with an emphasis on Colonie and southern Clifton Park.

Immediately, Mike Lisuzzo issued a press release. The Clifton Park Republican Committee was offering a $200 cash reward for "information which leads to the arrest and conviction of those responsible for stealing Republican candidate lawn signs." A lot of GOP signs were being stolen or destroyed,

Lisuzzo announced. Surely, Lynch knows who the vandals are, the press release charged.

"We are asking Lynch," Lisuzzo said in his press release, "to stop the dirty tricks so residents can focus on the real issues of the campaign."

I realized immediately what that press release was all about. Lisuzzo had ordered his 62 committee people to destroy my Clifton Park lawn signs and had issued a pre-emptive complaint of his own to blunt the effect of any complaint I might make about the vandalism. Lisuzzo was notorious for stealing and destroying the lawn signs of opposing candidates, Jan Lemon told me.

That night, as I cruised along a main road near my house, on my way home from four hours of walking in Colonie, I found all my signs along that stretch missing or trashed. Warned by that press release, I had a dozen more signs in the back of my car. With a hammer, in the darkness, I got out of the car at each corner and replaced every sign that had been stolen, ripped apart or driven over.

It was the beginning of a nightly ritual.

Bill Hammond was on the line. Had I enrolled as a Democrat, he wanted to know?

No, I told him. To please some of the party people, I said, I'd filled out an card that would make me a Democrat, and it was in the hands of Tom Bayly, the Saratoga County Democratic chief. I wasn't yet sure what I would do with it, I said. I would decide after the election. It would be my preference to serve in the Assembly as an independent, I told

Hammond, but I wasn't certain I could gain admission to the majority conference without submitting that card.

Hammond told me that he'd spoken to Ron Canestrari. Canestrari, Hammond said, had told him that he would sponsor me for membership in the conference regardless of whether I was enrolled as a Democrat.

"Well," I responded, "I haven't had any conversations with Ron on the topic, so you know something I don't know."

I couldn't figure out just what Hammond was trying to get at. Whatever it was, my guess was that it wasn't anything good. I'd said in my announcement speech that I was an independent and that I would enroll as a Democrat if I needed to take that step to get into the Democratic conference. Everybody had printed that months before this conversation, including the *Gazette*. There was nothing new here, no legitimate news, and I decided to follow my new policy with reporters—to talk to them no more than was absolutely necessary.

I had someplace to go, I told Hammond, and got off the phone.

At the monthly breakfast of union leaders at the restaurant at the Albany Municipal Golf Course, I again cornered Mike Burns. I'd brought Cardboard Bob as my breakfast guest. Cardboard Bob was making a big hit with the union guys.

I told Burns precisely what I'd told Jennings. Questions about the Albany machine's lack of support for my campaign were sure to start coming from reporters—probably Hammond, who was exhibiting a morbid interest in every dime I collected rather than in my political positions. When the questions came, I told Burns, I most assuredly would not lie. So, what was Burns going to do?

Burns hemmed and hawed. Burns did that a lot, I noticed. He simply lacked the basic integrity to say it to my face—that the machine was now terrified that I might actually win this thing and wasn't giving me a dime. Well, he told me finally, he had an executive committee meeting the following morning. He would raise the matter in that setting. I should call him, he said, so, I did—six times over that weekend.

And, of course, Burns failed to return the calls.

After seeing my letter to Prentiss inviting him to pick any debate moderator he pleased, the *Record* was back on the debate story. Bob Spearman, Prentiss's campaign manager, was saying this was a non-issue—that Prentiss had accepted the WMHT debate, that we would be doing that candidates night together at the Methodist church, that at least five other debates were being set up by independent groups. He cited the Jaycees, the Clifton Park Sportsmen's Club and so forth.

"We are working with legitimate and long-standing good government groups to line up debates and candidates nights," Spearman assured the *Record*.

It was the same fiction, repeated over and over. None of those groups ever invited me to take part in any debate. Meanwhile, the *Times Union* was reporting that Prentiss had accepted an invitation from the League of Women Voters to debate me before that group. Now, the League was saying, all they had to do was find a time and place acceptable to both candidates. I, of course, would be no problem.

"Do you think Prentiss will actually go through with this League of Women Voters debate?" Mike Mann asked me.

"Sure," I told him, "when pigs fly."

"I'm down to five grand on hand," I was telling Neil Fisher over the phone to DACC headquarters. "Despite what Jennings promised me, Burns is quite clearly not going to come up with a dime."

"You have to raise money for broadcast ads," Fisher said. "You've got to do it. Call the lobbyists."

At my end of the line, I slowly ran a hand over my face. If DACC had given the signal before my fundraiser a few weeks earlier, as I'd been led to believe they would, then I wouldn't be in this fix. Now they were telling me that my only recourse was to get back on the phone to the pressure groups and beg some more. I was not pleased.

DACC had been reviewing press coverage of the campaign with Matt what's-his-name from Kiley & Company, the pollsters. It was everybody's opinion, Neil Fisher told me, that I'd done real damage to Prentiss on the issues of his trustworthiness and credibility but that any more criticism on those issues, no matter how fair or accurate, would turn off voters.

"Voters have to be able to see their own interests in every dispute like this," he explained. "If they don't see their own interests at stake, then they see all this just as two politicians bickering over something that doesn't concern them. They shut it right out."

I was upset with the Democratic machine. I also was upset with DACC. Then DACC's first mailing went out. It was a smooth, slickly prepared, eight-by-ten brochure that portrayed me as a fighter for ordinary people. Briefly, it told the story of how I'd stood up for John Bove when the State Transportation Department had taken down his sign and damaged business at his restaurant, the My Way Cafe. The brochure featured a photo of me and John standing outside his restaurant. The headline read, "Taking on the bullies."

It was a nice job, a wonderful introductory ad. Maybe these guys knew what they were doing, after all.

Meanwhile, a Prentiss direct mail ad also went out, a full-color broadside. Despite his dismal rating by the League of Conservation Voters and that group's support of me, he was portraying himself as a friend of the environment.

"Assemblyman Bob Prentiss recognizes that New York's residents deserve simple things like clean drinking water and breathable air," the mailing read. "That's why he helped pass the Clean Water and Clean Air Bond Act."

In actuality, the sole extent of Prentiss's "help" had consisted entirely of voting for the measure, which virtually every other member of the Assembly also had supported. In one corner of the mailing, there was a paragraph headlined: "Democrat Dan Lynch? Wrong on the Environment." The paragraph read, "As a newspaper columnist for the Albany *Times Union*, Dan Lynch spoke out against the federal Clean Air Act. This important program is already making a huge difference in the air we breathe and the water we drink. Dan Lynch even questioned if global warming exists."

I'd never spoken out about the federal Clean Air Act. I'd never written a word about it, in fact. What I had done was question a Pataki administration initiative to make auto emissions testing a standard test adding to the cost of state car inspections throughout the state when air quality was a problem only in the New York City area. I'd also never questioned whether global warming was occurring—only whether human involvement was driving it instead of natural climactic evolution. Nobody could say that for sure, I'd written; the data were insufficient for firm judgment. Also, as Prentiss well knew, I wasn't a Democrat.

I could have issued a press release complaining about the latest lies in the Prentiss mailing. The fact was, though, that it was unlikely that any news outlet would use any story on my complaint. Like so many ordinary people, reporters and editors simply expected politicians to lie. They accepted that lying as a fact of life, like gravity. Any release I put out probably wouldn't be considered news. And, even if it did get some news play, the voters would ignore it, Neil Fisher assured me.

This was a RACC mailing, prepared by John Faso's Republican Assembly Campaign Committee. Those two mailings, Prentiss's and mine, set the tone for the rest of the campaign. DACC never once asked me to lend my name to any ad that wasn't meticulously accurate and fair. I'd made it abundantly clear to DACC that I wouldn't lie, and the DACC people never even hinted that they viewed lying as an acceptable campaign tactic.

Throughout the campaign, however, Prentiss's RACC mailings were crammed with distortions and outright lies like this. The mailings represented a stark contrast between the ethical standards and cultures of the two statewide campaign organizations. It wasn't a question of party, and it wasn't a question of liberals versus conservatives. It was a simple matter of the personal style and class of the individuals involved in each campaign. Bob Prentiss had demonstrated that he had absolutely no class.

Neither, apparently, did anybody in John Faso's campaign organization.

Bill Hammond from the *Gazette* was on the phone again. From his questioning, I now was beginning to figure out where he was trying to go with this sudden fascination with my party enrollment. He seemed to be planning a story designed once again to link my name to Shelly Silver's. The purpose of this piece, as near as I could determine, would be to convey to readers that I was lying to the voters when I informed them in my campaign literature that I was an independent—that I really planned to enroll as a Democrat as soon as I won election.

There was nothing remotely subtle about this. Yes, by this point I was admittedly paranoid. I still suspect, however, even though I had a high alarm rate at this stage of the campaign, that I wasn't uncovering all the plots against me. While I knew from long experience in newspaper work that it was always a mistake to attribute to conspiracy that which could be more readily explained by mere ineptitude, the *Gazette*'s conduct had become pretty blatant. The newspaper was roundly ignoring every distortion and lie associated with the Prentiss campaign and was, instead, bent on presenting me as somebody that nobody should trust. At this point, with only a few weeks left in the campaign, the *Gazette* seemed to be abandoning all pretense about the newspaper's purposeful bias in its news coverage.

Oh, sure, the *Gazette* would neither endorse or oppose candidates on its editorial page, where readers have a perfect right and legitimate expectation to encounter opinion. This newspaper, however, clearly had no reservations about using its news columns to support or oppose candidates. The *Gazette* would push or punish candidates under the guise of presenting readers with objective news reports. It was a fairly flagrant violation of basic journalistic ethics, but this was the way the *Gazette* was doing business in this campaign.

"I might at some future point join a party," I explained to Hammond. "I might also join the circus. The point is that I want no shackles on me, and no obligations to anybody but the people of this district when I serve in the Assembly."

The story ran under the headline, "Lynch insists he's not a Democrat." The subhead read, "Despite backing, he claims to be independent." The story began:

> ALBANY—Assembly candidate Daniel Lynch is running on the Democratic ticket, has gotten financial help from the Democratic Party and plans to join the Assembly's Democratic majority conference if elected.
>
> But that doesn't make him a Democrat—and he doesn't want his Republican opponent, Assemblyman Robert Prentiss of Colonie, calling him one.
>
> "I see Robert Prentiss in his latest literature is saying 'Democrat Dan Lynch'—which is not true, and he knows it," Lynch said. "Misleading people like that is absolutely reprehensible."

The story quoted Prentiss as saying, "It sounds to me right now like he's attempting to deceive the voters of the 107th Assembly District. It's an insult to their intelligence. . . . He's clearly in Shelly's pocket. He's bought and paid for by the Democratic Assembly Campaign Committee. . . . He'll sell the voters of the 107th Assembly District down the river to Manhattan."

Basically, the story was a Prentiss campaign ad.

The message groups were on the job.

Mine produced brief letters to the editor attacking Prentiss for his voting record on some state employee issues and on his refusal to debate. Prentiss's message group produced a letter to the editor saying that Prentiss had been an unusually effective legislator and that I wouldn't accomplish anything in office.

One more time, I placed a call to Tom Woodman, the *Gazette*'s managing editor. He didn't get back to me, so I called back the following afternoon and finally got him on the phone.

"What was the point of that story?" I asked him. "There was nothing in there that I hadn't said last May. I can't figure out the purpose of your decision to run that piece."

Our coverage has been just fine, Woodman said in response. We think it has been well-conceived and eminently fair. Some of my specific complaints, he acknowledged, had been on the mark, but not any complaint I might have about the newspaper's coverage in general.

"Then why is all your newspaper's scrutiny directed toward me?" I asked. "Every story you do seems purposefully designed to do damage to me. You never look at the difference between Prentiss's handouts and the reality of his record. You never say anything about his refusal to debate. What's that about, Tom?"

"What we're doing is just fine," Woodman insisted.

I got off the phone with Woodman. Not two minutes later, the phone was ringing again. Now, I was on the line with Bob Conner, a *Gazette* editorial writer who also produced an occasional signed column. He'd called to take me to task for my criticism of Prentiss's anonymous faxes and Mike Lisuzzo's press releases.

"Don't you think that words like 'slimy' and 'reprehensible' are over the top?" Conner demanded. "I mean, what would you say about Hitler?"

"Something considerably worse," I responded.

There was no question about what was going on here. I could have hung up the phone or responded merely with a written statement. Instead, I decided to play along. After all, it wasn't as though anything I might say in any written statement would inspire this newspaper to cover this campaign fairly. I had little doubt that these guys were operating on instructions from higher-ups in the *Gazette* organization, possibly even from Jack Hume, the newspaper's proprietor.

The plan was obvious—to find ways to criticize me relentlessly at every opportunity, no matter how tortured, and to provide pretexts for Prentiss to link me to Shelly and the New York City Democrats in the *Gazette*'s news columns. With election day nearing, the pace of these activities was stepping up sharply.

"There exists a sharp and clear moral distinction between a guy whose campaign would produce material like the Prentiss campaign has produced and a guy willing to criticize that material forthrightly," I told Conner. "I'm disappointed that the distinction seems to elude you."

I pointed out that Prentiss's attack on me in the previous

day's *Gazette* was a classic example of what Conner was trying to accuse me of.

"I'm 'bought and paid for?'" I said to Conner. "I'll 'sell the voters of the 107th Assembly District down the river to Manhattan?' And you're contending that I'm out of line for describing Prentiss's conduct with the threats to the charity groups and the attacks on my daughter and the poison faxes as 'reprehensible?' You're kidding, right?"

That's when I told this guy that the coverage of his newspaper had become fairly transparent.

"I competed against your newspaper for more than 20 years," I told him. "I now perceive a clear pattern in your coverage. I don't know anything for sure, of course, but I've been around long enough to conclude that if it walks like a duck, quacks like a duck and looks like a duck, the odds are overwhelming that you're dealing with a duck."

Conner chuckled into the phone. "Well, we hear from a lot of people who have conspiracy theories."

I had no doubt that they did. What was most interesting to me was that Bob Conner wasn't even bothering to deny the validity of this one.

What followed was a *Gazette* editorial headlined, "Lynch doth protest too much." It read:

> OK, so Al Gore and George W. Bush are uninspiring, but they sound like Founding Fathers compared to Dan Lynch and Assemblyman Bob Prentiss. While Prentiss and his supporters are partly responsible for the low tone of this Assembly race, Lynch bears more of the blame.
>
> For example, when some Italian-Americans objected to a satirical column Lynch wrote earlier this year for the *Times Union*, Lynch accused Prentiss of running "a vicious, totally dishonorable smear campaign," making a "slimy, utterly unfounded attack," and engaging in "quite

simply, the vilest sort of political warfare."

It's hard to know how to react to this kind of rhetorical overkill. . . . The most reprehensible thing about this campaign is Lynch's hysterical overreaction to the occasionally crude attacks of Prentiss supporters.

DACC was upset with my wife. Donna had something she wanted to say to the community we lived in. Using about a thousand bucks of her own money, she placed ads in two of the weeklies to publish a letter to the voters. It read:

In 1963, two events occurred that changed my life forever. I was just short of my seventeenth birthday when John Fitzgerald Kennedy was shot down in Dallas. His candidacy three years before introduced me to the world of politics and the realization that a world existed beyond my own.

I began to look forward to my Social Studies (then called History) classes. I was being challenged to think, to be aware but most of all to become involved. My own teaching is today reflective of those days so long ago when President Kennedy challenged us to ask what we could do.

It is, however, the second event of so long ago that has had the most impact on me and the one I'd like to share. It was meeting Dan Lynch.

We were both seniors in high school and he attended a party I was having. Several months later, he called and asked me to a movie. My life had never been the same.

It's not the husband or the father I want to tell you

about. It's about caring and commitment and intelligence and integrity. It's about helping right injustices, raising our level of consciousness, it's about challenging us to do our very best, to be the best we can be. It's about providing our children with role models and people teens can be proud to emulate.

Many of you have read his column over the years. Some of you have listened to his radio show. A few of you have disagreed with him (so have I, on occasion) but NO ONE can ever challenge his desire to get to the truth, to hold us accountable for our actions or inactions or his demand that we all stand up and do the right thing.

I am proud to be married to Dan and have had the privilege to stand beside him in so many causes he has penned. I am proud to share a home with a man who has meant so much to so many of you. I know that when he is elected to the New York State Assembly from the 107th District, he will continue to be that man, the one I met so very long ago. I know he will serve you and care about you and do his very best to help make our part of the world just a little better than it is today. And he will do this with integrity. A vote for Dan Lynch is a vote for all of us to get involved. A vote for Dan Lynch is a chance to return to the days when commitment and dedication was the driving force behind all our decisions. A vote for Dan Lynch will tell me that you, too, share my belief in him.

Thank you, Dan, for changing my life.

A total waste of time and money, DACC pronounced. It's too long, and nobody will read it. I would have been better off, I was told, to have put the cash that had paid for that ad toward buying radio time. That might have been true, but the criticism completely missed the point of what my wife had been reacting to with that open letter to the voters. She was wounded by DACC's assessment.

"Don't worry about it," I told Donna. "The hell with DACC."

Then I added, "Come to think of it, actually, the hell with a lot of people."

17

BAG OF TRICKS

"In the Bible it says they asked Jesus how many times you should forgive, and he said seventy times seven. Well, I want you all to know that I'm keeping a chart."—Hillary Clinton

Not good.

We were throwing another fundraiser, this one a buffet dinner. Attorney General Eliot Spitzer had agreed to host the affair and was saying nice things about me in his talk. We might as well have staged this event in a phone booth, however. No more than 30 people showed up. One of them was Mike Burns, with a check for $500 from the Albany County Democratic Committee and a coy smile on his face.

Did I accept the check? Without the slightest hesitation. I'd now collected a grand total of $750 from the Albany Democratic machine. Again, Jennings was conspicuously absent.

"Tell me," I asked Ron Canestrari as we gazed about at the light turnout, "do you see anybody's fingerprints on this?"

"Oh, yes," the assemblyman said.

I later was told that a figure in the Albany County Democratic Party inner circle had put out the word to potential

contributors—don't attend Lynch's fundraiser.   It was three
weeks and five days before election day. We'd run a few radio
ads, but I needed to begin my broadcast advertising in earnest.
Meanwhile, the Albany machine was knocking itself out to
keep me from raising any more money—all the while pretending to support me, of course.

We responded in the best way we could think of to
throw the machine off its stride. We took on the problem directly. The following afternoon, Donna called Jennings at his
office in Albany City Hall and requested that he host a fundraiser for my campaign.

Oh, sure, the mayor assured my wife, he would be
delighted to help us.

I was at DACC's basement headquarters, ready to look
at the television commercial they'd put together for me.

"You'll like this," Ron Canestrari was assuring me as the
tape went into the VCR.

We'd shot the commercial a few weeks earlier, at the
same time we'd taken a ton of still photos for the mailings.
We'd gone into Colonie's West Albany neighborhood late on a
sunny morning. We'd been met by a squad of CSEA people—
young and old, short and tall, male and female, white and
otherwise—to pose with me in the photos. We later did another such shoot at a playground in Clifton Park, with me and
some kids and a couple of young mommies. The still photographers and the film crew from New York City had shot me
shaking hands, talking to groups in the street. I wore a suit and
tie in some shots and, in the others, golf shirts that Mary Gilson

had hustled off to buy at a nearby shopping center. I'd stood there in the street stripping to the waist and changing clothes all morning.

The TV ad was deftly crafted, filled with quick cuts and bearing a strong message—namely, that I would stand up against the political hacks and work instead for the benefit of ordinary people. Canestrari was right; I liked the ad a lot.

"If we can get this on the air," Ron was saying, "you'll win hands down."

As I watched the commercial, though, I knew I would never see it on the air. With money this tight, I couldn't afford television time—not when so many viewers wouldn't be voters in the 107th Assembly District. We would be better off with radio advertising running on some of the metro area's 38 radio stations. Vastly cheaper radio ads, on stations targeted to the demographic groups that the poll had told me I needed to reach, would give us far more bang for the buck than this terrific television commercial. My campaign, unfortunately, didn't have a dime to waste.

As I watched the ad, Mike Mann called me on my cell phone. Bill Hammond was trying to reach me, he said. I returned Hammond's call from a phone in the DACC print shop. What do you want, I asked him? He'd been digging through the financial filings again. Prentiss had seven times as much money on hand as I did. What did I want to say about that?

I'd been telling this guy for months that I would be outspent in this race. I'd told him that I'd refused to fill out most of the pressure groups' questionnaires and refused to sign on to specific language in their bills because I was determined to remain independent. Hammond had printed none of that, however; he seemed too bent on portraying me as Shelly's creature in bed with the left-wing special interest groups.

The fact was that Shelly had managed to raise a few

grand for me from some trade groups and through transfers from the campaign committees of a couple of Democratic assemblymen who had no competition in November. When it came to fundraising, however, the only thing going on now that I hadn't expected from the start was the active opposition of the Albany machine, and I wasn't prepared to mention that to any reporter—not at this precise moment and certainly not to the *Gazette* in particular.

Hammond was grilling me on the latest financial filing, on DACC's expenditures on my behalf. At this point, I'd had it with this stuff. Just that morning, I'd fired off press releases on a bill I would introduce in January, if I ended up sitting in the Assembly. It was the proposal most important to me. It would create a new financial aid program for New York college students similar to the defunct federal program that had gotten me through college so many years earlier. It was the one thing I really and truly wanted to push through the Legislature if I could manage to get into office and get a chance to work on it. And here was Hammond, focusing still one more time on the minutiae of this race—stuff that concerned voters not at all and that would neither touch nor interest them in the slightest. Moreover, he was doing this while utterly ignoring the substance of what I had to say and the total paucity of substance in Prentiss's campaign.

I said to him, "I sent to you this morning a proposal that I'll introduce in January. If it becomes law, it'll have a hugely beneficial impact on the lives of thousands and thousands of people. Are you going to do anything with that?"

"Yes," Hammond said, "at some point."

At some point? The election was three weeks away.

I told Hammond, "Well, when you want to talk about that—when you want to talk about the issues in this election and my ideas on how to make life better for people—then feel

free to call me, and then we'll talk. But that's all I'll talk about
with you or with anybody else associated with your newspaper.
Have a nice afternoon."

I then hung up on him.

Way to go, John Longo told me. You stayed on message. Stay cool, though, Longo advised me.

That afternoon, I placed a call to both Dave White, the
Times Union's publisher, and to Jeff Cohen, the paper's editor.
This isn't an ordinary race, I told both guys, after informing
them of my adventures with the *Gazette*. This is the only truly
competitive election contest in the Albany metro area, and it
deserves more coverage in the *Times Union* news columns and
on the editorial page.

Each guy listened politely. There was sound journalistic logic in what I was telling them. It was clear, however, that
they were concerned about anybody accusing the *Times Union*
of favoritism in this race and that my contest would get no special attention.

Walking door-to-door in Colonie. A guy came to the
door. He recognized me when I said hello.

"Hold on a minute," he told me. "I want to help."

He disappeared into the house. He came back with a
check. I took it, stuck it in my wallet, shook his hand and
thanked him. As Mike Mann and I moved on to the next house,
I looked at the check. This total stranger had contributed $500.
I responded with a letter. It read:

> I was simply overwhelmed when I strolled to your
> door and, my jaw agape, walked away with a $500 cam-

paign contribution. I deeply appreciate your generosity. I also feel obligated to warn you that once your name shows up in my next financial filing it's certain to find its way onto any number of mailing lists, so brace yourself.

Their names were Jeanine Gomez and Wendy Quinn.

Jeanine was in her late 20s, dark and pretty and an experienced hand in Assembly campaigns. Wendy was several years younger, freshly out of Mount Holyoke, ruddy and thin and quiet. These were the DACC operatives that Neil Fisher brought to my campaign headquarters one afternoon three weeks before election day. They would be there every day, running things, he told me. As far as you're concerned, Neil Fisher said, Jeanine is now DACC. Wendy, he told me, would do the campaign's writing. I would have no more time to do my own.

Donna and Mary Gilson appraised these women young enough to be their daughters and assured me that they were fine with this. I had my doubts. I was aware that DACC staff and volunteer staff in Assembly campaigns generally got along badly. The volunteers were there because they believed in the candidate. They'd been in the war since the opening shots. The DACC people were disinterested pros, working only in tight races and coming in late. They went out of their way to avoid getting too chummy with either the candidate or the candidate's volunteers.

I told both Mary and Donna privately that Jeanine was to be completely in charge. The DACC people were keeping their word to help in this campaign, I said, whereas Burns and company were, at best, offering little help. Even if these DACC people end up rubbing you the wrong way, I urged Donna and Mary, just remember that we need these friends.

Neil was warning me that CSEA was falling behind on phone calls. We would have to throw volunteers into the effort to help CSEA staff the union's phone banks. We did that, and we also threw volunteers at the phone banks at the National Education Association headquarters in downtown Albany. Doing that cut down on our ability to put big crews on the streets to walk door-to-door with me and Mike Mann, but Tony Catalfamo was supplementing the door-to-door forces with Tim Lane and other committee people. Clearly, once Tony gave somebody his word, it meant something. The contrast between the Colonie Town Democratic chairman and Burns and his top people at the county level was nothing less than startling.

Unfortunately, not all Tony's committee people could be counted upon, despite his best efforts. One of them, Cindy Dott, operated a T-shirt business. Prentiss's campaign filings showed that he'd bought his campaign T-shirts from her. Moreover, as Mike and I and a few other people walked door-to-door in Cindy's neighborhood, where she was supposed to be pushing my candidacy, we spotted signs on her family's lawn. According to the signs, the Dott family was for Al Gore, Hillary Clinton and Bob Prentiss.

At Neil's suggestion, I called Shelly and brought him up to speed on my fundraising efforts. Dismal, I described them. I'm holding a fundraising affair in a few days, I informed the Assembly speaker, and I've dutifully called all the lobbyists. Shelly told me that he'd now confirmed that Jennings, working at Sweeney's request, had shut off the spigot to local campaign cash for me. The speaker said I would end up with a total of two grand from the Albany County machine; that would be it.

That meant another $1,250 to go from Mike Burns, assuming that whoever had made that commitment to Shelly was prepared to keep the promise—which I doubted.

Jeanine's first official act was to inform me that I needed to raise more money.

"If you can't raise it," she told me, "then you'll have to use your own."

I explained that I'd kicked in $2,500 in cash already and that my major financial contribution had consisted of going seven months thus far without income and burning up my savings to support my family. My contribution already had been many, many thousands of dollars. My name was Lynch, I explained to her, not Rockefeller. Jeanine then called Longo.

"He won't do it," she said.

Which, I thought, tended to lose just a bit in translation.

The *Spotlight* newspapers finally had figured out they'd been snookered by the Prentiss campaign on the debate issue. He had, as I'd predicted to Mike Mann, backed out of a debate sponsored by the Southern Saratoga Chamber of Commerce, and invitations to all those other debates he'd touted had never appeared.

The *Spotlight* responded by running a story headlined, "Prentiss avoids one-on-one debates." The story ran without comment from Prentiss. This time, he'd refused to return the weekly newspaper's phone calls.

In keeping with the theme of the campaign—that I could be counted on to stand up for ordinary people against the bureaucrats and the power-abusing politicians—DACC sent out a direct-mail piece to voters about how I'd fought the previous year for John Bove when the State Department of Transportation had tried to take down the sign on the Northway for the My Way Cafe. The mailing showed me and John, standing outside his restaurant and in the kitchen. The headline on the mailing proclaimed: "He'll fight that hard for your family too." The text of the slick, two-color glossy, eight-by-ten direct mail ad read:

Tackling Problems

John Bove owns the My Way Cafe in Malta. When he opened in 1985, John had a sign placed on a pole at Exit 12 of the Northway, so travelers would know his cafe was nearby. Every year, he paid the state department of Transportation (DOT) $250 to rent the space to advertise his cafe. And business was good.

Then, in April of 1999, DOT informed John Bove that his sign was coming down—some new fast food restaurants wanted to put their signs on that pole. That summer, usually John's busiest time of the year, business plummeted 60%.

Tracking down the held you need

John needed help quick, so he called Dan Lynch. Dan turned up the heat in his daily column and called the DOT. In a few short days, John's sign went back up, and so did his business.

A fighter in our corner

When John Bove needed help, Dan Lynch was there.
And John's just one of the many people Dan has gone to
bat for over the years. In the Assembly, he'll keep fighting for working men and women when others let them
down.

Dan Lynch was there for John Bove and he'll be there
for your family, too.

Not days after that ad hit mailboxes in the 107th
Assembly District, DOT cars rolled into John Bove's parking
lot.   Department officials personally handed him a letter
informing him that his sign was coming down again—and, this
time, the sign was coming down for good. It was an obvious
act of retaliation by the state's GOP administration against John
for permitting his name, face and story to appear in my ads. I
cranked out letters to both the New York state transportation
commissioner, Joe Boardman, and the Assembly transportation
committee chairman, David Gantt of Rochester.

"It's not right," I wrote Boardman.   "Nothing has
changed since the last time DOT tried to do this except Mr.
Bove's support for my election to the State Assembly. Please
restore John Bove's sign, Commissioner, and do the right thing
by a local small businessman."

To Gantt, I wrote, "Please look into this matter. If any
citizen of this state can be subjected to this sort of abuse, then
none of us is safe."

We put out the whole nasty business as a press release—
one heavily rewritten by Neil Fisher at DACC headquarters
before it was distributed—and scheduled a press conference at
John Bove's restaurant. Precisely two news media representatives showed at the press conference at the My Way Cafe—A
photographer for the left-leaning weekly, *Metroland*, and Mike

Fricano of the *Times Union*. Fricano did a six-inch piece and
Metroland gave the story a decent shot. DOT was saying that
John Bove's restaurant no longer met the department's criteria
to have his sign on that pole. The timing of this decision, DOT
insisted, was pure coincidence. A few days later, in a *Gazette*
story, Prentiss proclaimed himself "totally unaware" of any of
it. Fred LeBrun wrote a *Times Union* column outlining what
had happened to John Bove after he'd appeared in my campaign
ad, but the column was decidedly tepid.

I felt just awful about what they'd done to John Bove. It
was in keeping, though, with what had happened to the charity
groups. This was how the Prentiss campaign did business. And
nobody seemed to care.

Each side was mailing now.

My direct mail pieces focused on the campaign theme—
that I could be counted upon to stand up for people—or, as the
DACC literature put it—"Dan Lynch for State Assembly—
Fighting Harder for Our Families." My next mailing featured
me and a woman named Mary Bissaillon, a crime victims
activist whose son had been killed by a drunken driver whose
parole I'd opposed in my column. The point of the ad was that
people could count on me to intercede on their behalf with state
government. They could count on me to provide vigorous constituent service.

Prentiss put out a mailing in which he took credit for a
Pataki property tax relief proposal. He also put out a mailing so
bizarre I couldn't believe it. It featured a cartoon of Shelly and
me on a bicycle built for two pedaling toward New York

City.   It told voters, "Dan Lynch says he wants to be our Assemblyman.   There's only one problem: Lynch has already sold out to the New York City politicians so they'll help him get elected. . . . Say 'No' to Sheldon Silver and his New York City political cronies. Vote 'No' on Dan Lynch."

Meanwhile, the *Gazette* finally had gotten around to doing a story on the substance of this race. Under a headline reading, "Legislative ideas point to differences; Lynch, Prentiss take opposing approaches to serving district," Bill Hammond did a piece tightly summarizing some of my positions and the proposals I'd put out—my plan to expand EPIC, my proposal to improve nursing home staffing, my proposal to aid volunteer fire company recruitment and my student loan program. He also included Prentiss's positions, all of which consisted of tax cut proposals that would save the average household in the district about $300 a year. I also was for several of them. The biggest proposal in that package, eliminating state taxes on gasoline and diesel fuel for a savings of $200 a year for each consumer, had zero chance of passage, and Prentiss knew it. The *Times Union* ran a similar piece, the usual campaign wrap-up in 20 inches or so. It mentioned the anonymous poison faxes. Prentiss told the *Times Union* he had no idea who had sent them out.

Mr. High Road added, "But when he chose to run for office, he has no privacy."

At my campaign headquarters, Mary Gilson and some of the other volunteers were now engaged in a running dispute with Jeanine and Wendy about the proper temperature at which to set the thermostat. In an effort to keep the warfare to a minimum, I grabbed Wendy and took her walking with me one afternoon in Clifton Park.

We walked in the October rain. To shed water, I wore a baseball cap and leather jacket—marching briskly across soaked lawns and bounding hedges, as was my habit. Wendy followed under an umbrella, clutching campaign literature and scrambling to keep up.

"Is politics fun, or what?" I asked her.

Paul Vandenburgh had me on his WROW morning drive-time program for a solid hour. It was the time he'd set aside for a debate between me and Prentiss, only Prentiss had never responded to the invitation. I took Cardboard Bob with me into the studio. The *Record* did a story on Cardboard Bob's appearance at WROW. In the story, Prentiss's campaign manager, Bob Spearman, said that Prentiss had refused the debate because Vandenburgh, the most visible conservative Republican in the Albany media, was biased against Prentiss and in favor of me.

The hour was heavily laden with commercials, but I felt I'd gotten my message out. Jeanine later advised me to lay off the, "I'm not a Democrat," routine. Not for that audience, I told her. Vandenburgh's listeners were 2-1 male, middle-aged and heavily Republican. They represented as many as 10,000 of the 60,000-plus voters who would cast ballots in the election in just a few weeks. That's Prentiss's base, I told her, and I needed to stress my nonpartisanship in front of that audience. Remember, I told Jeanine, I need to take Republican votes away from this guy; I won't accomplish that by waving the flag of the Democratic Party on WROW radio.

I also, early in the program, dealt with Vandenburgh's questions about the tone of the *Gazette*'s coverage.

"Look," I said, "I began serving the *Times Union* as managing editor in 1979. The *Times Union* had roughly 82,000 daily circulation, and the *Gazette* had about 70,000 circulation. When I left the *Times Union* this spring, the *Times Union* had roughly 100,000 circulation, and the *Gazette* had 60,000 circulation. Those numbers represent many, many millions of dollars in revenue. And anything you see in the *Gazette* about this race has to be filtered through that reality—that I was their most ferocious competitor for two decades. The tone of the *Gazette*'s coverage of this race is nothing more than a reflection of that history." I then added that I was not running against the *Gazette* and would rather talk about the issues in the campaign.

DACC was distinctly nervous about Cardboard Bob. At Neil Fisher's urging, I left Cardboard Bob in the car when I appeared at Channel 6 for a five-minute interview with Liz Bishop during the evening news.

"Where's Cardboard Bob?" Liz asked me. "I would have loved a live shot of him."

"He's a little camera-shy," I explained.

We threw a fundraiser. Five hundred invitations had gone out. Six people showed up. We made $1,500. The next day, I took Jeanine for a cup of coffee at a McDonald's down the road from campaign headquarters. It was time for a heart-to-heart conversation.

"I'm hurting for money," I told her. "It looks to me as though I won't be able to scrape together more than another couple grand before election day. I've raised 40 grand in cash in my first run for office, and I've raised another 40 to 50 grand in in-kind services. I've done it with virtually no help and in a very short period of time. Unlike most guys who run for this office, I haven't been out there for a solid year shaking down people.

"The well now seems pretty much dry," I said. "Other candidates for other offices have been raising money like mad, and there's only so much available. Prentiss's financial filings say that he's sitting on $50,000. I expect him to advertise heavily during the last weeks of this campaign. I can't answer back. It's not my fault. Jennings has shut me down locally. The Albany machine endorsed me and is now stiffing me. And DACC failed to support my fundraiser in September, when there was still money out there and I still had a chance to get some of it. So, what now?"

She understood the question perfectly. If DACC really was in this race with both feet, then what was DACC going to do to dig me out of this hole?

Well, Jeanine told me, DACC had fronted me some money for my first round of radio ads. I still owed 2,500 bucks on that.

"If that gets paid," she told me, "then we might front you for the next round of radio advertising."

"I'll get it," I promised. "I can always stick up a payroll truck, I suppose."

❖   ❖   ❖

With 17 days to go before the election, Neil Fisher was at campaign headquarters. He, Jeanine and I were sitting around a table. Neil had a memo from Kiley & Company. The campaign's second poll had been taken. Four hundred likely voters had been sampled. The memo began:

> Bob Prentiss continues to hold a significant lead over Dan Lynch—in fact, Prentiss' margin has increased slightly since August.
>
> The tracking survey shows Prentiss with a 53% to 33% lead over Lynch, a net increase of five points from the August benchmark.
>
> Prentiss' unaided awareness and reelect numbers are both up as well.
>
> —Unaided awareness is up 41%, from 37% previously.
>
> —His reelect score now stands at 50%, up six points from August.
>
> Prentiss' favorability rating (61% to 16%) is about what it was two months ago.
>
> Lynch's favorability rating is 46% to 20%, compared with 33% to 15% in the benchmark. (Note that we identified him as a journalist in his favorability question this time around.)
>
> Almost four-in-five (79%) of voters feel they know at least a little about Bob Prentiss, including 36% who say they know 'a good deal' about him and where he stands on the issues.
>
> By comparison, two-in-three (66%) voters say they are at least somewhat familiar with Lynch and where he stands, including 22% who feel they know 'a good deal' about him.

The key factor in those numbers, the pollsters said, was advertising. Prentiss was doing more direct mail than I was. He'd reached 74 per cent of the electorate with it while I'd reached only 58 per cent. Moreover, among voters who'd seen mailings from each side, he led by 56 per cent to 35 per cent. Television news was doing virtually nothing on the race. Meanwhile, print and radio news coverage was being roundly ignored by the public. I'd done well with what DACC called "earned media," but it hadn't seemed to make much difference in the polls.

I'd heard rumors from the lobbyists and others in the loop in state politics that the Republicans had different numbers—that the GOP polls showed this closer. If this poll was correct, though, then DACC's involvement had helped me not at all in this race. In fact, given the thrust of Prentiss's advertising—his ceaseless attempts to portray me as Shelly's henchman—DACC's involvement might even have hurt. The poll also had me down 15 points in Colonie, although Mike and I had, by now, knocked on nearly one in four doors in town.

"Well," I said, "now what?"

DACC was still with me, Neil Fisher assured me. Believe it or not, he said, it was still early. This was mid-October, and people were just beginning to pay attention to politics. You got started late, he pointed out, and so did DACC. This was always going to be a tough race, but it was a race that could be won with enough advertising volume.

"You have to raise more money," Neil Fisher told me.

❖ ❖ ❖

We put out a new mailing. So did Prentiss. Ours said that I would vote for more aid to local schools, for "common sense gun safety measures" and for expanding health care to the uninsured. It pointed out that Prentiss had voted against all three.

Prentiss's mailing had a drawing of some machine gears on one side. On the other, it said, "Dan Lynch wants to represent us in Albany. But will he protect our interests? He's already sold out to Sheldon Silver and other New York City Democrats to finance his campaign. Dan Lynch will be just another cog in Sheldon Silver's political machine—a machine that works for New York City—not us."

The *Gazette* ran a story headlined, "Second Prentiss-Lynch debate goes by wayside." Prentiss had made a big show of agreeing to participate in a debate before the League of Women Voters. He'd told reporters he definitely would be there. Somehow, though, every date the League came up with was unacceptable to him. Aimee Allaud, the League official charged with organizing the event, finally got the picture when the Prentiss campaign stopped returning her phone calls.

"It's not going to happen," she told the *Gazette*.

Scheduling conflicts, explained Prentiss's campaign manager, Bob Spearman, when the *Gazette* ran him down. However, Spearman insisted, Prentiss definitely would be on hand for the half-hour WMHT television debate. That would be taped Friday morning, October 27th, and would air twice. WMHT would run it at 6 p.m. the next day, opposite a few football games, and again the following night, a Sunday, at 11:30

p.m. Prentiss apparently figured that the air times would mini-
mize the viewing audience and that any newspaper story that
resulted from the debate itself would be buried in the Saturday
newspapers, traditionally editions with lighter readership than
Sunday papers and the bigger weekday editions.

I wasn't at all sure that he actually would show for the
WMHT debate. He most assuredly wouldn't show unless I
made a huge issue of his ducking all the others. There was only
one way to make certain that Prentiss couldn't afford to duck
that last debate. Cardboard Bob was going back out on the
street.

Whether DACC liked it or not.

Walking in Colonie.

Mike and I were going door-to-door in the darkness.
Reception in this new, treeless, suburban neighborhood was
good, even though this election district was down low on the
DACC list of swing districts. Each district we'd walked, we'd
noticed, had seemed considerably less swingy than the preced-
ing one. Knock on 10,000 doors, and you can begin to tell the
difference.

And that's how many doorsteps that Mike and I had
stood on personally at that point, separate and distinct from the
other houses visited by volunteers who walked the streets of the
district both with us and without us, conducting what the organization people called "lit drops." We kept count of the pieces of
literature we handed out and the post cards sent to friendly voters thanking them for their time. We were now hitting roughly
2,000 homes a week, allowing for nights off for appearances

before this group or that one and for my constant fundraising phone calls—"Dialing for Dollars," the organization people called it.

As we marched from one house to another, a guy approached us. We'd seen him earlier, walking around the neighborhood alone in sweat pants and a hooded sweatshirt. He gave us his name, Chuck something. Then he said, "You're Dan Lynch, aren't you?"

"Yeah," I replied. "Glad to meet you."

"Well, I'm not glad to meet you. I'm voting against you. I don't vote for ultra-liberals."

"Really?" I said. "Do you know where I stand on a single issue?"

"I just know you're an ultra-liberal."

"Have a nice evening, Chuck," I said.

Mike was taken aback. Chuck had seemed furious and ready for a fight. When we left him, Mike said, "What the hell was that about?"

"Maybe he was having a bad night at home," I speculated. "Or maybe his medication isn't quite right. Some people are just nuts, that's all."

And, maybe it was true. Maybe this guy had merely been demented. We later checked his enrollment and learned that he was a Democrat. I suspected, though, that if this guy thought I was an ultra-liberal that our real problem was our failure, so far, to reach enough voters in this district with our advertising. Prentiss was outspending me 3-1, according to the financial reports at the New York State Board of Elections. Our friend, Chuck, clearly would have been a tough sell under the most ideal of conditions. What it seemed to boil down to was that without big money—much more than I would ever be able to come up with—this district seemed to constitute a steep, steep hill for any candidate who wasn't on the Republican line.

More like a cliff, actually.

Upset with the *Spotlight* story on his continued ducking of debates, Prentiss had Spearman fire off a letter to the editor. There's a debate set at WMHT, Spearman wrote—and Lynch is a liar when he says that Prentiss is ducking debates. Spearman ended the letter with, "I want to thank the *Spotlight* for allowing me the opportunity to respond to Lynch's untruths."

I fired off my own letter to the editor. It read:

> Prentiss has demonstrated his terror of facing the people by ducking all but one debate at the very end of the campaign. It remains to be seen if Prentiss actually will show up for that debate, by the way. He has, after all, refused to appear or canceled out of seven other debates, using one lame excuse after another.
>
> I've urged Prentiss for two full months to stand next to me before the people. He has fled from every opportunity to do that. The presidential candidates have debated three times. The U.S. Senate candidates have debated twice. But Bob Prentiss can't find the time?

I also threw in some stuff about his record and his fear of having to defend his votes in the Assembly. That was right on message, the DACC people told me. I was less concerned with their verdict, however, than with the pressure I was putting on Prentiss to actually show up at this one, final debate. I wanted him too frightened of this issue to duck my last chance to have voters in the 107th see us side by side and to understand what a totally duplicitous, substandard character their assemblyman really was. I wasn't worried about being able to show him up as that. The trick, I realized by now, would be getting people to watch the event.

    And making the complacent, conservative voters of this district even care about the quality of whoever was representing them in the New York Assembly.

18

EYEBALL TO EYEBALL

"That's not a lie. It's a terminological inexactitude."
—Alexander Haig

❖ ❖ ❖

The *Gazette* was at it again.

Just in case any inattentive Republican voter in the
107th Assembly District had missed Prentiss's mailing featuring
Shelly and me on that bicycle built for two, the *Gazette* was
stripping an AP story across five columns on an inside page on
the Republicans' efforts to "appeal to upstaters' fears of New
York City, personified by the Manhattan-based speaker of the
state Assembly. . . ."

"Mailings last week from the state Republican
Committee to voters in this affluent suburb north of Albany
depicted Speaker Sheldon Silver and the Democrats' local candidate for Assembly, Dan Lynch, riding on a bicycle built for
two," the Associated press reported.

The headline the *Gazette* chose? "GOP raises specter of
Sheldon Silver in Assembly race."

The *Record* also ran a brief item based on the AP story.
That newspaper also reported, however, that Prentiss had
ducked out of the League of Women Voters debate and was

hardly a sure thing to show up for the debate at WMHT.

"If he does," the paper quoted me as saying, "then we're going to have a 'Cardboard Bob' retirement party right afterwards."

The *Record* also was running its wrap-up piece on this race on its local front, jumping inside. The story was headlined, "Prentiss and Lynch have contrasting styles; Lynch has been on offensive for months." The story began:

> ALBANY—There are distinct differences, both in style and substance, between the two men running for the Assembly in the 107th District.
>
> The race pits a three-term incumbent against a former Clifton Park journalist, running as an independent on the Democratic line.
>
> The thrust of Assemblyman Robert Prentiss's re-election campaign has been to tout his record in office and emphasize tax cuts. Prentiss says, as an assemblyman, he has voted nearly 150 times to cut taxes, fought to enact tougher criminal laws and sought to protect the environment.
>
> His opponent, Dan Lynch, contends that Prentiss has "grossly distorted his true voting record" and has taken credit for legislation that he played little, or no, role in advancing.

The story detailed my various proposals and Prentiss's platform of assorted tax cuts. It made reference to Prentiss's overwhelming enrollment advantage, and it pointed out that Prentiss had not only been dodging debates with me but also had refused to speak to the *Record* reporter doing this story.

"While some observers believe that 'bunker mentality' indicates he is worried about his opponent, others say he is con-

fident the power of incumbency will return him to office," the
Record reported. I'd gotten out my message in this story, but
what I had to say ended up on the jump, deep inside the newspaper.

"There are so many people who seem to think it doesn't
matter who represents them in office," I told the *Record*.
"They're wrong. It matters enormously what kind of person
represents you. It matters enormously whether that is a person
you can trust to stand up for your interests or whether it's a person who is basically in this for a paycheck and goes along with
the party program. There's a radical difference between the two
candidates and the degree of personal honor that they exhibit in
dealing with voters in telling them the truth."

The day after that story appeared, Prentiss ads blos-
somed all over Albany radio. An announcer intoned,

> Assembly candidate Dan Lynch claims he's inde-
> pendent. But who's he kidding? From day one of the
> campaign, Democrat Dan Lynch has been bought and
> paid for by the New York City political bosses. Lynch is
> already taking orders from Assembly Speaker Sheldon
> Silver, a tax-and-spend liberal from Manhattan. Boss
> Silver urged Lynch to write a letter to lobbyists and spe-
> cial interest groups, asking them to funnel money to his
> Assembly campaign. Now Silver is pumping tens of
> thousands of dollars into Lynch's campaign himself.
> What does that mean for families in Colonie and
> Southern Saratoga? It means that if Silver and his cronies
> can get Lynch elected, they'll have one more willing vote
> for higher taxes and more New York City spending pro-
> grams. It means more school aid for New York City and
> less for Colonie and Southern Saratoga schools. And it
> means Dan Lynch will be a partner in Sheldon Silver's
> agenda of higher taxes and wasteful spending. Dan

Lynch for Assembly? Great for New York City. Bad for
us.

As near as I could figure, the letter the ad mentioned had
been the invitation to my first fundraiser, back in July. Bob
Berry had composed it, I'd approved it and it had mentioned
that Shelly was backing me. Beyond that, though, the sheer
scope of the lying in Prentiss's radio ad was astounding. Shelly
had played no role whatever in the phrasing of that fundraiser
invitation. I wasn't a Democrat. Both Shelly and Denny Farrell
were acutely aware that I would represent the interests of my
district, first and foremost, in any floor vote. And the only candidate in this race who'd actually voted against an extra million
bucks in school aid for the 107th that very year had been
Prentiss.

The ad was totally negative. It turned out to be the only
radio ad Prentiss ran for the entire campaign. The stuff was so
nasty that I suspected it might even cost Mr. High Road a few
votes. I hoped so, at least.

DACC checked. Prentiss had made a buy totaling nearly $40,000—or, roughly, as much cash as I'd raised for my
entire campaign thus far. He would be running these ads, as bad
as they were, every five minutes on every radio station in the
market, Jeanine told me.

"You have to answer back," she warned me. "It's political suicide not to."

Walking door-to-door in Colonie, and the cell phone on
my belt was ringing. It was Jeanine, and she was butting heads
with my wife.

DACC had persuaded its Manhattan-based media-buying firm to front the campaign 2,500 bucks to air that first round of radio ads. Now DACC wanted that money back. Donna was afraid that the minute she turned it over, DACC would go back on the air with another $13,000 in broadcast ads, and the campaign would find itself deeper in the hole than ever. We had heavy debts and only $3,800 in the bank. I'd told Donna to hold off paying the $2,500 until I'd spoken to DACC. I wanted to make sure the ads didn't go back on the air until I'd raised more money.

When pressed for the $2,500, Donna had told that to Jeanine. Jeanine had responded, "We don't care about that. Running for office is expensive. That's your problem."

What had followed the utterance of that delicate bit of phrasing had been, as the diplomats like to say, a "frank and open exchange of views." Jeanine was upset and complaining to me over the cell phone about "dramatics in the headquarters." I pointed out that this was a time when Jeanine reasonably could expect the candidate's wife to be a trifle on edge. I suggested that some small measure of tact on Jeanine's part might have deflected the confrontation. Jeanine did, however, now understand my position on all this. We'll give you the $2,500, I told her, but be sure not to put us into the hole by buying more radio ads until I okay it.

From there, Mike Mann and I moved on to the candidates night at the Newtonville United Methodist Church. About 60 people were gathered in the church's basement meeting room—or, more precisely, .0006 per cent of the Assembly district's electorate. Reporters were present, but so were State Senator Neil Breslin and his opponent, Joe Sullivan, which meant that my race would have to share news space with a race in which the outcome was already set in stone.

The *Spotlight* newspapers had previewed the event with

a terse editorial headlined, "Face to face." The editorial had read, "The Newtonville Neighborhood Association should have a full house for its meet the candidates night Monday at 8 p.m. in Newtonville United Methodist Church. That's because the opponents in this year's closest and nastiest political race— between Assemblyman Bob Prentiss, R-Colonie, and his Democratic challenger, Dan Lynch of Clifton Park—are scheduled to finally meet face to face before an audience of constituents.

"We hope they will address the real issues facing the 107th Assembly District, rather than give us more talk about which one is running the dirtier campaign."

Contrary to the repeated claims of Prentiss and his campaign manager, this was no debate. The candidates would not directly address one another. We simply would stand up, deliver brief versions of our stump speeches and field a few questions from the crowd—most of which directed at me would come from Prentiss plants in the audience, I was certain.

The candidates were seated at a table facing the crowd. One by one, we stood up to deliver our spiels. When Prentiss's turn came, he threw open his arms and said, "Well, here I am, Cardboard Bob, in the flesh." He spoke from a manila folder crammed with notes. After a few moments of rambling, he lost track of what he was trying to say. There followed a silence of 30 seconds or so while he stood at the table, mutely digging through his notes. Then he mumbled out a closing and sat down. When my turn came, I managed to get a few laughs with my opening.

"Nice of you to drop by, Bob," I said.

I delivered my rap, beginning with the need for state government to pick up more of the cost of education to provide better programs, reduced class sizes and to alleviate soaring local property taxes. Our base poll had told us that education was the number one issue for voters in the 107th, and it had been my number one issue even before the poll had been taken. During the question and answer period, somebody asked me about the need for better mass transit in the booming northern portion of the district.

The *Record* story the following day paraphrased my response. The paper reported, "In the Capital District, Lynch said the state has not done enough to develop a 'sensible' mass transit solution. The state also needs to create more tax credits for homeowners who use alternative energy sources to power their homes."

"Off message," Jeanine pronounced after she read the *Record* piece.

I explained to her that the reporter had taken a two-hour session involving four candidates and had boiled down everything that had been said to a 15-inch story. Most of what I'd said at the session, I assured her, had dealt with the campaign's message issues—education, health care, economic development and the difference between Prentiss's real voting record and the fictional one he was claiming for himself in his mailings and press statements. One person in the crowd had asked a direct question on mass transit, I told Jeanine, and I'd answered it.

"Don't ever do that," she advised me sternly. "When they ask something about mass transit, answer on education. Limit what the reporters have available to use to only what you want used."

"You're telling me to avoid answering direct questions, then?"

"Yes," she said. "That's exactly what you do. Education, health care, economic development, you'll fight harder. That's all you talk about no matter what they ask you."

And, as I looked over the story again, I had to admit that I could see her point.

Jeanine was all over me about the need to raise more money. We have to get back on the air, she was saying; it's crucial.

I told her, "I know you're only carrying messages, but all this conversation does is take up your time and mine. I've done everything possible to raise more money. I'm continuing to do so. Nagging me about it, and pretending that there's some other step I can take, is really useless. This is like gravity, and there's no point in railing against it."

"Well," she told me, "we've done what we promised to do."

Which wasn't quite accurate. DACC had been a great help in terms of direct mail advertising and production for radio advertising. I was reading DACC-prepared scripts for my radio ads in an old church converted to a slick, computerized sound studio, and DACC was picking up those costs. I remained amused at the irony of what once had been a house of worship serving as a site for the creation of political advertising— although another old church in the Albany metro area was now home to a particularly salacious strip joint. Both locations, I hoped, had been properly de-sanctified.

DACC had, however, raised only a few grand for my campaign directly, as opposed to the $100,000 or so they'd promised to raise, and the lobbyists were still holding back. Also, if there was DACC pressure on Jennings and/or Burns to lift the machine-imposed embargo on my local fundraising, I wasn't aware of it. Aside from my refusal to sign on to specific bills for the lobbyists, that was the real problem in my fundraising—the reluctance of contributors to come on board in the face of the machine's steadfast opposition.

It was another gathering of candidates. This event was being held outside the 107th Assembly District, at a branch of the Albany Public Library. Legislative candidates from five of the metro area's Assembly districts were on hand. The audience was the disabled community. The event was sponsored by the Center for Independence, one of the two charity groups Prentiss had threatened early in the campaign.

We candidates were seated in chairs in a library meeting room facing a group of attentive listeners, some of whom were wheelchair-bound. Some of the other candidates—the ones with no chance of winning, who were running merely to serve the party—I was meeting for the first time. One of those was Bruce Trachtenberg, a Schenectady County lawyer who apparently hoped to become a judge someday. He was running against Assemblyman Jim Tedisco, a strong Republican incumbent with a 2-1 enrollment edge. His only chance to win, Trachtenberg had conceded to a friend of mine, would be Tedisco being caught in bed with either a dead girl or a live boy.

Prentiss showed up late and prattled on so long and so aimlessly that the session's sponsors had to ask him, twice, to cut it off and let the other candidates speak. My mood wasn't good that day. I was tired and frustrated with both the press and the hassles involved in raising money. When my turn rolled around, I got up and said, "I'm here to tell you what I'm for and what I'm against. Here's what I'm for." I then set forth my positions on a number of issues important to the organized disabled community.

Then I said,

> Now, let me tell you what I'm against. I'm against dishonesty. I've spent my professional life telling people the truth. That's what I'll do after election day, whether I'm in the Assembly or in some other form of public life. I'll never lie to you.
>
> At the moment, the airwaves are filled with commercials attacking me as a slave to the special interests. These ads have been paid for by a man who has raised four times as much money as I have—by a man whose financial reports contain page after page of corporate and special interest contributions. The cynicism and dishonesty of this ad campaign, financed by the special interests, is simply breathtaking.
>
> I've covered three state capitals—Albany, Harrisburg and Trenton. I've covered Washington. I know and understand the system as few people outside it do. The New York Legislature contains some fine people. Some of them are in this room. But the system is essentially flawed and frozen with partisanship. That's why I'm trying to get into it and make a positive difference.
>
> What this election is about is whether somebody who has achieved a certain level of visibility and distinction in a private field of endeavor can come into this system against the professional politicians who kow-tow to the special interests, take their money, use it to lie to the voters and then vote as their campaign contributors obligate them to vote, rather than in the interests of the people who vote for them.

> Basically, this election is about who you can trust to
> look after your interests—somebody like me or some-
> body who would take special interest money to run ads
> like the ones on the air right now. Thank you.

When I sat back down, Trachtenberg leaned over and whispered, "You don't mince words, do you?"

The fact was, though, that I had minced words on occasion during this campaign, and DACC still was urging me to do so. Now, however, with the campaign dead broke and a poll that showed me down 20 points, what was the point in diplomacy?

Walking in Clifton Park with Mike Mann. This time we had Fred LeBrun in tow. The *Times Union* columnist was doing a piece on this race. His reporting technique was to walk with each candidate and to scrutinize their styles at voters' doorways, although none of that ended up in the column he wrote later.

Generally, I walked in casual clothes, often aided by a squad of volunteers, and moving at a snappy, ground-eating pace. This evening, however, I had an appearance to make in front of a business group, so I was in a suit and tie. Moreover, since this walk was mainly for show, Mike and I were out alone with LeBrun and moving at a leisurely rate of speed. Prentiss, LeBrun told me, literally ran from door to door in his campaign T-shirt, grinning, shaking a voter's hand and then running off to the next house.

I was sure that was exactly how Prentiss did it—whenever a reporter or news camera was around.

When LeBrun's column finally appeared, its contents

came as no surprise to me. I'd known the man for two decades. LeBrun was a liberal Democrat, but he virtually never criticized the Republicans on the state or local level—only the GOP's stances in Washington, which was a long way off. He seemed determined that nobody would be able to call him biased in this race, although his job description as a metro columnist required him to express personal opinions in print. Moreover, LeBrun, who was nearing 60, enjoyed affecting the pose of the perpetually amused, world-weary cynic who'd seen it all and deemed all that he'd seen essentially meaningless.

The column took shots at both me and Prentiss—alleging that my status as an independent was "a fiction so thin as to be transparent, although the strategy is understandable." Yes, LeBrun wrote, Prentiss was ineffective in the Assembly because his party was outnumbered and because "Bob is Bob." I would be, too, LeBrun wrote, because all legislators were ineffective. The thrust of his piece, however, was a repetition of the theme of his earlier column on this contest—that it really didn't matter which of us won the election, that it really doesn't matter who's in office and who's not.

"Fortunately," LeBrun wrote, "all this sound and fury is over an inconsequential office as far as the affected public is concerned, the folks of Colonie and Clifton Park. I'll bet if voters of the 107th District were given a choice between Bob, Dan and simply doing away with a taxpayer-supported sinecure costing us about $80,000 a year after the perks and add-ons, there would be a landslide for the last. Dan acknowledges, going door to door, how he's been struck by a startling lack on interest in the electoral process."

Yes, LeBrun acknowledged, the press was doing a fairly crummy job of covering this race—the same rotten job the press generally did on such races. That didn't matter, though, he wrote.

As for better serving as a truth squad than we have, how quickly Dan has forgotten his newspaper life. Wading into the deep shades of political claims and counterclaims in ever-changing literature is dangerous work. To do it even half right would take a staff 10 times our size, considering all the races we cover. . . .

Dan ascribes this to the media doing a lousy job of airing the issues and not acting as a truth squad for the claims of candidates. He's got a point, but a smaller one than he thinks. Yes, we should do more to bring light to all local political races, which are enormously important in the aggregate. But, frankly, there are no burning issues, or even smoldering ones, in his district. Life is good for those in the 107th. There's nearly full employment, a work force heavily larded with well-paid state workers who know the system. The last person many in the 107th would call for their help with a 'government matter' is their assemblyman. . . .

So there you have it. Dan is in actuality a clean slate who's never been in politics, a bright guy full of promise while Bob has never not run or accomplished much and yet the Republic survives. I have this tingling feeling that after this race is over, either way, the Republic won't even wobble for an instant.

Finally, things were looking up on the fundraising front.

A trade group, the independent auto repair shops, was throwing a fundraiser for me. They were pushing a bill that Prentiss had opposed. The bill would have placed limitations on big oil companies opening up company-owned gas stations within a certain distance of the independents. The practice of the oil companies was to sign up these independents to buy gas wholesale at a set price. Then the oil companies would open up a gas station-mini-mart nearby that would sell that same gas for a lower price than the independents could match. When the independent station went under, the oil company would grab its location, establish a monopoly in the neighborhood and raise the price of gas at both stations.

I was for the bill for several reasons. One, my grandfather had operated a garage, and it had broken his heart when the business had failed. Two, the oil company stations didn't offer repair service, and the death of the independents meant hardship for consumers. Three, I wanted to see small, independently owned businesses continue operating in the 107th Assembly District, and the oil companies were simply killing off these small enterprises, right and left.

We raised a few thousand dollars at that cocktail party. Also, Shelly sent in $4,100, transfers from the campaign committees of two downstate assemblymen who were shoo-ins on election day. Now, the campaign finally had some cash to get my ads back on the air. Prentiss still would be running three ads to my one, but we would be able to answer back.

In a quiet voice, anyway.

Walking door-to-door in Colonie, and I was growing more disturbed by the minute. I didn't like what I was seeing. Mike Mann saw it, too.

That week, the Yankees and the Mets were going at one another in the World Series. Normally, I paid some attention to baseball as the series rolled around. This year, though, for understandable reasons, I'd ignored the game, as I'd also ignored the NFL. Now New Yorkers had two New York teams in the World Series—the first subway series since Dwight D. Eisenhower had occupied the Oval Office.

As Mike and I marched along the streets of Colonie, it seemed that the entire 107th Assembly District had lost its collective mind over this development. Yankees bumper stickers decorated cars in every fifth driveway. As we walked from house to house, people were coming to the door in Yankees T-shirts and caps, clearly annoyed at being pulled away from ESPN's Sports Center, where they were spending two hours before the game would begin at 8 p.m. The 107th was caught up in Subway Series frenzy, and the poll had told me that I needed to make inroads with male voters. As near as we could determine, every male voter in this Assembly district was glued to the TV set every evening, watching the Series and its pre- and post-game coverage.

"This is not good," I told Mike Mann as we walked. "These guys are just coming to the door, grabbing the palm card and probably tossing it in the kitchen garbage as they scurry back to the TV set."

"There does seem to be a lot of interest in this series," Mike agreed.

"Just one more reason to hate George Steinbrenner," I said grimly.

Jeanine Gomez was no fool. She had a pretty good idea of what was on my mind. We were standing on the sidewalk outside WMHT's downtown Albany studio, almost directly across the street from the building that housed DACC. With us was a volunteer, Jan Jones, who'd once worked in Prentiss's legislative office. Jan was a staunch Republican, but she knew Prentiss well and disliked him intensely. Jeanine, at this point, knew me, and she was aware that I viewed this debate as our last chance to provoke any real interest in this race.

"Just be cool and calm," Jeanine was counseling me. "And, whatever you do, stay on message."

"I can't call him a vile, vicious, lying, pin-headed scumbag?" I asked, trying to provoke her into a smile.

"No," Jeanine said grimly.

"How about a despicable, dishonest, moronic half-wit? Can I call him that?'

"No," she said, not entirely certain that I was kidding.

Jeanine was worried. While I hadn't told her directly, she well understood that my plan was to make this debate as big a news story as I could manage. I knew that few voters in the district would watch this thing on television when it aired at 6 p.m. the following day, a Saturday—unless, of course, prominent stories appeared in the newspapers that morning reporting it as a raucous, entertaining confrontation. DACC wanted this to be a conventional political debate. I wanted it to be anything but conventional.

As we spoke, a car pulled up to the curb. Prentiss got out of the passenger side, glanced our way and nodded. Then he went into the building.

I smiled at Jeanine. "Well, it's time to rock and roll."

Reporters from all three daily newspapers were waiting in the studio, which cheered me. Prentiss's campaign manager, Bob Spearman, extended his hand. We'd never met. Spearman was a graying, bespectacled man in his 60s, a Republican legislative worker doing his political duty so he could keep his job.

His candidate was clearly jumpy. Prentiss was sweating and solemn. We sat facing one another in chairs, my right side to the camera, Prentiss's left facing it. A small table separated us. To my left and to Prentiss's right sat Gary Carter, the WMHT television personality who would moderate this session. I'd appeared on Gary's program several times before I'd become a candidate, making observations on the news from my now former positions as a newspaper columnist and broadcast commentator. Behind each candidate was a clock.

The debate began with Carter explaining the rules to the viewing audience. Each candidate would begin with a one-minute opening. Each would have a total of 10 minutes to respond to Carter's questions. Then, if time permitted, the debate would end with brief closing statements. Prentiss went first. To my delight, he started out nasty.

"Well, Democrat Dan," the assemblyman said, "here I am, Cardboard Bob, in person. You can pinch me all you want. I'm all flesh and blood, the real person. And you know something, Dan? That's who the voters want to see at their doorstep, the real person—not some picture in a brochure."

Prentiss was unable, however, to pronounce the word, "picture." It came out, "pitcher." In a perfect world, I would have preferred that he drone on simply forever.

He then went into his rap about voters telling him as he went door-to-door that they wanted lower taxes and energy costs. He said he'd given them that via Pataki's property tax program—although he failed, somehow, to mention the governor's name in connection with the program for which Prentiss had merely voted. He also said that he'd cut sales taxes. Again, Prentiss had cut precisely nothing. He'd been only one vote among many. He prattled on with this sort of smoke until Carter finally had to shut him up.

Now, it was my turn.

"Bob," I said, "it's good to see you here. You have ducked conversations like this for the last seven months. You've turned down challenge after challenge to appear with me in front of the voters. You've agreed to one half-hour here toward the end of the campaign. I think that's unfortunate. I think it's a betrayal of your constituency, but it's not the first one."

I went on to say, directly into the camera now and to whoever among the 107th's voters might be watching, that this campaign was about who would fight harder on their behalf and to protect their interests.

"Who can you count on," I asked, "to vote for your schools, and to vote for your health care and to vote for economic development for your community—and not for the special interests? Who can you count on to look out for you and not for the people who give him campaign money? This campaign is about trust. It's about competence, and it's about who will better serve the people." I urged the voters to watch and listen closely and to "make your judgment at the end of this conversation."

Carter started out with questions about energy policy. Prentiss was now describing himself in the plural, referring to himself as "we" and talking about "our legislative record." He said he wanted to cut two state specific taxes on energy. When my turn came, I said I also was for cutting those taxes.

"There are some things that Mr. Prentiss and I agree on," I said. "There are some things we don't agree on, as relates to this issue. We have the highest electrical rates in America, in this state, because of decade after decade of shoddy regulation."

I then blamed all that on Bob Prentiss, who took contributions from the utility companies. That wasn't fair in the slightest, but I was trying to anger him. I wanted to be sure, when I really ripped into him, that I wouldn't seem to "be kicking the family dog," as Mike Mann had put it. I wanted to be seen as kicking a pit bull, which is what this guy really was. It worked. When Prentiss replied, he was mad and was now stumbling over his words.

"That's an obvious distortion of my record," Prentiss said, "just as he's been very deceptive in, uh, distorting, uh, uh, my charge, his charge, uh, my record as to being available, uh, for debates."

He then began saying that he'd refused to subject himself to "a Jerry Springer type of sideshow" in accepting unmoderated debates. He said he'd refused to do the WROW debate because I'd worked at that station.

Carter wanted to go back to the energy issue. No, I said, I want a chance to respond. Looking directly at Prentiss, I said, "Very quickly, you refused a debate with a moderator. You refused a debate without a moderator. When I said, 'Pick your own moderator, bring in anybody you want,' you still continued to hide, refused to participate. You turned down the League of Women Voters debate. You have been in hiding for seven solid months. It's just that simple. And the fact that you lie about it so openly is an indication of the way you deal with your constituents. You've lied about your record on issue after issue after issue. Your portray yourself as a friend of education. You voted against an extra million dollars in state aid for the school districts in Colonie and Southern Saratoga County last year. You portray yourself as a tax cutter. You voted for an extra billion in sales tax increases across New York over the past six years—$220 million alone this year. You are not a man to be trusted. You put your mailings out replete with lies. You do it repeatedly. And then you disguise your record and hide from an open debate on it. *That* is your record, Bob."

"You're a better fiction writer than a reporter," Prentiss

shot back, "because the fact is that the League of Women Voters debate was scheduled the very same night that you and I were faced in a debate at the Newtonville Methodist Church in Colonie—"

"—That's not true," I broke in.

"You're interrupting me," Prentiss was complaining as I explained the details of this latest lie—namely that the League debate he was referring to had been held well outside the district and that he'd refused to agree to the League debate inside the district, that the event at the Methodist church had been a meet the candidates night and not a debate. Prentiss started complaining about Jerry Springer again, and I told him that all he had to do to avoid interruptions was to tell the truth. We were both talking at the same time, and Gary Carter was fighting to regain control and keep the debate, as he described it, "on point." As far as I was concerned, Prentiss's repeated lies were precisely the point I wanted to stress. That point, however, had been made nicely in that exchange.

Carter asked, and Prentiss and I both responded to, a question about a transportation bond issue that would be on the general election ballot. We were both for it. Then Carter asked about New York's high debt load and rotten credit rating. I responded that the Legislature had permitted too much debt and should focus on pay-as-you go programs. I was worried that this conversation was getting too sedate to be worth much coverage in the newspapers. Mr. High Road, though, was still bent out of shape about the battering I'd just given him and was eager to get in his own shots.

"It took a long fight because it was blocked by the Assembly majority of which Democrat Dan would want to become part of."

"I'm not a Democrat," I said, breaking in again.

Prentiss smiled nervously. He began, "Dan, uh, you're

interrupting again. There you go again."

"Every time you lie," I said, "I will interrupt you. That's correct."

"The truth of the matter is this," Prentiss was saying angrily, "that all you are is a registered blank! Are you ashamed to be a Democrat? You're ashamed to be a Democrat!"

It was wonderful stuff. He'd been forced to admit that the thrust of his ad campaign—that Democrat Dan stuff—was totally fraudulent. And he'd managed to insult every independent in a district where independents outnumbered Democrats. I let him go back to answering Carter's question while I awaited another opening. Prentiss still was using "Democrat Dan," though. It had been scripted for him, and he wasn't quick enough on his feet to avoid it now that he'd just admitted it was a lie.

When Carter turned to me with another question, I responded in a sentence or two on the issue and then said, "Once again, we see the pattern emerging. For one thing, Bob knows I'm an independent. He knows I'm not enrolled in a party. He knows I'm backed by four parties, including the Democratic Party. And yet he repeats, "Democrat Dan, Democrat Dan, Democrat Dan.' He knows what the truth is. He doesn't care what the truth is."

Carter kept trying. He asked me another question on the transportation bond issue. I was still for it, I said, because the work needed to be done on the state's bridges and highways and because the Legislature and "the professional politicians, like Bob Prentiss, have not been supportive of these projects."

Now, Prentiss was openly livid and stumbling over his words again. When Carter turned the question to him, Prentiss said, "Well, the need came about because of the tax-and-spend, uh, uh, policies of the Democrats that he would be part of, uh, blocking, uh, pay-as-you-go all of these years. And, uh, uh, the fact of the matter, Dan, is this: If it, uh, uh, if it walks, uh, like a Dan Lynch-Shelly Silver duck, and if it talks like a Dan Lynch-Shelly Silver duck, and if it quacks like a Dan Lynch-Shelly Silver duck, and if it takes money. . . ."

That was my opening. Now I was in his face again, as he ranted in a raised voice. I was pulling out his financial filings, and saying, "Let's just see who's bought and paid for here."

". . . and it takes money from the Democrat, the Democrat Assembly Campaign Committee and Shelly Silver . . ." Prentiss was shouting.

"Okay," I said, reading from his campaign filings, "Bob Prentiss, New York State Right to Life ...

". . . then it must be, it must be, a *Dan Lynch-Shelly Silver duck!*"

"NIMO PAC," I said quietly, making reference to the political action committee of Niagara Mohawk, the Albany-area gas and electric utility.

Carter was waving his hands, trying to regain control. Prentiss was now openly furious, shouting at the top of his lungs and managing to drown me out nicely. "Why are you lying to the people and deceiving them?" he was bellowing. "Because you know—."

"That's why I've got four lines, right?" I was saying, holding up four fingers.

"—that you are going to be beholden to the New York City Democrat tax-and-spend liberals!" Prentiss was roaring and waving around a piece of paper. "And this says here that it was paid for by Shelly Silver."

"Knock it off," I told him.

But by now Carter was saying, "We have to move on. Let's move on." And I was leaning back in my chair, giving Prentiss a hand sign to shut it off.

"And that's the reality," Prentiss was yelling.

"Mr. Prentiss. . . ." Carter was saying.

"Accept the truth for what it is!" Prentiss was yelling at me.

"You wouldn't know the truth," I pointed out, "if it came up and bit you in the behind."

Now Prentiss was still shouting, but he'd plastered a phony grin on his face. "There you go again! There you go again, Danny Boy!"

Carter was saying, "Gentlemen, gentlemen, gentlemen, let's try to—"

Prentiss was bellowing, "Whoa, now!"

It was simply priceless stuff. I knew that the reporters in the next room, watching a television monitor, would be scribbling furiously in their notebooks. I would get my newspaper stories, all right, and this debate might actually attract enough audience to get me moving in the polls.

Carter moved on to a question on economic development. I used my time to point out that during the six years Prentiss had sat on the Assembly small business committee the average wage earner had lost income in adjusted dollars; that upstate New York, with 39 per cent of the state's population, had received only 26 per cent of the job growth, and that manufacturing jobs had diminished as a percentage of the employment mix to be replaced by lower-paying retail and service jobs. Heeding Jeanine's advice, I then shifted the topic to education, saying that it was crucial for New York to improve its schools and to turn out a more highly skilled workforce as a mechanism for economic survival.

Prentiss again accused "Democrat Dan of distorting my record." He admitted voting against—which he pronounced, "aginst"—the extra million in state aid to the district's schools—which he pronounced, "skoos"—the previous year.

But that had been a "Democrat bill," he explained, and he'd voted for a later bill that the Republicans had gone along with. It had been "the same amount of dollars," he insisted, which was simply untrue.

"The fact is," I responded, "that the bill you voted against contained an extra million dollars in aid for the school districts in Colonie and Southern Saratoga County, and the bill you voted for did not contain that aid. Bottom line. And you didn't vote for it, you didn't vote against it, because of any conviction. You voted against it because you were told to. That's what your voting record consists of—voting the way you are ordered by the people who finance your campaigns—that's who you are—and voting against the interests of your district."

"Guess how you would vote," he snapped. "Who would be your first vote for the speaker of the Assembly? Shelly Silver. And that's the one that's running your campaign and financing your campaign, and that's—."

I broke in, "If that's true, then how come you have four times as much money as I do?"

He was trying to talk through me. "That's who you're beholden to," he was saying. "There you go again, Democrat Dan."

"Answer the question," I demanded, jabbing a finger in Prentiss's direction. "How come you have four times as much money as my campaign does?"

"About half of it," he said, "is right out of my own pocket. Check the financial disclosure statements. You'll see how much I've loaned my campaign."

"How come, if I'm the candidate of the bosses, you have so much more money than I do? *You're* the guy."

Carter was again fighting for control. This exchange seemed to be a dead heat, so both Prentiss and I sat back and gave it to him. Carter then asked me if I really could be effec-

tive in the Assembly after spending so many years being so critical of the Legislature in my newspaper column.

"Yeah," I replied. "I've known the leadership in both
parties for a long time. We have a mutually respectful relationship. The problem with the Legislature is the election of sec-
ond-rate people—like this—who don't understand issues, who
don't have a shred of integrity, who take the special interest
money and then lie about it, and vote the way the special interests want them to. And they vote against the interests of their
districts. This man has a record of voting against education, of
voting against the environment, of voting against health care for
the elderly and of voting in favor of the big monied interests
who finance his campaigns. This is the candidate of the bosses
and the special interests right here, not the candidate of the
people."

That, as it turned out, was my last word. Prentiss then
delivered a rant on Democrat Dan selling the 107th Assembly
District down the river to the New York City tax-and-spend
liberals. In so doing, he managed to chew up all the remaining
time. I later told Carter he'd screwed up by failing to give me
time for a closing. He agreed but assured me that it hadn't
made any difference in the outcome. I'd won big, Carter
assured me.

After the debate, three reporters from the three daily
newspapers did brief, separate interviews with Prentiss and
with me. He has been lying in his advertising, I said, and I was
determined not to let him lie with impunity in this setting. Bill
Hammond of the *Gazette* was on his usual kick—trying to play
up Prentiss's claims that Shelly Silver owned me. Hadn't
Silver's campaign committee spent a lot of money on my
behalf, he demanded?

"Well," I said, "you're so enthralled with stories on the
financial filings. How much has Faso reported spending on
Prentiss?"

"Twenty-eight thousand dollars," Hammond replied.

"How much has DACC reported spending on me?"

"Seven hundred dollars," he said.

"Next question," I told Hammond.

Actually, DACC had at that point reported $7,000, not $700, in expenditures on my campaign. It wasn't my fault that Hammond couldn't read. The important thing was that this debate had provoked sparks, Prentiss had come across as a ranting, lying fool and I figured I could count on prominent stories in all three papers that might prompt some voters to actually watch this debate.

Outside the studio, I asked Jeanine how she felt it had gone. She was non-committal. I knew that she had to go across the street and give her report to Longo and company before she could offer me the official DACC verdict on the debate's value, or lack thereof, to the campaign. Later in the day, I spoke to her by phone. She said that I'd appeared too angry and had gone off message several times. I disputed her assessment that the message, as defined by DACC, hadn't been delivered. I'd simply had other points to make as well. What had bothered DACC, I was sure, was my harping on the relationship between votes and campaign contributions. On that issue, each party lived in a glass house and preferred that candidates never talked about it.

The following day, the *Record* ran the story on page one. The paper characterized the debate as "one of the year's most combative exchanges between political rivals." The *Times Union* and *Gazette* each ran the story on the front page of their local sections. The *Times Union*'s headline called it a "fiery face-off." The *Gazette* called the debate "a verbal donnybrook" and quoted Prentiss as calling me "a bully." I was thrilled with the coverage. Now, I knew, the airing of this event would attract viewers. It did, apparently. Kiley & Company polled the day after the debate aired. I'd picked up five points.

Now, with slightly more than a week to go until election day, we were moving in this campaign at long last.

19

HELL-BENT FOR ELECTION

"The most successful politician is he who says what everybody is thinking and in the loudest voice."—Theodore Roosevelt

❖ ❖ ❖

Walking in Colonie.

It was now two Sundays before election day. Mike Mann and I were accompanied by a large team of volunteers. Now, after stalking neighborhoods in the blistering heat of summer and the crisp chill of autumn, it was snowing. We went door-to-door with the stuff swirling around us in a bitter, icy wind. After a few hours, perhaps an inch of snow blanketed the lawns and pavement.

We were closing in on 11,000 houses—most of them in Colonie, as DACC had instructed. Using the walk teams, we'd handed out nearly 40,000 pieces of literature. Stops at all those doorsteps had produced some interesting conversations.

A few months earlier, while walking a busy road in search of lawns on which to place our signs in the closing days of the campaign, we'd walked to a doorstep in Colonie and spoken to a woman in her 60s named Hilda. Hilda had talked our ears off, prattling about her health problems and her son who'd served in the Gulf War. It had been impossible to get away from her without being rude, and it took 20 minutes before we could manage it. Can we put up a lawn sign, we'd asked? Sure, Hilda had told us. Mike had suggested that I drop her a personal note, thanking her for her time, which I'd done.

So, now, the day's walking complete and a dozen signs in the back of my car, we were cruising to Hilda's house, which was nearby, to place that sign on her lawn as the snow fell. As we arrived at her home, however, we saw a lawn sign already in place—a Prentiss sign. Hilda, apparently, had been a Prentiss activist whose goal in running her mouth so vigorously that day had been to keep me on her doorstep and prevent me from knocking on the doors of other people who might actually vote for me.

It was an old trick, and perhaps a half dozen people had tried to pull it on us out of all those houses we'd visited. Garrulous, grandmotherly Hilda, however, had been the only person who'd managed to actually pull it off.

Hy Rosen was on the phone.

For four decades, Hy had drawn editorial cartoons for the *Times Union*. Now retired from the newspaper, he was doing books and turning out serious art, mostly public sculpture. He'd created bronze statuary for a women's war memorial next to the New York State Museum and for the lawn outside the New York State Police Academy. He'd done a marvelous piece of work downtown, a statue that had captured the images of the Dutch patroon and the Indian that adorned the official seal of the City of Albany.

Hy was upset with Prentiss's radio advertising. These

relentless swipes at Shelly Silver, he felt, were distinctly anti-Semitic in tone. The subtext of every Prentiss ad, Hy was saying, was, "Watch our for those New York City Jews."

"Well, of course," I told him. "And, also, watch out for those black people. Watch out for those Latinos. Watch out for those new immigrants from the Mideast with their funny accents. That's the whole point of that kind of advertising."

From the start, I'd toyed with the idea of saying that publicly. Ultimately, I'd rejected doing it. Yes, an attack like that had the virtue of being true. Prentiss was race-baiting with his ads, appealing to the very worst instincts of the basically conservative, white-bread voters in this district. I didn't want my campaign to go there, however.

If the voters of the 107th couldn't figure out what Prentiss was doing with those ads on their own, or didn't care, then there was no point in my making an issue of it.

Cathy Woodruff of the *Times Union* was on the phone. She was putting together some sort of post-debate story. Prentiss, she told me, had called me a bully when she'd spoken to him. Did I want to call him any names?

He'd behaved like a total fool, I told her, but I didn't want to call him that. Aside from my pointing out that Prentiss was a professional liar, he could have the name-calling franchise all to himself. Well, she asked, did I want to hit him on his trip to Cuba?

Prentiss had made a jaunt to Cuba in January at the behest of some Cuban-American political contributors and had missed a few key votes in the Assembly as a result. I'll talk about the Cuba trip only in that context, I said. What I did want to talk about, I told her, were my policies on education, health care and economic development and his votes on those same issues. Woodruff wasn't interested in holding that conversation.

The brief item she ended up running was a classic example of the sort of silly, hopelessly shallow news coverage that, over the long haul, has the effect of turning readers into non-voters.

"Friday's taping of a debate between Republican Assemblyman Bob Prentiss and challenger Dan Lynch was as rough-and-tumble as it gets," Woodruff wrote in the *Times Union.* "Prentiss complained later: 'This was not an organized mugging here, but without a moderator, the next thing I know my opponent probably would have took a swing at me.' Lynch, a former *Times Union* managing editor and columnist, would neither apologize for nor talk about his debate tactics, saying it would distract from criticism of Prentiss' record.

"'This other stuff is childish nonsense, and I'm not going to participate in a discussion of it,' Lynch said."

The press was driving me crazy with its relentless focus on the campaign as theater and the refusal of reporters and editors to deal with issues of more substance in this race—or even with the truth, for that matter. Prentiss had spent much of the debate he'd struggled so hard to avoid screaming "Democrat Dan" at the top of his lungs. And my debate tactics—my pressing him on his record and the lies in his literature—required a defense? He was afraid I was going to take a swing at him? The story was brief, but it was ludicrous beyond belief.

Watching news coverage from this side had turned out to be nothing less than a revelation for me. I'd never expected special handling because of my media background. If anything, I knew, my professional history would work against me, not for me. Everybody in the media who knew me would take special care to ensure that nobody could accuse him or her or their institutions of bias in my favor.

I hadn't expected, however, that the *Gazette* would function essentially as the Prentiss campaign's attack machine. When that had begun happening I'd clung fiercely to the belief that the skew of that newspaper's coverage was the product of mere incompetence. It had taken me months finally to admit what everybody else in my campaign had seen from the start—that my years of competition against that organization had been taken personally at its top levels and that the *Gazette* was utterly untroubled by journalistic niceties like fairness and equity in its campaign coverage. At least as far as any race involving me was concerned.

I also hadn't expected that the news coverage across the board would be so painfully superficial. Yes, the *Record* and *Times Union* and, to an even greater degree, the *Spotlight* newspapers, were now doing stories on where Prentiss and I stood on some of the issues in the contest. Those stories tended, however, to be once-over-lightly jobs, too brief and seemingly written just to get them out of the way. Television was doing, quite literally, nothing on the issues. In short, I was astounded and disappointed at the rather stark inability—or, in some cases, the blatant unwillingness—of reporters, editors and news directors to actually tell their readers what Prentiss and I stood for and what sort of human beings we seemed to be in terms of integrity, honesty and basic character.

Even allowing for the unavoidable—and totally rational—paranoia that afflicts every candidate in every race, I felt able to detach enough from this process to make a dispassionate judgment based on three decades of professional training and experience.

In general, when it comes to covering political campaigns, the news media really suck.

Donna went out to the mailbox and found a direct mail piece from the Prentiss campaign that totally misquoted a column I'd done five years earlier. So, I figured, where's the surprise? However this election turned out, I could always take pride in this much:

None of the material I'd put out had been in any way untrue. I'd told the truth in every piece of direct mail and in every bit of political advertising on the air. The contrast between my campaign material and what Prentiss had put out—lie after lie after lie—was the difference between night and day. However, that and a quarter, I now realized, would get me a cup of coffee.

And nothing more.

Now the *Gazette* had a story critical of Prentiss. Bill Hammond's steadfast fascination with the financial filings finally had turned up some genuine news. Prentiss had failed to include the names of whatever contributors had given him roughly $30,000. A clerical error, the Prentiss campaign explained.

After I'd worked him over so fiercely on this topic during the debate, Prentiss was obviously worried that I would research and reveal any connection between his votes in the Assembly and whoever had given him this latest chunk of money. So, he wasn't going to reveal the names of these contributors until after election day. Hammond had called for my reaction. I do believe, I told him, that this is a violation of the law.

It was, in fact, a particularly damning story, but no other news outlet picked it up. Also, since the story could hurt Prentiss, the *Gazette* had made it a point to bury the thing in the deepest hole the editors could find in the newspaper—way back inside the classified advertising section. If I'd pulled a stunt like this, the *Gazette* would have plastered the story all over page one.

In red ink.

Jeanine Gomez was agitated over the story. My remark in the *Gazette* piece, she told me, had been off message, and DACC was getting severely annoyed at my off message tendencies.

Off message how, I wanted to know? She had no clear response. Apparently, when Hammond had asked me what I thought about Prentiss's failure to report the names of political contributors, I should have promised to fight harder for education and health care.

The Albany County Democratic Committee was throwing a $500-a-head breakfast to squeeze money out of union leaders. Jerry Jennings was on the line with Donna, my chief fundraiser, telling her that I should show up at the event and that Burns would have some money for my campaign.

Also, the mayor was saying, Donna should meet him outside city hall and pick up a check transferring $3,000 from his bulging campaign warchest to my campaign. Whoa, I thought when Donna recounted that conversation to me, what

the hell had happened here? My best guess? A personal phone
call to the mayor from a much-perturbed speaker of the New
York Assembly.

Which, I later learned, had been precisely what had
occurred. Lynch might win this, Shelly had told the mayor; you
might think about doing the right thing.

Jeanine was calling. The new numbers are in, she said.
We need to get together.

She didn't sound too cheery. I drove to headquarters and
walked with her along the shopping center to a breakfast joint.
Over coffee, she told me what Kiley & Company had found
with the most recent poll. Prentiss stood at 51 per cent, I
stood at 42. Seven per cent were undecided. We'd moved, and
moved big, in less than two weeks. We'd had no movement
during World Series week, though, when nobody had been
paying attention to politics, and now we had only a week to
go.

"It can be done," she was telling me. "Also, the numbers might be off a bit."

"I doubt it," I said. "I've had some experience with this
stuff. The sample of only 400 gives you a wider margin of error
that a larger sample would provide, but this methodology gives
you a 95 per cent confidence rate. That means there's only a
five per cent chance that these numbers are wrong. That tells
me, basically, that in the next week I have to pick up nine
points, while we've been averaging a gain of roughly a point a
day, and I have to get three points away from him at the same
time. I have to take all the undecideds and, at the same time,

give his more weakly committed voters a reason to abandon him. That's a real chore."

She was right, though. It wasn't impossible. Despairing finally of getting any press coverage on the matter, we'd just put out a mailing to 60,000 homes in the district slamming Prentiss for loaning his campaign many thousands of dollars while, at the same time, refusing to pay property taxes in the community he was supposed to represent in the Assembly.

He also had sent out a mailing we felt could damage him. It was, by far, the scummiest stunt he'd pulled in the entire campaign. On one side of the slick mailing was a photograph of a black man laughing under the headline: "Did you hear the one about Dan Lynch?" On the other side, superimposed over the face of a child with a troubled expression, was text painting me as a bigot.

It quoted from the Sons of Italy newsletter critical of my Godfather column. It quoted from a column I'd done four years earlier critical of excess in the celebration of St. Patrick's Day in the form of "all the slurping of green beer and bellowing in phony Irish brogues and singing 'When Irish Eyes Are Smiling' over and over again." It contained a totally fictitious accusation from something called the "Polish American Journal" stating, "On his radio show, Dan Lynch said, 'Polish women are repulsive and even Polish men can't stand them.'" That bore virtually no resemblance to anything I'd ever said.

Prentiss's name was nowhere to be found on this slimy ad. The mailing had come out from the New York Republican State Committee, which meant it had been created by John Faso's Republican Assembly Campaign Committee. The main headline read: "Dan Lynch for Assembly? That's not funny!"

The text read,

> If you're Italian, Polish or . . . Dan Lynch has a joke
> about you! Most of us would agree it's wrong to use eth-

nic slurs. And most of us would agree it's wrong to tell derogatory jokes. Not Assembly candidate Dan Lynch. He used ethnic slurs to describe Italian-Americans, Polish Americans and Irish Americans. And he told derogatory jokes about the same ethnic groups.

The mailing then pulled out a quote from one of my columns in which I'd written that Irish jokes on St. Patrick's Day were no real cause for alarm for people of my Irish ancestry. That was portrayed thusly: "So what did Dan Lynch have to say for himself? 'I don't get that worked up over jokes like that'" (The *Times Union* 3/15/96).

The direct mail piece finished up with,

Do We Really Want Someone Like This Representing Us? We deserve better than Dan Lynch. Colonie and Southern Saratoga deserve an Assemblyman who doesn't make fun of the very people he's supposed to represent. Your vote is no joke. November 7. Vote "NO" to Dan Lynch.

It was bizarre that Prentiss would try to portray me, of all people, as a bigot and, especially, as anti-Irish. Already, in going door-to-door, Mike Mann and I had encountered people who'd told us that they were switching their votes from Prentiss to me after receiving this slimy thing in their mailboxes.

It was unlikely that Prentiss's polls were telling him anything much different from what we were getting. He knew that I was picking up votes but also that I had to step up the rate of that process during this final week. He knew also that voter perceptions of my integrity and independence were my strongest selling points. The "Democrat Dan-Shelly Silver" mantra had been designed to attack voter perceptions of my independence. If our polls were correct, that plan of attack had failed miserably with everybody except Fred LeBrun, my old column-writing colleague at the *Times Union*—and, of course, the entire editorial staff of the *Gazette*. This shoddy piece of advertising was designed to attack my integrity, pure and simple, and it had heavy potential to backfire on Prentiss. Finally, Mr. High Road might have gone too far.

The bigot mailing also attracted some news coverage. I told the *Times Union* that, "I was waiting, frankly, for something like this." The *Times Union* story quoted Prentiss defending "the tone and accuracy of the mailing and [he] said it struck a nerve with voters as he went door-to-door campaigning this week.

"'It's not funny, no matter what the intent,' Prentiss said of Lynch's remarks. 'A Polish woman came to the door along with her husband and said they were on the fence and now they're voting for me.'"

Tom Kelly, a Siena College history professor and co-director of the college's polling operation, told the *Times Union*, "I would say it indicates unease on the part of the Prentiss campaign."

The *Gazette* story took the opportunity to re-hash the Sons of Italy flap and quoted Bob Spearman, Prentiss's campaign manager, as saying, "Some are saying, 'Thank God somebody said this. It is something the public should be concerned about.'" When Hammond had called me for response, I'd refused to play ball with him. The only quote he got from me was, "Everything he does in this campaign is designed to distract attention from his record. I will not play this game."

As we left the restaurant, Jeanine handed me an envelope. It contained a $3,100 check transferring money from Shelly Silver's campaign account to mine. Like Jennings, Shelly had maxed out, giving me all the law permitted him to donate personally to my campaign. Now, though, I would be able to get more ads on the air. DACC was running some warm and fuzzy stuff about how much help I'd given to individual people in my column over the years. Armed with these poll numbers, I knew I needed something tougher.

I went back to my home office and cranked out some copy. The following morning I went into the sound studio in the converted church and read it into the microphone. The copy read:

> The following has been paid for by the Committee to Elect Dan Lynch:
>
> I don't know for sure why Bob Prentiss voted last year against an extra million dollars in state aid to schools in Colonie, Clifton Park, Malta and Stillwater. I don't know for sure why he's voted repeatedly during the past six years to shift the tax load from people with money to the shoulders of ordinary property taxpayers. I don't know why he voted against the interests of seniors. I can't imagine why he voted for nearly a *billion* dollars in local tax increases.
>
> I can only tell you this: Bob Prentiss is no friend of the community he's supposed to represent. He votes time after time *against* the interests of the people. Then he dodges debates, over and over again.
>
> I'm Dan Lynch, and I won't do that. I'll represent *your* interests in the State Assembly. I'll stand up for *you*, and nobody will own my vote but you. Remember that, please, in the voting booth on Tuesday.

Now Carl Strock, the *Gazette*'s daily columnist, was in the paper with a column proclaiming that "Lynch really gets insulting with Prentiss." Strock also was saying that even though I was an independent, I'd accepted $66,000 in services from DACC and was engaging in "a bit of have-your-cake-and-eat-it-too that others have a hard time swallowing." On the jump of the column, Strock told his readers that, on Paul Vandenburgh's program on WROW, I'd accused the *Gazette* of bias because of the circulation the *Gazette* had lost during its years of competition with the *Times Union* and the millions of dollars in revenue represented by that lost circulation.

"The reader is so cautioned," Strock wrote. "I am writing about our most ferocious competitor, who buried us for two decades. I try to write accurately, but millions of dollars are millions of dollars, so when I say he's the candidate of the Democratic Party, has stated his intention of joining the Assembly's Democratic bloc, and has accepted $66,000 worth of help from the Democratic Assembly Campaign Committee, you better check it out, just to make sure."

Finally, some good news on the media front. While the *Gazette* didn't endorse political candidates—not openly, at any rate—both the *Times Union* and the *Record* did. Each newspaper's editorial board had interviewed me and Prentiss separately, and both papers were out with editorials calling for my election.

"Lynch for the Assembly," read the *Times Union*'s headline. The subhead read, "The challenger offers a strong agenda for helping his district and upstate."

The text of the editorial read,

> The race for state Assembly in the 107th District . . .
> presents us with an awkward situation but an easy choice
> nonetheless. The incumbent, Republican Bob Prentiss, is
> being challenged by Dan Lynch, who's running as the
> Democratic Party's nominee. Both also have several
> other lines on the ballot.
>
> We've never endorsed Mr. Prentiss, who first was
> elected in 1994. This year will be no different. Our
> resounding choice is Mr. Lynch.
>
> We must concede that we know Mr. Lynch as a for-
> mer colleague at the *Times Union* far better than we know
> him as a politician. A certain predisposition to his candi-
> dacy might have been inevitable, then, but Mr. Lynch has
> earned our endorsement, and the votes of his potential
> constituents, for one reason above all others. He'd be a
> considerably better legislator than Mr. Prentiss has been.

The editorial praised me for my knowledge of government and the quality of my legislative proposals. I would be a
strong advocate for upstate New York interests, the editorial
said.

> And Mr. Prentiss? Mr. Lynch's harsh criticism is still
> fair and accurate. This Assemblyman hasn't been part of
> a serious discussion about public policy. Mr. Prentiss
> instead has been an ineffective member of the Assembly
> minority. He's not above taking credit for legislation, like
> an increase in the state's college Tuition Assistance Plan
> funding, that he had no personal role in passing. Nor,
> alarmingly, does he see anything particularly wrong with
> himself, or any other legislator, doing just that. . . .
>
> The sorry truth is that the Legislature is not an

especially distinguished institution. Too much power is concentrated in too few hands. Far too many of its members are career politicians. The Legislature would be a much more effective and representative body if it counted among its members more outsiders like Dan Lynch.

The *Record* editorial was not entirely laudatory. It assailed Prentiss for "a very mean-spirited campaign marked by apparent lies and misrepresentations. His opponent, Dan Lynch, running on the Democratic line although he labels himself an independent, carries some baggage also, mostly in an air of superiority and being above it all. But he clearly is the better candidate. . . . We believe old-style politicians such as Prentiss have served their purpose, but times call for more forceful visions and aggressive activism, attributes we believe are held by Dan Lynch."

The *Record*'s columnist, Doug DeLisle, came out with his own endorsement in the form of a poem. DeLisle wrote:

> Dan Lynch can be smug and an arrogant twit,
> But he's also got style, deep knowledge and wit.
> In talk of Bob Prentiss, call him a wit, you're half right,
> He's a back-room politician, who's not terribly bright.
> At the risk of incurring a counterattack,
> I say come Tuesday morning, let's Lynch the old hack.

At the $500-a-head union breakfast the Albany machine
was throwing to raise money, I found Jennings warm and supportive, in keeping with the three grand he'd donated to my
campaign. Burns took me aside at one point and promised that
the county party would give me another $1,000. It was a small
enough sum, only a fraction of what cash-poor Tom Bayly had
given on behalf of the Saratoga County committee.

At this point, though, I was too weary to fight about it
any more.

The Friday before election day, I walked into the monthly union breakfast at the restaurant at the Albany Municipal
Golf Course. The place was filled with what had, by now,
become the familiar faces of the metro area's union leaders.
John Bulgaro of the Teamsters greeted me with a check for
$2,000.

"Good news," I told Mike Mann later in the day. "Now
we won't have to break Bulgaro's kneecaps after all."

Jennings was there. He took me aside and told me that
he'd ordered Burns to kick in a few thousand dollars. He asked
how much the Breslin brothers had donated. A few hundred, I
told him; not much.

"That's wrong," the mayor said. "They have tons of
money. They should have given you the max—like I did."

Jack McEneny and Neil Breslin, safe from harm next
Tuesday in their overwhelmingly Democratic districts, each got
up to speak. They thanked the union leaders for their support.
When my turn came to speak, I took a long moment to gaze
around the room at these people, some of whose unions had

stayed out of this race and one of which, the Service Employees International Union, actually had supported Prentiss.

"Unlike Jack and Neil," I said, "who have 2-1 Democratic districts, I'm running in a district with a nearly 2-1 enrollment disadvantage. So, I'm in a tight race, and this campaign has been an ordeal. However, one of the compensations for all this frustration and effort has been the opportunity to get to know some of the people in this room.

"Some of you have backed me," I said, "and some of you have been less supportive because I'm not an incumbent. Well, don't worry about it. If I win this thing on Tuesday, whether you did or did not back me will make no difference at all in how I vote. If I win and take office in January, you'll find no more loyal a supporter of organized labor. That's because I believe in the movement. I believe in it because organized labor has made life better for my own family and millions of other families.

"Yes, the presidential race is important, and so is the race for the U.S. Senate. But, for the people you represent, the state legislative races are paramount. That's because the Republicans, if they retain control of the State Senate and keep me and one other Democratic Assembly candidate from winning and giving the Democrats a veto-proof majority in the lower house, will very quickly go back to being who they've been all through the 1990s—except for this past year when they began to sweat the elections of 2000.

"They are who they are," I told the union leaders. Then I gestured to McEneny and Breslin. "And we are who we are. There's a big, big difference for working families between them and us."

I sat down to applause. A union leader at my table, a guy visiting from out of town, asked for my card. I gave it to him. His union later sent my campaign a check for $1,000.

The next morning I swung by Albany County Democratic Committee headquarters on Colvin Avenue. Waiting for me was a check for $1,500. Combined with what Burns already had given, this totaled slightly more than the two grand Shelly Silver had told me the machine would contribute. Mike Burns was keeping none of his big promises to me.

Apparently, though, he wasn't prepared to break any commitment to the speaker.

To the *Gazette*, Prentiss now was accounting for some of the 30 grand or so he'd reported to the state board of elections without the names of donors. We couldn't get the information on the others from our bank, Spearman was saying.

Prentiss was reporting a grand from the National Rifle Association and $1,900 from the Medical Society. He'd also collected another grand from the campaign committee of another GOP assemblyman. For the rest of the contributors' names, though, everybody would have to wait until after the election.

Should we say something about this, I asked Jeanine? No, she said. DACC despised the very idea of any candidate saying anything whatever about campaign contributions.

Our mailing on Prentiss's failure to pay his property taxes was hitting mailboxes now. You'll get press calls on this, Jeanine was telling me. No, I won't, I assured her. DACC was superb at producing advertising, reading polls and providing guidance to candidates. But the DACC people didn't understand squat about how to make news. For whatever reason, every news outlet in town simply had refused to do a story on this. Maybe it just wasn't sexy enough.

Or dirty enough.

On my way home from going door-to-door, I swung by campaign headquarters and picked up more lawn signs—both for my own campaign and a few of the ones for Al Gore and Hillary Clinton we had laying around.

As had become my nightly custom, I cruised along the main road near my house, stopping to replace the lawn signs that had been stolen or destroyed by Mike Lisuzzo's merry band of vandals while I'd been out walking in Colonie. That chore complete, I then swung off the main road and parked quietly in the darkness in front of the home of Paul Vandenburgh, WROW's program director and the loudest conservative Republican voice in the local media. When Vandenburgh emerged from his house the following morning, he would find his lawn adorned with signs for Gore-Lieberman and Hillary Clinton.

What the hell. It was time to have a little fun.

20

TOUGHING IT OUT

"The voters have spoken—the bastards!"—Mo Udall

❖ ❖ ❖

Walking in Colonie.

It was a sun-splashed Saturday afternoon in early November. Reporters had joined us for a while, doing work for their "last weekend of the campaign" wrap-up stories. Tim Lane was fighting a fever as we walked door-to-door. Mike Mann, at long last, was dragging badly. After several hours of banging on doors, we finally stopped at the big, old wooden frame house that was home to Mike Conners, the Albany County comptroller. He was in the front yard, raking leaves.

We heard a rumor that you're hoarding beer, we told Conners. This completely imaginary rumor turned out to be accurate. Gratefully, we sucked down Conners' beer as we sat on his front steps in the pallid autumn sunlight, catching our collective breath.

"How does it look?" Mike Conners asked me.

"Tight," I told him. "We've been moving up for three weeks. The question is whether we'll have enough time to pull it off. That goddamn Subway Series didn't help a bit."

I took the occasion, sitting on Conners' front steps, to

call the *Times Union* on my cell phone. That morning, utterly ignoring DACC's insistence on approving every word I sent out, I'd fired off press releases from my home office fax attacking Prentiss on the property tax issue. The headline on the press release had read, "Lynch Assails Prentiss For Putting Campaign Finances Above His Duty to Neighbors."

I got Rex Smith on the phone at the *Times Union*. Another *Newsday* alumnus, Smith had taken over the job as managing editor/news that I'd abandoned to begin my daily column for the newspaper. At the time, Smith had been editor of the *Record*, and I'd recommended him for the job I was leaving. Are you going to use that press release, I asked? It's in the wrap-up, he assured me.

Not good enough, I told Smith. You ran 15 inches on Prentiss calling me a bigot, yet you won't devote a separate story to this—when it's both verifiably true and highly revealing of the man's character? That's totally inequitable treatment, I told him. After all, hadn't the *Times Union* deemed Prentiss's failure to pay his taxes a legitimate story in the spring?

"But when you learn the weekend before the election that he was pumping money into his own campaign instead of paying his taxes," I said to Smith, "you don't think that's worth a separate story? Not right, Rex."

Smith was non-committal. Think it over, I advised him. Somehow, though, I doubted that he would. I then called Jeff Cohen, the newspaper's editor and Smith's boss, at home. Cohen was out. I left a message on his machine. He got back to me later that evening. He was in Houston, his home town. Cohen said he would call the paper and see that the story got proper treatment.

"What do your polls show?" Cohen asked me.

"That this'll be close," I told Cohen. "Getting this story out to people could make all the difference."

Ultimately, though, the material I'd released appeared only in a few sentences in the *Times Union* wrap-up story, deep inside the newspaper. In the story, Prentiss characterized my criticism as "negative campaigning" and "mudslinging."

In its final story on the race, the only reference the *Gazette* made to my statement was, "Lynch issued a press release highlighting the fact that Prentiss has been late paying his property taxes." It was a characterization that illustrated a rather startling facility, intentional or otherwise, for missing the point entirely. The *Record* and television ignored it entirely.

With total predictability—I'd been expecting something along these lines for weeks—the only newspaper in town too fair to endorse candidates weighed in on the Sunday before election day with another broadside against me.

Bob Conner, the *Gazette* editorial writer who'd attacked me in an editorial a few weeks earlier as out of line for complaining about Pentiss's anonymous poison faxes, had a signed column in the newspaper that day. It stressed the *Gazette*'s supposedly principled policy of not endorsing candidates. It attacked me for failing to quit my WROW program until I was about to announce my candidacy and pronounced that I'd "received favorable coverage on WROW's other shows ever since." The most bitter criticism, however, was reserved for the rival *Times Union* for endorsing me for election.

"In this case, for example," Conner wrote, "the *Times Union* has left the impression that if any of its bigwigs quit and run for office, they will get favorable treatment from the newspaper, irrespective of their politics or anything else."

Conner went on to say that, "Lynch is even more thin-skinned than the average media type, able to dish it out but not take it. While Prentiss has run an uninspiring campaign, Lynch had contributed more than his share of vitriol. Between them, with Lynch leading the way, they have set a new and abysmal low for political discourse in the Capital Region."

Conner went on to accuse me of "a sort of condescending indignation. He sounds the same tone when he accuses the *Gazette* of conspiring against him because he was our 'most ferocious competitor for two decades.' But that's not much of a motive, and he provides no evidence for any such journalistic malpractice."

Prove that we've been unethical, Conner was saying. Prove that we're out to get you, Lynch. Despite everything that had come before, I was astounded to see the *Gazette*'s final salvo in this campaign framed precisely in those terms. Just who was this guy and the newspaper he worked for trying to kid, I asked myself?

Only their readers, apparently.

The day before election day, Donna and I were out in the pre-dawn darkness shaking hands in the fall chill with school bus drivers in Clifton Park. At the same time, Prentiss had a crowd of volunteers standing near a Northway exit with signs proclaiming me a "New York City liberal."

We'd each sent out our final mailings. Mine had been to Democrats, urging them to turn out to vote. In his mailing, Prentiss once again had taken personal credit for the increase in the state's Tuition Assistance Program, for which he'd done no more than cast a vote. It was just one final lie, printed in living color with John Faso's RACC money and delivered to everybody's mailbox. The sheer scope and breadth of the untruths Prentiss had produced in this campaign had been nothing less than staggering, but the news media had paid only scant attention to them.

After shaking hands with the bus drivers, I took time out to screen tapes of the Sunday morning news programs aired the day before and evening news reports I hadn't yet seen. On John McLoughlin's Sunday morning local news talk show on Albany's Channel 10, McLoughlin had decided that this would be the perfect occasion to ridicule the *Times Union* for endorsing me on its editorial page. *Times Union* columnist Fred LeBrun, who'd now written two columns on my race stressing how inconsequential the character, ability and integrity of anybody serving in public office might be, told McLoughlin in response that the *Times Union*'s endorsement had been entirely justified—that Prentiss had accomplished nothing in office, that I was by far the better candidate and would make the better state legislator as well. McLoughlin seemed displeased with LeBrun's assessment. He turned to another member of his program's panel, Paul Vandenburgh of WROW.

"Those endorsement editorials don't mean a thing, do they?" McLoughlin demanded. "Lynch can't possibly win this, can he?"

"He can win," Vandenburgh responded. "It's an uphill fight, but he could pull it off."

Annoyed, apparently, at the very prospect of my winning this race, McLoughlin moved along to another topic.

A Channel 6 report the previous evening had featured tape of both me and Prentiss going door-to-door. With the cameras rolling, there was Prentiss jogging from house to house in his campaign T-shirt while his wife, Albany County Legislator

Marlene Prentiss, cupped her hands around her mouth and shouted, "Go, Bob, go!" It was a profoundly weird bit of television news footage.

Then there was tape of me walking up a set of suburban steps, talking seriously to some guy who'd asked me why he should vote for me. The clip also featured talking head bits with both me and Prentiss being interviewed separately. He was prattling on about tax cuts, and I was saying that this election was really about whether an outsider could overcome the professional politicians to get into the system and make life better for ordinary people.

That night, after walking in Colonie, I got on the phone with a number of people. I called Tom Bayly, the Saratoga County Democratic chief, and gave him the latest poll numbers.

"Well," he said, "a few things have happened since that poll. You got endorsed by the *Times Union* and the *Record*, for one thing."

"Yeah," I said, "and Prentiss sent out that nutty mailing—the bigot thing."

"Oh, that was awful, just awful. They do that stuff all the time. It'll hurt him."

"Yes," I said, "but will it hurt him enough? That's the question."

I also called Mary Gilson to lay it all out for her. She'd been in this since the very start, the most devoted of the volunteers, and she deserved to know precisely where we stood. Nobody can tell for sure where this'll go, I told her.

"Either way," I said, "despite the huge enrollment edge Prentiss has, it'll be only a few percentage points—no more than five for him and, if it goes the other way, no more than a point or two for me."

That night, I went over my schedule for election day, the one that had been faxed to all the news outlets from headquarters. I would start out shaking hands with sleepy, probably hostile commuters at a park-and-ride lot before dawn. It would get progressively crazier as the day wore on. I would go to polling places all morning, waving to strangers and begging for votes. Jeanine wanted me walking the streets of Colonie until 8 p.m. I'd told her that she was in Dreamland. One in three of the houses she wanted me to visit wouldn't even contain voters, I pointed out. Past elections results had shown clearly that fully a third of the enrolled electorate in the 107th would fail to cast ballots in my race.

I would be cooperative, though. I would do a few hours of door-to door. Anything beyond that, however, would simply be nutty. Jeanine's goal, apparently, was to keep me busy all day, but I'd already done what I could do, and the voters of this Assembly District would do what they were going to do— whether I knocked on a few of their doors or not. I was scheduled to vote with Donna at our home precinct polling place in mid-afternoon. After that, I was inclined to head home to field phone calls, watch television and catch what would be a much-needed nap. I'd been sleeping fitfully for weeks, with thoughts of the campaign dancing relentlessly through my skull as I'd struggled to drift off. As soon as the polls closed, I would drive to headquarters to await results with our volunteers.

However this turned out, I was glad I'd done it. It had turned out to be a fascinating experience—if not a terribly pleasant or entertaining one. And it certainly had been a costly experience. Our liquid savings were nearly gone. After election day, we would be restructuring our family finances to reduce monthly cash outlay. I should have done that before I decided to run, but I hadn't made a final decision on running until fairly late in the game. After that, I'd simply been too busy.

I would never do this again, though. Win or lose, this

was my first and last election. The process simply was too distasteful, and so were too many of the people involved in it. The people who worked in the mud, walking the streets—the Tim Lanes and the volunteers like Kathy Strait and Pam Murphy and Brendan Pendergast and Rick Canfield and Roy Pfeil and Donna Langdon and Norreida Murnane and all the others— were first-rate human beings. I simply was awed by the commitment of the volunteers and the rank-and-file party workers I'd dealt with—by the people who really performed the work of politics. I'd been horrified, however, by the behavior of the bosses and most of the money people. With only a few exceptions and to a startling degree, I'd come to realize, the people who tend to rise to positions of real authority in this system are duplicitous back-stabbers conspicuously bereft of anything that resembles personal honor.

Also, the performance of the media had been a terrific disappointment to me. If anybody had reason going in to appreciate the shortcomings of the news-gathering process, it had been me. Seeing it from this side, however, I'd developed a far sharper grasp of how inept, superficial and venal the media people could truly be. Could it be that this is what the framers of the First Amendment had in mind? Was the *Gazette*'s naked bias in this contest what James Madison, et al., had been thinking of? The answer, of course, was yes. Those guys had created the First Amendment for a blatantly partisan colonial press that would have made the *Gazette* seem a model of journalistic objectivity by comparison. The framers of the U.S. Constitution had been able to find no better solution to the problem of guaranteeing that voters would have access to independent information on the democratic process.

I'd come to realize by now that, in politics, you couldn't count on anybody to do the right thing—well, damned few people who were important, anyway. The treachery and sheer pettiness I'd witnessed during this adventure had been nothing less than breathtaking. Running for office does nothing whatever to bolster anybody's faith in the ultimate worth of the human species.

Finally, I'd learned that the people deserve what they get. Ignore government, and you end up with a Bob Prentiss in office, term after term after term. Across the nation, lawmaking bodies in every state overflow with these dim-witted, lying, unprincipled, classless people making decisions that have enormous impact on the lives of others. Churchill had said that democracy was the worst of all political systems—except for all the others. Winnie had nailed it. I'd now seen this system and its participants from the inside, and neither it nor they were pretty sights.

Hillary Clinton had come to town the day before the votes were to be cast. I failed to show at the rally with her on the steps of Albany City Hall. I suspected that, in my district, she would end up with her butt up around her neck when the votes were counted, and I was keeping my distance from her to the very end. Her husband had been rumored to show up at this rally. As it turned out, however, the only Bill she'd brought with her had been a guy named Cosby.

Instead of hanging out with Hillary, Mike Mann and I walked all afternoon in Clifton Park and got a good response. I then whipped down to Albany for a county committee election eve rally. I stood on the stage and told the party workers that I was proud of my support by the Democratic party and proud to stand for its principles. I said I was proud to represent a party that believed that government can make people's lives better and provide those at the bottom of the heap with hope for the future.

What I didn't say was this: With a lot of the people involved in this game, in either party, the nearest they can come to telling the truth is a fib.

Election day was gray, grim and chilly.

I had Wendy Quinn, the other DACC operative in my headquarters, with me at the park-and-ride lot at 6:30 in the morning. To my surprise, people were polite and gracious. Several of them told me that they planned to vote for me. From there, I dropped Wendy back at headquarters and picked up Mike Mann. We spent the next few hours shaking hands and handing out copies of the *Times Union* endorsement editorial in front of a Colonie supermarket. One older guy made it a point to tell me that he'd already voted for Prentiss.

"Your mistake," I told him. "Let's just hope that you don't get what you deserve."

Mike was working the cell phone, keeping in touch with headquarters. At one point, we learned that some residents of a senior citizens home needed rides to the polls. In my car—with a couple of large, magnetized, green and white "Dan Lynch for Assembly" signs on each door—we provided chauffeur service. Then Mike and I finished off walking the single election district on our list that we'd failed to complete. Reception was terrific. Of course, this was a district with more Democrats than were found in most other neighborhoods in Colonie.

I got back to the house in time to pick up Donna so we could vote at 3:30 p.m. in front of the television cameras. Walking into my neighborhood polling place to be blasted by TV lights was an unsettling experience. I spent some time in the voting machine, casting my ballot first for myself on the Independence Party line—those guys had been with me early on, and at some cost—and then in every other race.

After that, I found myself too wired to simply go home. Because Donna's mother and sister were coming up from New

Jersey for election night, I knew that my house would contain people, and I was too stressed that afternoon to be decent company in that setting. So, instead, we fired out a revised schedule to the press. Then Mike Mann and I and a group of volunteers went roaring off from headquarters to a busy intersection in Colonie to do The Wave one last time. TV news cameras showed up—just what I needed at a time when most of the votes in the district already had been cast. Also, Prentiss showed up with a squad of his own volunteers to do The Wave at precisely that same location. I figured that was what happened when you sent out notices telling the press and the world where you would be on election day.

For 90 minutes or so, as the sky grew dark, we stood side by side, two separate regiments of political warriors. My people waved "Lynch for Assembly" signs. Prentiss's people wore his campaign T-shirts and were waving signs about state tax dollars being shipped off to New York City. Car horns honked. Each of us got the finger from this driver or that. At 6 p.m. or so, I thanked my people and let them go. Then I walked over to Prentiss and shook his hand.

"Well, Bob," I said, "it has been a war."

Prentiss seemed flustered. He took my hand and said, incongruously, "It's been fun."

He asked where my headquarters was located. I told him. He then said that he would appear there later to congratulate me. I went away puzzled. I'd presumed that he'd had the same polling numbers I'd had. If so, then he must have known that I was closing in on him, but he also must have known that the odds were slim that I would pick up the full nine points in that last week that I would need to beat him. I had no idea what to make of what he'd said to me—unless his numbers had shown me closer than the DACC numbers had me.

I then drove home for a much-needed nap. I crashed on

the family room sofa while friends and family gathered elsewhere in the house. My mother-in-law and sister-in-law, up from Jersey, were glued to the living room television set, watching cable reports on the first, dribbling results in the presidential race between Al Gore and George W. Bush. Exhausted, physically and mentally, I slipped off to sleep.

Donna awakened me shortly after the polls closed at 9 p.m. Early returns had Prentiss leading, she informed me. I rubbed my eyes and shook off the cobwebs. Now it was time for me to shower, shave, put on a fresh suit and hustle over to campaign headquarters, where people awaited me.

Finally, it was election night.

We arrived at headquarters just after 10 p.m. I pulled around to the rear of the shopping center, and we entered headquarters through the rear door. I'd figured that TV cameras and photographers from the various newspapers would be hanging around the front entrance, and they were.

The official Albany County Democratic Committee election night headquarters was in the city, so only a few of the Colonie Democratic Party people—the ones who'd worked like dogs on my behalf—had made the journey north to my headquarters in suburban Clifton Park. The other 50 or so people in our storefront headquarters were Lynch campaign volunteers, finally off the phone lines at CSEA and NEA and nervously watching returns on a television set in the headquarters reception area.

Wendy Quinn was at the office of the Saratoga County Board of Elections to get numbers. Jeanine and a few other people—DACC operatives, I figured—were in a small room at the rear of headquarters using a laptop computer to crunch numbers as they came in by phone. Those numbers would then go on big sheets of cardboard on the wall in the reception area, election district by election district.

Paul Clyne was winning his race for district attorney in Albany County, although he wasn't at 50 per cent. Mark Mischler's third-party candidacy was giving Clyne the election—that and all the money that Mike Burns had thrown into that race while stiffing me in mine. Both Hillary Clinton and Al Gore were running better in the 107th than anybody had anticipated. On the other hand, the Albany County Democratic machine had gone all out for them, as it most assuredly had not done on my behalf.

In my race, from the start, the trend wasn't good. Around 10:30, we learned from television, Prentiss had claimed victory. He's crazy, Jeanine assured me; these numbers don't support any such verdict. That's what I told reporters, both on live TV and the print people who called me. I made it a point to return every call but Bill Hammond's of the *Gazette*. There was no way, win or lose, that I would speak to anybody from that newspaper on election night.

By 11:30, I had enough in the way of numbers to make a decision. There had been some chicanery in Saratoga County. Voting machines had broken down in Stillwater and in certain sections of Clifton Park—a sure sign of vote fraud with paper ballots being used to pad the outcome. But, even assuming thievery—a totally rational assumption in those two communities, by the way—they hadn't managed to steal enough in those isolated precincts to make it worth my while to challenge the count and to have those ballots impounded.

Fred Altman was a Colonie Democratic committeeman, a lawyer and an all-around good guy. He'd been poised to han-

dle such a challenge for me. I told him by phone to forget it—
for the night, at least. With nearly all the votes counted,
Prentiss had roughly 30,500 votes. I had 27,500. And the
Green Party candidate, that Republican stalking horse named
Kimberly Audi-Desorbo, had 660. The percentage breakdown
was Prentiss 53, me 47 and her one per cent. The Greens had
only 35 or so members in my district, but Ralph Nader had been
on their presidential line, and he'd brought votes to Ms. Audi-
Desorbo that otherwise would have gone to me.

 These were big numbers for an Assembly race. In losing, I'd polled more votes than had been cast on both sides in
the McEneny race, which he'd won with nearly 80 per cent of
the vote. I'd also attracted more votes than had been cast on
both sides in John Faso's race. I'd polled more than twice as
many votes as Bruce Trachtenberg had polled in losing to Jim
Tedisco.

 I'd polled 200 per cent of the district's Democratic
enrollment. Prentiss had polled 125 per cent of the Republican
enrollment. From the start, enrollment had been the key to this
thing—that ferocious determination of so many people to vote
party rather than candidate. That had been the hurdle for me to
clear from the very beginning. I'd nearly pulled it off, too. In
that last week, I'd picked up another five percentage points.
Prentiss had managed to get the votes of one in three of the
undecideds in that last poll, enabling him to pick up another
percentage point.

 Prentiss hadn't won on the money that Faso had thrown
in at the last minute for those horrible "Democrat Dan" ads.
That money, although there had been a lot of it, had been spent
unwisely and had ended up having no real impact on the outcome of the election. In actual fact, the polls had shown,
Prentiss could have stayed home, watching Oprah every day,
and I needn't have begun my campaign until October 15th. If

any of the newspapers had given big play, however, to the story that final weekend about Prentiss financing the early days of his campaign with his own cash while refusing to pay his property taxes, we might have pulled this off.

Basically, it was the Subway Series that had done us in. It had illustrated the ultimate expression of public disinterest in politics in general, and in a race at this level in particular. We had no movement in the polls during that entire week. The series had distracted voters, especially male voters, from anything else—except, possibly, sex. They'd paid attention to the presidential and U.S. Senate races, but they'd ignored everything lower on the ballot until the Yankees had won. After that week, we'd begun moving up in the polls, but it had turned out to be too little, too late.

If I'd had another week—despite the enrollment disadvantage, the *Gazette*'s purposeful bias, the treachery in the Albany County machine, the endless stream of Prentiss lies and all the money thrown his way by Faso—we would have won the election. The campaign would have peaked not quite a week after election day.

Years earlier, as I'd worked as a reporter for the *Philadelphia Inquirer* covering the early days of the presidential race of 1972, Hubert Humphrey had told me one night in his hotel room, as we shared a chicken sandwich, that if the presidential election of 1968 had been held two weeks later, he would have been elected President. I hadn't fully understood what he'd been saying at the time. Now, I did.

Interestingly enough, I'd won every district where Mike and I had walked. I'd never quite figured out why people would vote for you just because you come to their door and beg, but they do. It made no sense whatever. I had the proof, however, before my eyes on the sheets of paper thrown about in abandon around Jeanine's laptop.

In another 10 minutes, I'd seen enough to conclude that I'd lost even if I challenged the paper ballots and won them all in court. I then called Prentiss on his cell phone, on the number I'd had for years in my reporter's phone book, and congratulated him. As it turned out, he hadn't even seen the numbers from Colonie. He'd simply figured that his margins from Stillwater and Malta had been large enough to carry him through. Essentially, when he'd claimed victory an hour earlier, he'd been guessing.

I went out into the reception area. My son, Kevin, had called earlier from Florida. I'd stood in the rear parking lot, on my cell phone, and had told him that things weren't looking good. By now, Kelly had finished up work for the night at Channel 13 and had arrived in the reception area. She hugged me.

"It's good to be able to see my family again," my daughter told me.

Now, came the hard part. My volunteers were gathered, grim-faced. Nobody was weeping, thank God, but most of them were obviously crestfallen. Jerry Vitagliano and Cynthia Pooler were especially down. I'd known for a week that winning would be a long shot. They'd had their hopes up until the very end, and I felt horrible for them.

We didn't make it, I told the crowd. I told them how much I valued my association with them. I thanked them for their dedication, commitment and hard work.

"It was humbling to watch that," I told them, "and humility doesn't come easy for me. Just ask the *Gazette*."

Mike Mann had known everything that I'd known. I'd never kept any secrets from him. Mike still was badly down over the outcome. He came up and hugged me. I didn't see it, but Donna later told me that there were tears in his eyes. Mike had been my loyal friend and companion throughout this whole nightmarish adventure. The man had worked like a galley slave. Having Mike Mann at my side, day after day, had made the entire ordeal bearable for me. Mary Gilson, too, had given her all to this effort. I felt worse for the two of them than I did for myself.

The place cleared out rapidly after that. Jeanine Gomez and Wendy Quinn, my DACC operatives, said goodbye and split. I hugged them both. I later sent Shelly a letter about how much help his DACC people had been. For all the friction, grief and aggravation, they'd behaved throughout the campaign with style and class—no lies, no down-and-dirty advertising, no slime.

Nobody on the other side could say the same.

21

PATRIOTISM IS NOT ENOUGH

"Government is too big and too important
to be left to the politicians."—Chester Bowles

The caller was adamant.

"You have to run again," he was saying. "You really owe it to people to give this another try. And this time, forget the Legislature. Run for Congress."

I was sitting on a wooden stool in the WROW studio in the Albany Broadcasting building, in front of the microphone. This anonymous caller's voice was coming to me through my headphones. I was doing the live, afternoon drive-time talk radio program that I'd begun toward the end of November. My plan after election night had been to rest and reflect for a while, catch my breath and then start a new novel, my first in nearly a decade. Paul Vandenburgh, however, had been steadfast in his insistence that I do this radio program, and that I start it right away.

"After all I've done for you already?" I'd said. "Who gave you the Hillary lawn sign? Who gave you the Al Gore sign? No gratitude, Paul; that's your problem."

"Yeah," said Vandenburgh, for whom Democrats represented all that was dangerous and misguided in American political life, "thanks a bunch."

Vandenburgh had his own reasons for asking me to do this program. His station needed stronger ratings during afternoon drive-time. Moreover, after pondering the offer for a week or so, I decided finally that I had my own reasons to accept it. For a while, at least, I felt the need for a public pulpit again. After all those maddening months of fighting to get out my words and thoughts through the frustrating filter of press coverage and via advertising financed by my own shameless, blatant begging, I had a few things I wanted to say. Also, I wanted to say those things directly, without the ferocious static of a political campaign obscuring the message.

It wasn't that losing the election had particularly bothered me. Given the enrollment disadvantage I'd faced and the re-election percentages of incumbents across New York, election after election, I'd figured from the start that a loss in this race had been likelier than a win. In fact, in New York State, only one of the 211 incumbent legislators in both houses had failed to win re-election in 2000—a single-term Republican from the Buffalo area who'd sneaked into office only two years earlier, during an off-year race.

The pattern, by the way, had been much the same in congressional elections. On election day, 2000, House incumbents had prevailed over challengers 394 to 6. All through the 1990s, more than 95 per cent of House incumbents were re-elected. For incumbent members of the U.S. Senate, the figure had topped 90 per cent.

During the final week of the campaign, as we'd slogged door-to-door, Mike Mann had asked me how I might handle a loss. I'd been an athlete as a kid, I'd explained to him, competing as a team player in football and individually as a wrestler. I'd also had six bouts as an amateur boxer. I'd won some of those contests and lost some, too. It's a cliche, but athletic competition really does build character. For me, the lasting value of competing in individual sports, I'd told him, had been the growth of the emotional armor that competitors need to get back out on the mat or into the ring. I'd learned early in life how to shake off a loss and to move on to the next contest.

I hadn't been looking for a career in the New York Legislature. I'd already had a career. Not that losing an election is ever fun, especially after all that work. In October, though—just a few weeks before election day—my cat had died. Tiger had been been my good buddy for twenty one-and-a-half years. I'd felt vastly more grief over losing that ancient cat than I'd felt over the election results.

So, I was going back on the radio for a while because I wanted another chance to talk to people about their government and the unique variety of human beings who run it. I wanted to share with them what I'd learned from my months on the inside of the process. Moreover, I wanted to do that at a time when nobody could accuse me of trying to gain politically by whatever I might have to say. I wanted the chance most of all to discuss with listeners the dark, disturbing culture of political life— to explain what there is about this process that gives us so many positively vile, woefully inferior people in public office in the first place. Moreover, I wanted to say those things clearly and at length—without interference, without editing, without distortion, without having to fret over staying on message.

So, here I was, on the air again, for three hours every afternoon. And here was this caller urging me to dive right back into the fetid political swamp from which a majority of the voters of New York's 107th Assembly District had just extricated me. Thousands of people were listening as I responded to the caller's comments.

"Not a chance," I told him. "I turn 55 years old tomor-

row. I have other things to do—like writing more books, playing some golf, spending some time with my wife. Running for
the state Assembly was a thing I did because the timing was just
right. I'd just finished a career. My kids were grown, through
college and into their own careers. I finally could afford to take
time away from working at a job and to make this run for a
position that would pay me less than I'd been used to making.
I did it solely because I was in a unique position to do it, and
because I thought it was the right thing to do. Frankly, I still
think it was the right thing to have done. If nothing else, it
probably shaved a few minutes off my time in Purgatory."

"So," the caller was saying, "why not do it again?"

I told him, "Because it's virtually impossible for anybody to come into this system from the outside—even somebody with a name as well known as mine is in this town. It's
virtually impossible for anybody from outside political life to
elbow his way in amongst the professional politicians and to
have any real chance of making a positive difference in the way
state government works. It's unfortunate, but the political system is firmly in the hands of a certain class of people—the
political class, as George Will likes to call them. They own the
system—lock, stock and barrel. Look, I gave it my shot. If
anybody else from the outside wants to take a stab at it, then I
wish them the best of luck."

The reality is that, in this country's currently complacent
environment, the odds of anybody from the outside cracking
this system are depressingly remote. About 7,500 state legislators are elected in this country every two years. Some of them
serve in small states where the Legislature meets only a few
weeks during each two-year legislative session. Those people
really are part-time lawmakers, and many of them are in politics out of some sense of civic obligation to their neighbors. In
the bigger states, though, the Legislatures are mini-congresses.

Most big-state lawmakers essentially serve full-time, with large salaries, and their campaigns cost many thousands of dollars, financed by special interest money and overseen by political bosses who control many millions of dollars in patronage.

Overwhelmingly, the bosses ensure that legislative districts are drawn to reflect the painfully partisan voting inclinations of the electorate, and too many voters in those districts are too busy working for a living, raising kids or merely living real life to focus on anything but blind party loyalty on election day. In races on the state level, party bosses tightly control the nominating process within the party structures and the flow of campaign cash as well. Few of those bosses are prepared to support anybody who hasn't come up through the system, knows the rules and is prepared to abide by them slavishly. The only people with any real chance of cracking that rigidly controlled nominating process in a primary election are people who've already been in the system for years—people who've already built personal political organizations and, more important, developed individual ties to the special interest groups who finance campaigns.

Sure, exceptions come along. Jesse Ventura demonstrated that a colorful celebrity, even a bizarre one, can sneak into office as a third-party candidate with less than a majority of the vote if a certain state's election laws are permissive enough to permit an outsider to pull it off. Minnesota is not New York, however. There, new voters can register and vote on the same day. Older, industrial states like New York have woefully restrictive election codes. Those laws are carefully designed to keep the system firmly in the hands of the political class.

People with great wealth sometimes can overwhelm the bosses with torrents of dollars. None of the political pros could stop the Rockefellers, for instance—not in New York and not in

Arkansas or West Virginia, either. It was money, pure and simple, that got the Kennedys rolling in Massachusetts, where they had strong family political connections as well. Jon S. Corzine, the U.S. senator from New Jersey, is a more modern and vivid example. Worth more than $650 million from his years on Wall Street, Corzine burned up more than $60 million of his own money to break into the political system from outside. Most people with that kind of money, however, are not about to soil their hands with politics—not when there are tropical beaches to lie on and fancy toys to be bought and played with. And who can blame them?

Also, is that who we want in public office? Should we be stuck only with political professionals or people with so much money that they're unlikely to be able to relate to ordinary citizens, no matter how hard they might try? Nelson Rockefeller was a unique and memorable governor of New York, but I had a veteran reporter working for me at *Newsday* in the late 1970s, the late Pat Brasley. Two decades earlier, Pat had been forced to explain to the governor of New York the meaning of the phrase, "take-home pay." Brasley had spent the rest of his life shaking his head over the conversation.

So, in politics and government above the municipal level in the larger states, the professionals run the show. And, as professionals, they tend to understand the unique culture of political life and to function freely within it without concern for the degree to which that culture conflicts with the basic values of the citizens they're pledged to serve and represent.

I just hadn't realized, when I'd first gotten into this and had joked to myself about how much this culture seemed to resemble the culture of the mob, precisely how on-target that observation had been.

We know—from the sworn testimony of mobsters beginning in the 1950s and from the way that testimony has been spun over the years into literary and theatrical works like *The Godfather* and the *Sopranos*—that classic mob culture tends to be startlingly violent but almost pathologically indirect. In mob life, you find out you have an enemy only when bullets begin flying in your direction or when the garrote slips over your head from behind. Political culture is distressingly similar in its essential indirection.

In mob life, no enemy will confront you face to face. Michael Corleone never engaged in any conversation for the purpose of solving a problem, only to mislead an enemy and to lull him into complacency before the fatal strike. Like the fictional Corleones, any political enemy you might have doesn't want a solution to any problem. What he wants is you out of the way, preferably by stealth. Politicians don't fight duels. When they wage war, they're more apt to function as snipers, firing at your back from the bushes. An example:

When I'd begun this campaign, I'd invited a few people in the Albany County Democratic Party to lunch—to break bread and to iron out differences. These were people I'd been told would not work to help me, and I both wanted and needed their support. In each case, I'd sat across a restaurant table and said to the guy, "If you have a problem with me as the party's candidate, tell me now, and let's see if we can work this out."

One of these people was a key figure in the Albany County Democratic Party. He was Frank Commisso, the party's vice chair and the majority leader of the Albany County Legislature. I'd written several columns critical of Commisso's conduct as a public official. In one case, I'd criticized him for accepting a private contract to perform work for the Albany area Off-Track Betting Corp. when the county's representative to that organization's board of directors was, essentially, named by Commisso. It just so happened that OTB's chief executive, a particularly sleazy lawyer named Davis Etkin, was a crook who later pleaded guilty to mishandling OTB money.

I'd known that the OTB chief was crooked. Commisso had known it. Everybody in town with even half a brain had known it. Commisso, I'd written, had been wrong in naming a board member who supported this guy, and Commisso been even more wrong in taking money from this same guy in exchange for providing Etkin with a pliable board member.

So, when I'd asked Commisso at lunch to tell me how we could work this out, I'd been well aware that he bore me a serious grudge. Rather than say that to my face, however, he'd told me simply, "No, I have no problem."

Immediately after that lunch, though, I learned that Commisso had then told a number of people in the party organization, "At first, I just wasn't going to do anything to help this guy. Now, I'm going to actively work against him."

Which he did, in various ways, throughout the campaign. All the time, Commisso was openly friendly to me, openly supportive and knocking himself out to convince me that we were now best buddies. Virtually nobody in political life would have been surprised by his conduct, and few would have disapproved. It was simply the way things are done in politics. Commisso's behavior was perfectly in keeping with a deeply rooted culture of deceit, dishonor and attack from ambush. As in mob life, virtually nobody in politics ever fights fair. The very concept of a fair fight, an honest conversation, a candid expression of point of view, is laughably foreign to the world in which these people live, operate and prosper at public expense.

Now, is everybody in politics like that? Of course not. Many professional politicians—and some quite successful ones, actually—are honorable men and women who value the truth and whose word can be trusted. They're decent human beings who deal fairly, openly and honestly with their col-

leagues and constituents. Looking in from outside, however—
as I did for years as a reporter—it's not possible with minute
precision for anybody not an active part of the system to determine which of these people retain any ethical roots in the larger world and which are thoroughly soaked through with the
political culture's unique value system.

From my experience as a candidate, people like Shelly
Silver, Ron Canestrari, Jack McEneny, Tom Bayly, Tony
Catalfamo, Mike Conners and a number of others clearly recognized and understood the prevailing political culture of
deception, betrayal and treachery. They'd managed nonetheless
to retain their individual identities as ethical human beings with
moral roots in real life. The problem with political culture in
general is that, just as NBA players tend to be tall, political life
tends to attract—and, over the long haul, also to produce—a
vastly larger percentage of liars, fakes, phonies, back-stabbers
and hypocrites than you'll find in virtually any other industry.

That's what politics in America is, by the way—an
industry. It's a multi-billion-dollar business in which participants collect taxpayer-supported paychecks to put bread on the
table, not unlike people who work in the law or real estate or
plumbing. Lincoln Steffens, the pioneering New York City
journalist of the late 19th Century, had taken note of that for his
readers.

"Politics is business," Steffens had written, "And that's
what's wrong with it."

The difficulty is that the people who tend to rise in the
business of politics attain success in an environment in which
personal integrity is not only a deviation from the norm, it's also
a decided disadvantage in winning elections. Generally, the
most successful politicians are those bereft of genuine political
convictions or any tangible sense of personal integrity. Their
promises and commitments mean nothing. They survive and

prosper by defrauding people relentlessly, year after year, election after election. Then, once elected, they place their hands on Bibles and pledge on a sacred honor they don't possess to keep faith with their constituents.

Bob Prentiss, for example—who campaigned as a tax-cutting conservative, anti-abortion activist and gun control opponent—had begun political life as an active Democrat, sitting on a local government in his home state of Massachusetts. Three decades later, as a Republican sitting in the New York Assembly, Prentiss delighted in confiding to Democratic colleagues that he was, deep down, really a Kennedy Democrat. Given his public political positions, it mattered little in terms of his integrity whether Prentiss was telling his colleagues the truth or lying to them. Moreover, genuine political conviction on the part of any professional politician is a decided rarity. While all too many of their constituents are guided by rigid political beliefs—often to the point of mindless fanaticism— most professional politicians operate without any hard core of conviction. Overwhelmingly, they tend to be pragmatic moderates—deeply cynical and profoundly contemptuous of true believers in the electorate.

Deception is not only the successful politician's most potent tool, it's an ingrained component of his essential personality. In Jimmy Breslin's raucous novel about mob life, "The Gang That Couldn't Shoot Straight," he noted that any mobster who spotted a sign forbidding him to spit in the subway always felt the saliva surge up in his mouth like a fountain. In too many cases, politicians lie because lying is a compulsion with them. They can't help themselves, and they feel no moral obligation to refrain from doing it. After a while, they're not only unable to see anything wrong with it, they come to view lying as a virtue. Bob Kerrey, as a U.S. Senator from Nebraska, once said of Bill Clinton, "He's an unusually good liar." In political culture, that wasn't an insult; it was a compliment.

If a lie works, then its effectiveness is its own justifica-
tion. If it fails in some public setting, then a show of contrition
is all that's needed before going on to the next—and, hopefully,
more successful—lie. All the professional politicians who
howled so loudly when Clinton lied under oath in the Monica
Lewinsky scandal understood perfectly how Clinton, the ultimate professional politician, could view such a lie not only as
acceptable but as actually laudable. What was disturbing and—
to me, anyway—surprising, was how many people in the general population seemed to see it that way, too. As the classic
manifestation of the American political overachiever, Clinton's
obvious lack of any personal moral compass neither surprised
people nor, in most cases, particularly offended them.

As a venerable and highly successful political organization that hadn't been forced by defeat at the polls to question the
quality or utility of its values, the Albany machine had developed its own unique sub-culture within the larger scope of political attitudes. The machine's culture wasn't radically different
from that of political organizations elsewhere, only more stark-
ly defined and deeply ingrained because the machine was more
successful and longer-lived than most political organizations.

I have no doubt that Mike Burns, the Albany County
Democratic chairman, felt no personal sense of wrongdoing for
promising to support me and then actively opposing my candidacy behind my back. Surely, his confessor never heard about
that. That's because Burns simply was unable to appreciate any
abstract concept of right and wrong when it came to giving his
word and then breaking it. He would have viewed those as two
completely separate acts, utterly unrelated to one another. In
that, he was not at all atypical of political leaders. To them, yesterday's promise is meaningless history and of no particular
moment today. In the culture of politics, no commitment lives

beyond its immediate usefulness. There exists no cultural stig-
ma attached to betrayal or untruth. In fact, just the opposite is
true. In the Albany machine I dealt with, anybody too stupid to
lie was considered too stupid and too undependable to be in
charge of anything.

The same was true of Bob Prentiss, only in wide-screen
Technicolor. He'd pledged, both to me privately and to the public, an honest, dignified campaign conducted, as he put it, on the
"high road." In his view, though, anybody silly enough to keep
those pledges would have to be deranged. As soon as the campaign began, Prentiss proceeded to engage in every vicious tactic he could imagine, no matter how many innocent people he
might hurt in the process and no matter how little those tactics
might accomplish in practical terms for his campaign. Never
for a moment did he exhibit a shred of guilt about his actions or
the flurry of lies that surrounded them. This was politics, he
told reporters.

He was right, too; that's exactly what it was. It was a
close contest in a sadly befouled environment in which honor,
honesty and integrity had long ago been banished from the cultural lexicon. The name of the game was flim-flam, pure and
simple. A professional politician, more often than not, wins
elections by pulling the wool over the eyes of those not directly involved in the political culture. He wins not by showing
people who he is and asking them to approve of him but by
showing them somebody who doesn't exist and hoping that they
won't catch on.

Grinning, grandfatherly Bob Prentiss had no chance of
convincing anybody that he was a genius, so his goal was to
convince them instead that he was a harmless, kindly, good-
hearted guy—sort of a cross between Elmer Fudd and your
favorite, slightly bewildered old uncle. As con artists go,
Prentiss wasn't bright enough to be anything but painfully trans-

parent, but neither the press nor the public expect more from political figures, and few of the media watchdogs in the Albany metro area charged with giving the public the truth displayed any particular indignation over the man's behavior.

Hell, they're all liars, the voters complain to one another. And, by the way, where's the remote? Too many reporters and editors adopt the same resigned point of view about the people who make laws and run government.

In recognition of how pronounced the problem has become, more than a half-dozen states—including Maine, Hawaii and, most recently, the Iowa House of Representatives—actually have passed legislation making it a crime for politicians to lie during campaigns. The Iowa bill would levy a fine of $1,500 or impose a year in jail for any politician on the campaign trail who says anything about his or her opponent that the candidate "knows to be untrue, deceptive or misleading."

These laws, of course, are not enforced because they run afoul of the First Amendment of the U.S. Constitution. Campaigns are about speech and debate—or, at least, they're supposed to be. Government can't really restrict that speech, even when it consists of lies.

The question is, what can be done to make any of this better? Another question is whether making it better is worth the effort to begin with? And a third, equally important question, is whether people really care whether it gets better or not?

My best instinct is that they don't. For all its warts, the political system devised by the framers of the U.S. Constitution has been good to Americans. By the standards of the world, we're rich, free of oppression and generally safe from external threat to our security and basic way of life. The essential American idea of government is that it should leave ordinary citizens the hell alone. If it does that, and doesn't pick our pockets too greedily in the process, then we're more or less unconcerned with what politicians do or don't do. If they're more likely as a class to be scum than most people—and they most assuredly are—they're at least scum who can be counted on to stay out of our hair if we vote a few of their butts out of office now and then during hard times.

We Americans are a conspicuously forgiving people with historically low standards for the conduct of our politicians. Only rarely do voters exhibit genuine outrage on a grand scale. It happened in New York City, at the end of the Roaring Twenties, when political corruption grew to such immense proportions that it began to touch virtually every citizen of the five boroughs. As Herbert Mitgang described the scope and breadth of that corruption in his wonderful book "Once Upon a Time In New York," virtually every public job, from janitor to judge, was for sale along with every city service.

"A permit to make a cut in the sidewalk for a gas station?" Mitgang wrote. "Fifty dollars. A variance to add another floor to a skyscraper without a legal setback to let a little sunshine in? That'll be $3,000 for the building inspector, plus another $5,000 . . . for 'the organization' at Tammany's impressive new headquarters. . . . What's the under-the-table payment for a pier on the Hudson River to dock your transatlantic liner? Well, how does $50,000 in unmarked, untaxed bills sound?"

Like the 1990s in general and the year 2000 in particular, the 1920s were good times, so New Yorkers blithely ignored the corruption until the police began raiding hotels for women and threatening to hit the landlords with criminal charges of promoting prostitution unless the cops were handed bribes. It got so bad that Governor Franklin Delano Roosevelt finally ordered hearings. Local politician after local politician came forward under oath to testify about the hoards of cash found in tin boxes under their beds at home. They came to be known as

"The Tin Box" brigade. Typical of them was New York County Sheriff Thomas M. Farley, who earned $8,500 a year and whose tin box contained nearly a half million dollars in cash. Farley testified that he had no idea how the money had gotten there. It was then and only then that voters reacted with anger at the polls.

After the trials of the Depression, the agonies of World War II and the ensuing period of prosperity in the 1950s, however, Americans pretty much resumed ignoring politics and the conduct of politicians until the Vietnam War. It took bloody years of pointless conflict, both in Southeast Asia and on the streets of every city in America—with tens of thousands of American soldiers dead or crippled for life—before most people finally had enough of the nonsense and demanded an end to it in 1968. Even then, Richard Nixon lied to them in promising to end the war with dispatch once he took office. In a dead heat with Clinton as the most deeply despised President of the 20th Century, Nixon took office in January of 1969. Sure enough, just like clockwork, the war ended only six years later.

By then, though, Nixon had been driven from office for obstructing justice and trying to subvert the U.S. Constitution during the Watergate Scandal. Americans had managed to rouse enough outrage over that turn of events to radically alter the face of Congress in the next elections. Few voters ever had harbored any illusions about Nixon's character until those elections. Nonetheless, it required an overwhelming display of venality, deception and dishonor to rouse them to action.

A few months before I announced my candidacy, I'd visited Nixon's burial site at his presidential library just east of Los Angeles. On the black granite stone atop his grave, Nixon had proclaimed himself a "peacemaker."

"Good God," I'd muttered to Donna. "He even had a lie carved into his tombstone."

It was only one more indication of how differently professional politicians view both the world and themselves, and it
was part of a long tradition of such twisted thinking. William
Marcy Tweed was the notorious leader of New York City's
notorious 19th Century Tweed Ring, which had robbed taxpayers for a decade with phantom companies raking in city checks.
Upon entering prison after years of the most spectacular political thievery in American history, Tweed had listed his occupa-
tion as "statesman."

That same disconnect from political culture was the
enduring hallmark of daily life throughout the Albany metro
area, where fully one in four workers held down government
jobs. Only a few times in the last half of the 20th Century had
voters rejected casting their ballots along party lines. Most
conspicuously, that had happened after Albany County
Executive Jim Coyne had been shipped off to prison in the
arena construction scandal. A Republican had been elected
Albany County executive to succeed him, but Albany County
voters quickly returned to party-line voting.

However, if ordinary citizens were to decide to improve
this slimy process and replace the substandard people in it, how
could they go about that task—both individually and collec-
tively?

For one thing, voters need to take their responsibilities
as citizens vastly more seriously. It's an oft-repeated platitude,
but it remains true nonetheless; all around the world, people are
dying for the right to elect their leaders. Here, in the world's
longest continuous democracy, too few people care who those
leaders are or what sort of human beings they might be.

According to a survey of 1,053 Americans conducted in
March, 2001, by the Medill School of Journalism, only 51 per
cent of the voting-age population had cast ballots in the elections of 2000, up slightly from the 49 per cent who'd bothered

to vote four years earlier. Voting has dropped steadily since a 60 per cent high in the elections of 1960.

In New York's prosperous, self-satisfied 107th Assembly District, where half the voters were college graduates or better—twice the national average—fully one in three enrolled voters stayed home on election day, 2000. This country has a drug problem because it has a demand problem; people want the drugs. It has a democracy problem because too few people will take the trouble to nurture the democratic process as it both needs and deserves; they're simply too lazy.

The Medill poll indicated that there are ways to improve those numbers. Fully a third of the voting age citizens who didn't bother to turn out in November said they would have voted if the election had been held on a Saturday instead of a Tuesday, if they'd been permitted to register and vote on the same day, if they could have voted by mail regardless of whether they were in town on election day and if the election had been conducted over two or three days instead of just one. So, there are practical, workable ways to make voting easier for citizens and to encourage them to participate. Professional politicians, however, have a vested interest in low voter turnouts, so all across the country they resist efforts to make voting easier and more convenient.

For another, voters have a duty to pay attention—and a solemn duty at that. They need to read newspapers, watch television, listen to the radio news and public affairs programming. They need to learn something about who these candidates really are as human beings, not just which political party they represent. Party is important, and partisanship has its legitimate place. But the quality of individuals, both in terms of their intellect and character, is ultimately what makes the difference between a good government and a bad one. That's true whether your priority is to have government do more or do less.

Citizens should vote for people determined to find solutions to problems, not for people bent on keeping those problems alive eternally for the purpose of squeezing campaign dollars out of special-interest contributors or votes out of an inattentive electorate. Each state should give its citizens the power to gather a reasonable number of petition signatures to permit grass-roots initiatives to appear on the ballot, both locally and statewide, to circumvent the self-serving, foot-dragging tendencies of the political class.

Voters also should remember, first and foremost, that most of the people in the system for any length of time become corrupted by its prevailing values. Any incumbent you're faced with probably is a liar. Some aren't, of course, but they'll be the exceptions rather than the rule. That's why each state also should have a recall provision, to permit voters to collect signatures on petitions so they can vote on an elected official's removal from office during his or her term of office.

Something must be done to improve ballot access. State election codes must be simplified and petition signature requirements must be lowered to weaken the control the bosses now enjoy over the nominating process.

Finally, it's also crucial to broaden the base of political contributors. Only two per cent of Americans ever contribute to political campaigns. Virtually every dollar collected by politicians running for Congress or for legislative office in big states comes from people for whom contributing is a calculated business decision. The goal of that contribution is to ensure that tax dollars are directed to the pockets of those contributors or that the apathetic sheep of the general population are herded into directions convenient for the money people. Moreover, few people understand how this situation affects them in countless ways.

Two quick examples:

Nevada is the only state that permits legal betting on college sports. A 1999 University of Michigan study made fairly clear that gamblers have managed to reach a disturbing percentage of college athletes and have affected their performances on the field or on the court. The National Collegiate Athletic Association is acutely aware that too many impoverished student athletes are vulnerable to bribes in ways that highly paid professional athletes are not, and the NCAA vigorously opposes betting on college games. Yet the "gaming industry," as it calls itself, had poured vast sums into the campaigns of both Nevada politicians and national politicians to ensure that betting on college games remains legal in America and, especially, in Nevada.

So, the next time you see a college player drop a sideline pass or miss a free throw, ask yourself if that kid is working for his team or for gamblers concerned about the point spread. And ask yourself if political money should be permitted to taint college athletics, as it clearly does now.

Also, New York State Comptroller H. Carl McCall set his auditors loose on one region of the New York State Department of Transportation. The auditors discovered during the Spring of 2001 that the regional office had given non-bid contracts worth $275 million over a 10-year period to engineering firms for work that easily could have been performed by state employees already on the payroll. It's no accident that engineering firms are major political contributors to New York politicians. McCall's report constituted a classic case of public money going down the drain in exchange for political contributions. For some reason, though, many conservatives oppose public campaign financing measures that would save them vast sums in taxes in the long run.

Bruce Ackerman, a Yale law professor and constitutional scholar, has put forth an interesting public financing scheme for federal elections. His idea? Give every registered voter a $50 voucher that can be spent to support candidates or political organizations. Each election cycle, that money could go to candidates or political organizations that meet some minimal threshold of support—possibly via the sort of signed petitions that give candidates ballot access. Each state, especially the big states, should consider something similar to minimize the effect of special interest contributions.

Partial public financing of campaigns does exist on the presidential level and in some localities—New York City, for instance. Each system has its flaws, but some system of public financing is desperately needed in every large state, where legislative races involve huge sums of money. Between us, Bob Prentiss and I, for example, spent more than $400,000 on our race—or, roughly, $6.50 for each vote cast. According to our financial filings at the New York State Board of Elections, I spent slightly more than he did, but I know that my finances were meticulously detailed, while I saw at the end of the campaign how he handled his.

Just what form that system of public financing might take could be argued forever—and probably would be before it ever could be adopted on a large scale in the bigger states. But without such a system to provide outsiders with access to campaign dollars without restricting their independence even before they cast their first vote in office, the lawmaking and budget processes of every major state will continue to be dominated by the money people and their bought-and-paid-for hired hands in political office.

One quick fix—especially attractive in New York but applicable nationwide—would be to force people running for legislative office to raise a certain percentage of their campaign money from individuals or businesses with addresses in their home districts. If a lawmaker had to raise, say, 50 per cent of his or her contributions from the community he or she seeks to represent, the power of the special interests hovering over the Capitol would be dramatically reduced.

Would that system solve all problems? No. Could it be evaded? Yes, there would be ways to evade it. But virtually any step taken to reduce the power of the special interest groups would deliver a tangible payoff to ordinary citizens. Any measure that would disrupt the current relationship between lawmakers and the money people would constitute an improvement.

Finally, the news media need to get better. Yeah, sure, journalism is a hard job, and nobody appreciates that more than I do. But, in creating the First Amendment, the Framers of the Constitution created special protections for the news media in general—and newspapers in particular—as businesses. The First Amendment insulates the press from government regulation or interference with the basic mission of the press, which is to inform voters and preserve democracy. When dealing with public figures, the First Amendment protects the press from libel suits—what in any other industry would be product liability vulnerabilities—even when the press is wrong and unfair in its coverage. It's hard for me to believe that those guys so long ago created those protections just so modern media conglomerates could produce pallid publications with bare-bones staffs and rake in 35 per cent pre-tax profits year after year.

No, it's not that the public in any way holds claim to a bottomless entitlement to the wealth of media company owners and stockholders. It's simply that, if you're going to invest in a journalistic enterprise of any sort—as opposed to a hardware store or a fast food restaurant—then you have certain civic obligations doing business in a democratic environment. Owning a news media outlet ought to be viewed by its proprietors as a bit akin to owning a proprietary hospital. You have both a right and a duty to make money, but you have other obligations as well.

Last, ordinary people have to be willing to get into this process and to fight the professional politicians who really are so different from the rest of us. Ordinary people have to stand up firmly for basic human moral and ethical values in the democratic process. They have to fight, on a large scale, to ensure that honest, competent people—with a crisp understanding of, and a vivid appreciation for, the basic concepts of right and wrong—hold down public office. Ultimately, citizens in a democracy end up with precisely the government they deserve. And, ultimately, all the problems of democracy have only one solution.

More democracy.

Who's Who in the Book

Major Players

Tom Bayly: Chairman of the Saratoga County, N.Y., Democratic
Committee.

Bob Berry: Manager of the Lynch for Assembly campaign.

Mike Breslin: The Albany County, N.Y. executive, a Democrat.

Neil Breslin: Democratic New York State senator and Mike's brother.

Mike Burns: Chairman of the Albany County, N.Y., Democratic
Committee.

Ron Canestrari: Member of the New York Assembly, co-chairman of
the Democratic Assembly Campaign Committee (DACC).

Tony Catalfalmo: Chairman of the Town of Colonie Democratic
Committee.

John Faso: Republican Leader of the New York Assembly.

Neil Fisher: DACC political operative.

Gazette, Daily **and** *Sunday*: The second-largest daily newspaper in the
Albany, N.Y. metro area.

Mary Gilson: Director of volunteers for the Lynch for Assembly
campaign.

Jeanine Gomez: DACC operative assigned to Lynch campaign.

Bill Hammond: The *Gazette* reporter assigned to cover the campaign.

Jerry Jennings: Mayor of Albany and the behind-the-scenes leader of the Albany County Democratic machine.

Jan Lemon: Chairwoman of the Clifton Park Democratic Committee.

Butch Lilac: Supervisor of the Town of Stillwater, N.Y., and an early Lynch political rival.

Mike Lisuzzo: Republican chairman of Clifton Park.

John Longo: Political director of DACC.

Donna Lynch: High school government teacher, the candidate's wife and the Lynch campaign's chief fundraiser.

Kelly Lynch: The weekend anchor for WNYT-Channel 13 television and the candidate's daughter.

Mike Mann: The Lynch campaign's press secretary, scheduler and walking boss.

Joe McElroy: Colonie Democratic activist and an early Lynch campaign advisor.

Jack McEneny: A member of the New York Assembly and an early Lynch campaign advisor.

Bob Prentiss: The incumbent Republican assemblyman in New York's 107th Assembly District.

The *Record*: The third-largest daily newspaper in the Albany metro area.

Sheldon Silver: The speaker of the New York Assembly and one of the three top elected officials in state government.

***Spotlight* Newspapers:** An influential chain of weekly newspapers in the 107th Assembly District.

John Sweeney: The Republican congressman whose district includes much of the 107th Assembly District.

Times Union: The dominant daily newspaper in the Albany metro area.

Paul Vandenburgh: Program director and morning talk show host on AM-590 WROW radio.

Other Significant Players

Adam Acquario: Regional political director for a major public employees union.

Dennis Anderson: Prentiss campaign operative active in a public employees union.

Kimberly Audi-Desorbo: Green Party candidate for the 107th Assembly District.

Phil Barrett: Republican supervisor of the Town of Clifton Park.

Antionette Biordi: A reporter for WNYT-Channel 13 television.

Liz Bishop: Anchor for WRGB-Channel 6 television.

John Bove: Restaurateur and Lynch backer.

Mike Bragman: New York Assembly majority leader.

Joe Bruno: Majority leader of the New York State Senate.

John Bulgaro: Leader of the Albany area Teamsters Union.

Gary Carter: Broadcast personality for WMHT-Channel 17 television.

Jeff Cohen: Editor of the *Times Union*.

Paul Conti: News director of WNYT-Channel 13 television.

Frank Commisso: Majority leader of the Albany County Legislature and a power in the Albany County Democratic party.

Bob Conner: Editorial writer and occasional columnist for the *Gazette*.

Mike Conners: Albany County comptroller and Lynch campaign advisor.

Jim Coyne: Former Albany County executive who served time in federal prison for political corruption.

Mario Cuomo: Former governor of New York State.

Kevin Dailey: Lawyer, former Clifton Park supervisor and unsuccessful Assembly candidate in 1996.

Fred Dicker: State editor, *New York Post*.

Danny Donohue: President of New York's largest public employees union.

Rose Egan: Lynch campaign treasurer.

Sol Greenberg: Albany County district attorney.

Laura Hagen: Executive director of the Center for Independence.
Kevin Hicks: Head of the Albany area Carpenters Union.
Kevin Hogan: Reporter for the *Record*.
George Infante: An Albany County legislator.
Mike Kane: Deputy political director of DACC.
Peter Kermani: Albany County Republican chairman.
Tim Lane: Colonie Democratic committeeman working with Lynch for
      Assembly campaign.
Fred LeBrun: Columnist for the *Times Union*.
Jim Mancuso: Retired college professor, active in the Sons of Italy.
Mike McNulty: Democratic congressman whose district includes most
      of the 107th Assembly District.
Al Paolucci: McEneny staffer and a volunteer for the Lynch campaign.
Cynthia Pooler: A key volunteer for the Lynch campaign.
Tony Potenza: Head of the Albany area Pipefitters Union.
Bill Powers: New York state Republican chairman.
Wendy Quinn: DACC operative assigned to Lynch campaign.
Paul Rickard: Saratoga County Democratic party official.
Larry Rosenbaum: Head of the Albany County Independence Party
      and vice chair of the state organization.
Chuck Schumer: U.S. Senator representing New York in Washington.
Bob Spearman: Manager of the Prentiss for Assembly campaign.
Carl Strock: Columnist for the *Gazette*.
Jerry Vitagliano: Lynch campaign photographer and volunteer.
Dave White: *Times Union* publisher.
Tom Woodman: *Gazette* managing editor.

INDEX